Leaders We Deserve

For Catherine, Eleanor and Isabel

Leaders We Deserve

ALISTAIR MANT

Martin Robertson

First published in 1983 by Martin Robertson &
Company Ltd, 108 Cowley Road, Oxford OX4 1JF.

British Library Cataloguing in Publication Data

Mant, Alistair
    Leaders we deserve.
    1. Leadership
    I. Title
    303.3'4   HM141

    ISBN 0-85520-625-X

Typeset by Santype International Ltd.,
Salisbury, Wilts.
Printed and bound in Great Britain by
Billing and Sons Ltd, Worcester

Contents

Acknowledgements

I would like to acknowledge the help of Professors John Adair, Charles Handy and John Morris, all of whom read the manuscript and made invaluable suggestions. I have extracted substantial chunks from four authors in particular – Professor Liam Hudson (on creativity and psychological development), Bruce Reed (on creativity and faith), Bruce Page and Paul Willis (on creativity and evil); my debt to their work will be obvious. Anthony Holden, previously Washington Correspondent of the *Observer*, also contributed a number of marvellous political anecdotes.

In the course of writing, two giants of epistemological theory died – Gregory Bateson and Wilfred Bion. Both of them were important fundamental sources for some of the ideas herein. (Coincidentally, Jean Piaget, another founding father of modern epistemology, also died during this period.) Grant McIntyre, who was originally to have published the book, was a most helpful critic in the early stages, and Edward Phillips, a busy professional actor and one-time Cat Correspondent on the journal *Dog International*, typed the manuscript with meticulous attention to detail and also contributed various erudite inputs. I am also grateful to the editor of *Private Eye* and to the cartoonist, Newman, for permission to reprint the cartoon on p. 78.

A.M.

Introduction

The origins of this book lie in a single throwaway paragraph of an earlier book.[1] That is as it should be. This book, that is to say, has not been put together by a committee of agents and publishers with a 'market' in mind. It represents a stage in the thinking of one person, supported by hundreds of conversations with colleagues, the responses of scores of audiences and the reading of many books on diverse subjects. Anyone who works in a consultative capacity knows that the point of departure for creative change is nearly always the throwaway remark or thought – something so taken for granted that its deeper import is not immediately apparent. So it is with this book.

The circumstances of its origin explain the content and the rather iconoclastic process. The content (of which more later) concerns the differences between people obsessed by winning/losing in life and, on the other hand, those who are always impelled to inquire 'What's it for?' We might well ask the same question about books. Some books, and particularly those in the 'management' field, represent attempts to find and satisfy a 'market'; the author will do any seductive thing he can to please. Others – books of poetry, for example – represent therapy; the act of writing is as necessary for the author as eating and sleeping. The audience, if it exists at all, can please itself.

As to process, this book veers towards the poetic – it is not dispassionate and it sets out to sharpen the appreciation of familiar objects rather than to inform. The content, however, is important because we do seem, as a species, so very inept at ensuring that our various human enterprises

[1] *The Rise and Fall of the British Manager*, London, Pan, 1979, p. 119.

are steered forward by leaders of vision, courage, humility and trustworthiness. There are serious books to be read on these matters, but they tend also to be rather worthy. They leave out sometimes the ludicrous, the exciting, the side-splitting and the maddening aspects of institutional life. As such, they are not much *like* life.

There are therefore certain advantages to books built on a stream-of-consciousness principle, but there are also compensating difficulties for which the reader should be prepared:

(1)   In the first place, this book although it is not essentially about political leadership, was written during the terms of office of Reagan, Thatcher and Fraser in those countries I know and love best (and in which I sell books). This represents a coincidence, and the reader would be wrong to detect political bias in what I have to say about them. Their political views are less important, in my view, than their essential dimness. (The *nature* of dimness is taken up in chapters 2 and 3.) In *The Rise and Fall of the British Manager* I was, for example, quite scathing about some of Sir Harold Wilson's actions, not for their socialism but for their fundamental silliness. For this I got into trouble with readers of socialistic bent. Since then the political pendulum has swung, but the silliness marches on. The point is that dim political leaders, whatever their politics, are invariably surrounded by quite sensible people. The issue is *why* these sensible people rise to supreme power so infrequently; why we can't *make* it happen.

(2)   In so far as the book is about certain modes of thought and therefore (at one remove) about personality types, it made a certain amount of sense to begin at the beginning – in the womb, in fact (chapter 2). this is not to everyone's taste because the process involves a certain messiness of conceptualization and is a long way removed, in time and spirit, from the nitty-gritty of management and leadership in the adult world. Those of my colleagues who have kindly perused the manuscript suggest that it makes no difference at all in which order the chapters are read. Therefore I have left the order alone, and I encourage the reader to approach the table in a smörgåsbord frame of mind or even,

to mix the metaphor, to begin with the pudding and work back.

(3)   To change the metaphor altogether (from the digestive to the perambulative), the broad thoroughfare of the content contains an inordinate number of side-alleys, some of them blind. One knows in advance how very irritating this is for critics of a certain cast of mind (their particular psychopathology is also dealt with in the book, probably in a side-alley): 'The whole could do with a certain amount of tightening up; moreover, much of the thinking is speculative and at times opinionated.' On reading this sort of thing about a book, I myself am always encouraged to plunge forward with keen anticipation, but the reader is warned: it is a matter of taste. One day I hope to goad some critic into saying, 'This is the most irritating book I have ever read!' (with those words blazoned over the cover, it will probably sell a million.

(4)   The book does not really set out to advise 'Three-part-man' how to get to the top, nor does it provide a scholarly overview of the 'leadership' literature. The latter can be found elsewhere, and the former cannot really be accomplished in a mere book. I hope this book is in the nature of a mutual exploration of a strange town. All the features are town-like, but the detail is new, and every side-alley is worth a foray just in case there is something wonderful lurking there. There is usually more to be discovered than even the author is aware of, as I well know from readers' letters past. Three-part man (and woman, of course) may draw strength from the contents, but it would be absurd to offer tactical advice on careers. That sort of thing belongs in a different sort of book.

The original throwaway paragraph concerned two modes of organization – the 'binary' (o─o) and the 'ternary' (⟨o─o). It had not then occurred to me that there might be two distinct modes of thought, or even two personality types, associated with these organizational dynamics. At the time a whole host of organizational 'raiders' emerged, or consolidated their hold, on the political scene: Charles Haughey in the Republic of Ireland, Robert Muldoon in New Zealand, Menachem Begin in Israel, General Galtieri in Argentina,

General Pinochet in Chile – not to mention the more egregious loonies like Idi Amin, Colonel Gadafi and the Ayatollah Khomeini. The point about all these national leaders is that they share certain characteristics with the leaders of humbler institutions – a noticeably pugnacious spirit, inexhaustible energy and a combination of short-term political cunning and intellectual cluelessness about any long-term, complex system (like, for example, a country).

At the same time, a new generation was growing up which was not only sceptical about the quality of its leadership but also downright cynical as to the possibility of doing anything to improve matters. That generation had experienced 'leadership' in many guises – in parents, teachers, bosses, preachers, union representatives and (vicariously) the managers and captains of sporting teams. Many of these leaders too were a disappointment on grounds of intellect and morals. For the most part they were perceived as misusing *power* rather than as exercising due *authority*. (Chapters 5 and 6 deal with a few of these manifestations in different walks of life.)

The connection with the book's original theme was clear; all these flawed leaders were of one psychological type. What started out as a more or less scholarly comparison of two ways of thinking began to turn into an examination of just one of them, as manifested in particular leaders. It became a book about leadership, bound (if every they read) not only to irritate but also to mystify the existing corps of leaders. On the other hand, one of the book's themes is that there is a veritable army of decent, purposeful and clever people in the wings of power who ought to draw succour from an analysis of why such awful people rise, with such regularity, to high office.

The first of the two modes of thought (the original subject of the book) is the 'binary', in which the individual is swamped, despite himself, by the interpersonal aspect of relationships. In this mode the main thing is to control, dominate or seduce the Other in the interests of personal survival. An awful lot of awful people are like this, through no fault of their own. The other, contrasted, mode I have dubbed 'ternary' (borrowing the term from Gregory

Bateson).[2] In this mode interpersonal power is regulated, some of the time anyway, by some 'third corner' – an institution, a purpose or an idea. People who think this way value the third corner, see it as what life is about. Their instinct is to ask not, 'Shall I win?' but rather, 'What's it for?' (The argument is set out more fully in chapter 1.)

These people, of whom there is a sufficiency, make good leaders precisely because they are not badgered by threats to survival. From the vantage point, or haven, of the 'third corner' they can run personal risks in the pursuit of some higher purpose and observe themselves, as from a great height, in their own interpersonal relationships. They can, in short, see the joke, which means they are capable of thinking at two levels of abstraction at the same time. Their brains may well be wired up differently from those of the 'Survivor' type; how they get to be this way is the subject of chapter 2. Ternary thinking affords a grasp of paradox – a persistent theme throughout this book. The truly clever grasp the scale of their own silliness; the 'Survivors' are usually dim enough to think themselves clever (after all, they tend to succeed in silly examinations).

DEFECTIVE LEADERS RISE VIA THEIR DEFECTS

Inadequate leaders do not rise by accident. The great French essayist Jean de La Bruyère expressed a similar idea in his satirical *Caractères*: 'Men fall from great fortune because of the same shortcomings that led to their rise'. It is a comforting thought that flawed leaders will inevitably self-destruct, as Richard Nixon did, for example. Perhaps they did in seventeenth-century France, but nowadays an astonishing number seem to survive and flourish, spewing their neuroses all about them right to the bitter end. It is what they have to do to achieve their ambitions that renders them unfit, in the end, to bear authority. And yet, from time to time, saintly geniuses do rise to the top, often

[2] Gregory Bateson, 'On Morale and National Character', in *Steps to an Ecology of Mind*, St Albans, Paladin, 1978.

by fortuitous accident. Chapter 8 examines this phenomenon and suggests one or two homely means by which these felicitous accidents may be replicated on an organized basis.

We face, some commentators advice us, a 'crisis of leadership'. The more our leaders clamour to expose themselves in the media, the more their frailties become apparent, especially to the young. Our current leaders may well be no worse than their predecessors, but they *seem* worse, which amounts to much the same thing. Scepticism about authority, an old and worthy Anglo-Saxon tradition, is healthy. Cynicism and its bedfellow, apathy, are dangerous; sooner or later somebody is going to start burning books and pining after a really strong leader. Then we shall have nobody to blame but ourselves. On polling day in the 1983 British general election most of the young unemployed, who above all had cause to vote for something or other, stayed in bed.

We have no business blaming the Nixons, the Chamberlains and others of modest ability who rise above their proper level of capability; they simply fill a vacuum created by the indifference of abler people. We can't, either, blame the Bhagwan or the Rev. Moon if the heads of families abdicate that role in favour of crude material pursuits. Nor should be blame the militant shop steward in a factory in which the first-line manager is stripped, by technology and management 'theory', of all realistic authority. Leadership, seen as a process, is caused by following and most people follow by instinct. It is time we thought about these matters and perhaps did something too.

The 'third corner', be it an institution, a higher purpose or just an engaging idea, affords a certain graceful repose. In the ternary mode, it is actually possible to stop and think. The temptation then, having seen the joke, is (in Peter Cook's immortal words) to 'sink, giggling, into the North Sea'. In the meantime the super-energetic 'survivors', rat-like in their primal cunning, grab all the best jobs. Deploring it all is easy and sometimes quite funny. *Doing* something to redress the balance is harder and calls for a sense of outrage, a fear for the future and a great deal of energy. A small beginning, herein, is to poke accurate fun at our current sad crop of leaders. Because everybody knows about the problem it ought to be easy to dislodge a few of the worst of them. They are, after all, no more substantial than Lewis Carroll's playing cards. It ought also to be easy to clear the way for less obviously 'charismatic' but altogether more admirable people.

We begin therefore with some kind of presumption that most people have at least a pretty good hunch who ought not to rise to high position, on account either of their stupidity or of their mendacity or, likely, both. There is not, that is to say, a great problem in the identification of awful people for what they are. People usually don't mistake awful people for nice ones or vice versa; they make allowances for certain kinds of awfulness on the misguided assumption that certain benefits may flow from certain peculiar gifts. This is unwise. Awful people are always a disaster in the end, though the more cunning they are (very cunning, as a rule), the more likely it is that their tracks will be covered by confusion or their guilt projected on to others a little less quick on their feet.

The ideas herein are not exactly new. For example, James McGregor Burns, the eminent American writer on leadership, has drawn the distinction between 'transactional' and 'transformational' modes of leadership.[3] The former exists entirely within a web of interlocking deals made by 'survival' personalities. The latter transcends interpersonal transactions in order to focus on some imagined or desired state which the various transactions suppose. Burns's descriptions, particularly of political leaders, are always illuminating, but he does not really attempt a psychological explanation of the ways in which 'transactional' and 'transformational' leaders actually behave or think, nor of how they got that way.

This book does essay a link between 'object relations' in early infancy and the mode of thought of the resulting adult. This is an engaging speculation, though strictly a background for useful action. The presentation of modes of

---

[3] James McGregor Burns, *Leadership*, New York, Harper & Row, 1978.

thought in graphical form (o–o vs. ⧓) also has certain advantages over the use of mere words. The symbol ⧓ looks like two people engaged in an interchange *in the context of* something or other. Because the 'third corner' is box-shaped and thus constitutionally different, it carries also the notion of an abstractional shift. But, best of all, a wordless image frees us to invest the image with our own unique and complicated feelings about power, survival, authority and abstraction, not to mention 'transaction' and 'transformation'.

If words are really necessary, I favour 'raider' as a description of the o–o-oriented person (because it suggests the interpersonal dimension in fight or seduction) and 'builder' as a description of the ⧓-oriented person (because it focuses attention on the separate and abstracted object).

The reader may hear an echo of Adorno's famous 'authoritarian personality' in the raiderly psychology.[4] The binary obsession with the Other and with the projection of badness on to scapegoats and out groups is a crucial element in the make-up of the authoritarian psychology, according to Adorno and his colleagues. In the binary mode you may be intolerant of the Other for what you take him to *be* rather than for what he does or what he states to be his purpose. Finding out about the latter calls for hard work, sympathy and a real curiosity about what on earth other people are thinking.

Accordingly, this is a sexist book. It is not that all men are authoritarians of stunted intellect, but that a startling number of those who rise to high position are. Any possessor of a womb has an intellectual short-cut, potentially at least, to the notion of the 'third corner'. Theology too expresses the same essential idea in a slightly different form. It is all fairly obvious if your mind works in a certain way. After all, most of us can recall good bosses, good teachers, (maybe) good parents and good chums. Their qualities are the very devil to define, but almost everybody seems to recognize them when he or she sees them. But if we want to do anything about all of this, some of the ⧓ men too are going to have to do some intelligent fighting.

[4] T. W. Adorno *et al.*, *The Authoritarian Personality*, New York, Norton, 1969.

1

Binary vs. Ternary Thinking (Raiders and Builders)

In this chapter the basic distinctions between binary and ternary thinking are set out. The symbols ∘—∘ and ⏝ are used throughout in order to keep the ideas open and flexible, at least for a while, and to emphasize that the essential argument has to do with the structure of thought, not with personality. However, the reader who finds this strange may prefer to think in terms of the 'raider' type (∘—∘) and the 'builder' (⏝), the latter distinguished by his or her need to know what things are for and the need to be occupied usefully. There is nothing new about the basic idea; this is simply a novel way of presenting it, and it is one that many people seem to find illuminating.

There are really only two kinds of people in this world, and one of them ought never to be promoted to high rank – a gross generalization and a useful one, once the complications have been ironed out. Most of us have no difficulty at all in determining whom we like, whom we trust, and whom we approve of. There ought to be a high concurrence between those three responses, though an astonishing number of people are perfectly prepared to be led by others who fail all three tests. Led towards *what*, we must ask? Many people, for example, regard business and finance as essentially crooked trades. They are content, therefore, to render up leadership positions to those whom they would prefer not to invite into their own homes. It is not that they are taken in by the wide-boys, but they conceive of business as a kind of badland and business leadership as demanding wide-boy instincts.

The purpose of this chapter is to describe graphically the difference between those it is safe to trust and those we ought to keep a weather eye out for. It is less a description of personality than of mode of thought, though in chapter 2 there is an examination of the possibility that the wiring circuitry in the human brain may lie at the bottom of the characteristic ways people think; it is a persuasive argument when we come to consider the difference between binary and ternary thought. We are concerned, at each stage, not simply with national or political leadership but also with the behavioural phenomenon of leading – a state which may be deduced when the phenomenon of following is observed. The instinct for following determines leadership – in families, schools, work places, communities, churches, street gangs, trade unions, armies, sporting teams and so on.

A continuum between the two principal modes would look like Figure 1. That is to say, there are two ways for human beings to interact: either in terms simply of the survival/dominance dimension or in a way which is modified, mediated or otherwise made sense of by some third and abstracted element. But a continuum is too simple because most of us oscillate between these states, both according to regular cycles and also according to environmental circumstances. If you are set upon by a mugger with a flick-knife, it is prudent to respond, and quickly, in the survival (∘–∘) mode. There is not a lot of point in trying to seek out the basis for the attack at that

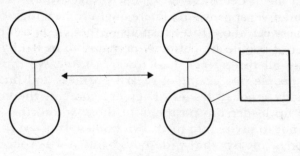

Figure 1

stage ('Look here, my dear chap, let's discuss . . .'). If you prevail, it is even more prudent to invoke the law (a third corner) and ultimately the judicial process.

The symbols ∘–∘ and ⌂ may be associated with a variety of opposed concepts, thus:

'Two-part'	*'Three-part'*
binary	abstracted/ternary
interpersonal	institutional
person	role/task
power	authority
fight/flight (survival)	dependence (work)
conflict	consensus
win/lose	share
defence	resolution
raiding	building

People who are able to cling to role in the context of task, to take a step backwards to make sense of events (or to see the joke in their own behaviour), to depend and be dependable, are safe to promote to high rank. Not everything they do will be informed by the ⌂ mode of thought, but they are capable of it and inclined towards it.

The others, those whose instinct is to see all interaction in terms of survival and dominance, tend to be locked into that mode of thought by the effects of their early primal experience. They do not – indeed, cannot – move readily between one state and the other. They are by instinct raiders rather than builders, but their survival capacity may well cloak them in a protective colouring; after all, it would be tactically foolish to reveal an intent to raid. To survive at all in the world (while clinging to normal human vulnerability and sensibility) means knowing how to tell the difference between true builders and raiders, however well camouflaged. Recognizing that people shift about on the continuum according to circumstance, most, by quite an early age, are already destined for a characteristic positioning – the artist consumed in his work at the ⌂ pole (where all interaction, even with family, is subordinate to relations with the object) and the paranoiac at the other.

For the remainder of the book, we shall be considering people in different walks of life as if they were relatively fixed on the continuum. That is merely a shorthand, although survival thinking is relatively rigid; it is much harder for the chronic survivor to retreat to a 'third corner' than it is for a ⊃o-thinking person to fight off a mugger on a street corner or in the boardroom. Later on we shall even consider the proposition that o–o-ness of mind and stupidity are actually the same thing.

BASIC ASSUMPTIONS

The ideas of *dependence* (where people behave as if they have to depend absolutely on someone or something) and *fight/flight* (where people behave as if they have to combat or flee from a terrifying enemy) have found their way into popular parlance since the late W. R. Bion discovered their significance in therapeutic groups after the Second World War.[1] He called these and other group phenomena 'basic assumptions'. They are, he said, 'instantaneous, instinctive and inevitable'. That is, they are not necessarily good or bad assumptions, simply omnipresent in the life of small groups. They may or may not contribute to the work the group has to do. Mostly, they are unconscious; anybody may slide, with bewildering speed, from one basic assumption to another, according to the emotional valency of the group. Leaders are particularly prone to such swings, and clever leaders learn to identify them and, as far as possible, to manage them. Some leaders are captured by basic assumptive emotions, as, for example, Baldwin and Chamberlain in flight, Hitler in fight and Jimmy Carter in expectant dependence.

The o–o and ⊃o states of mind may be seen as a personal, cognitive equivalent of basic assumptive life. o–o is a fight/ flight (or survival) mode and ⊃o a dependent one, in the sense that there is something or someone else to provide coherence for interpersonal relationships. Religion is a

---

[1] W. R. Bion, *Experiences in Groups*, London, Tavistick, 1961.

dependent system because God regulates human relations. So too is democracy, where the constitution performs a similar function. It is the 'third corner' that distinguishes human society from the jungle.

We shall return, later on, to the matter of constitutions. For the moment, the clearest possible illustration of the theme can be found in the remarks of Dr H. Coombs, formerly Governor of Australia's Reserve Bank and economic adviser to Prime Ministers of all political colours. Coombs, commenting on PM Whitlam's spectacular political demise, knew what happens when ∘–∘ brawling drives out ⊱⊐ structure:

When the constitution becomes a weapon used by one side, there is a serious risk that the procedures for the management and resolution of conflict will break down, leaving violence the only option open to the dissatisfied. I believe that in November 1975 Australia was brought closer to such breakdown and therefore to serious civil strife than at any time in its history. The breach at that time of widely held expectations of political behaviour changed the Australian constitution from a symbol of national consensus to a weapon to be used by whatever interests possess the legalistic cunning, political opportunism, and/or access to power to do so. Until the constitution regains a form and status that is substantially *neutral* [my italics] to political interests, and those interests can be relied upon to respect it, Australians will be divided by deep distrust – a distrust intensified and embittered by each succeeding evidence that our constitution is ineffective for its basic social purpose.[2]

Dependence (on some 'third corner' or other) is thus a perfectly normal state. After all, we all have to depend on others right from the beginning of our lives. But sometimes we use the term to denote a childish or resourceless state in adults. As such, it is a survival state because there is no higher-order logic to make sense of it. This is really *inappropriate* or *immature* dependence. Bion delineated a variant on dependence, the state of expectancy or pairing. Here group members behave as if two individuals can

[2] Maximilian Walsh, *Poor Little Rich Country*, Harmondsworth, Penguin, 1979, p. 99.

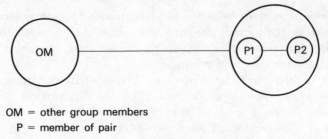

OM = other group members
P = member of pair

Figure 2

somehow be depended upon to mate, as it were, in order to sire a better tomorrow. This is sometimes going on when two members of a meeting, perhaps the chairman and one other, begin to talk together interminably. The test of the basic assumption is not the behaviour of the two (on whom all hope is projected) but the passive, voyeuristic behaviour of all the others. This too is a binary state (see Figure 2).

ABSTRACTION

It is important to recognize that the ternary mode involves an abstractional shift. The 'third corner' pertains to the relationship between the other two. We are, therefore, dealing not with a simple triangular relationship between three elements but with a binary relationship *made sense of* by some other type of element. 'Class' is a binary/power model, in the sense that it divides everybody into 'them' and 'us'. Elizabeth Bott's important studies of class perception distinguish between 'two-part power models' and 'three-part prestige models'.[3] But the latter is simply a three-decked societal hierarchy in the middle of which middle-class people locate themselves. Even her 'many-valued prestige models', sometimes with seven or eight strata, were a way for working-class people with middle-class pretensions to represent themselves as one step up from the bottom of the pile.

[3] Elizabeth Bott, 'The Concept of Class as a Reference Group', *Human Relations*, vol. 7, 1954.

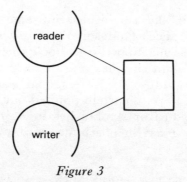

Figure 3

I have borrowed the word 'ternary' from Gregory Bateson,[4] who used it in the context of the strange relationship between infant/nanny/parent in the British middle- to upper-class family. At one level, that relationship is simply triangular, but, as Gathorne-Hardy points out (see page 117), it is a rare thing for the child's relationship with mother and nanny to be qualitatively similar. One of those relationships usually provides the context for the other. 'Ternary' isn't quite right either but will have to do; the best solution, perhaps, is simply to employ the symbol ⌐.

The symbol then becomes a mostly empty receptacle for the reader's thoughts on the subject matter of the book. By the end of the book, the symbol (by collecting fragments of reader ideas projected on to it) will have taken on a fuller and rounder meaning. No writer puts ideas into readers' heads; he strikes chords, if he is lucky, in harmony (or dissonance) with existing themes. He says, in effect: 'Come over here and look at these familiar objects from *this* angle!' This particular writer wishes to avoid a seductive o–o relationship with the reader; better by far to establish some kind of 'third corner' as a frame for the joint invention of new thoughts (see Figure 3). The 'third corner' is then both the book itself and the symbols which stand for the book's open-endedness.

Books are never completely set out in the mind's eye before the writing begins; they invent themselves as they

---

[4] Bateson, 'On Morale and National Character'.

go along, rather like a painting. Supreme storytellers like Dickens and Frances Hodgson Burnett actually wrote, to deadline, for serialization. For a book such as this, words are overloaded with complex and dissonant meanings. But the symbols o–o and ⌇, at this stage anyway, are relatively pure of meaning. Wittgenstein pointed out that the precise meaning of a word or symbol lies in its *future* use, even though we may grasp 'in a flash' its present use.

THE RAIDER, OR TWO-PART MAN

In the nature of things, a very high proportion of people in high office think most of the time in a o–o way, precisely because one of the best ways to prevail in competitive systems is to approach all activity in a binary/adversarial fashion. Once o–o people achieve high office, they screw up everybody else by squeezing institutional purposes, which are always ⌇ in character, into a crude o–o logic. They also, of course, contribute to gross inefficiencies. None of this is done wilfully; indeed, the o–o senior executive is usually well-intentioned and capable of great kindness (provided he gets a kickback of gratitude). His problem is that his predicament (which he does not see as a predicament) cannot be comprehended from the o–o vantage point. Instead, many of those around him – subordinates, members of his family and so on – experience his predicament for him.

Although he is capable of concentrating on issues, he is not consumed or taken over by them. His concentration is limited to the usefulness of the issue in sustaining his personal position. If he is a production manager, he will attend to quality because his job depends on it and not because he cannot bear to allow an inferior product out of his factory. If she is a mother, she will discipline her children in order to preserve her reputation as a good mother and not because the discipline is child-centred, part of her love and duty in the interests of the adult that child will grow into. Of course, production workers and children sense the difference between the two approaches and respond accordingly.

If I seem to use the royal 'he' rather a lot, I intend no disrespect to feminists of all sexes. Men, it seems to be the case, are far more likely to become entrapped in the ○—○ mode of thought than women. The reasons are twofold.

Evolutionary inheritance

Blessed with daughters, I have observed too many children's parties to believe that the thuggish, hyperactive brawling of little boys is entirely attributable to patterning on similarly disposed fathers. It is in the blood and based on hunting; it even leads otherwise rational and kindly men to mount excursions to shoot lovably furry animals, often with huge, soulful brown eyes. Meanwhile, back at the children's party, the girls have accepted the convention of party *society* and are playing the game(s).

Conditioning

Even without the inheritance, little boys are got at, not least by other little boys, but also in the nicest possible way by fathers. From these beginnings stem the intellectual biases of the sexes – boys towards the logic of numbers and girls towards the logic of words. Language is quintessentially a layered system. If I draw attention to the previous sentence ('Language is quintessentially a layered system') *as a sentence*, I withdraw to a higher abstraction, not separate but containing the idea of layering, at a higher layer.

Lyn Carlsmith, a research student at Harvard, pursued a typically feminine hunch during the 1960s. She reasoned that the (all-male) class of '64 at Harvard, born near the beginning of the Second World War, represented a research gold mine. She

looked up their scores on the Scholastic Aptitude Test (SAT), and compared their verbal scores with their mathematical scores. She then matched two groups of students, twenty in each. The first was of students whose fathers had been away for at least two years during the subjects' infancies, and had then permanently returned. The other was of students from similar social backgrounds, whose fathers had stayed at home. Eighteen out of the twenty in the 'father-present' group had the typical male bias towards the mathematical part of the SAT; only seven out of the twenty in the 'father-absent' group did so. Rather, their SAT scores looked like those of highly intelligent young women. Carlsmith found, too, that the earlier the father had left home, and the longer he was away, the more marked this effect became.[5]

There is no companion study of female children of the same vintage, those young women who, at an impressionable age, observed a previously omnicompetent mother reduced to a dithering travesty of her former self by the return of a usually less than wonderful male. It was enough to turn you into a feminist. The general rule is that the very best men manage to preserve their feminine instincts (without loss of masculinity), just as the best women harbour decisiveness, nerve and ambition. (It would be proper to confess at this point that this very book is being written by a male born at the beginning of the Second World War and exposed to male role models only in 'latency' (cf. page 73). This may well account for the elliptical style and the occasional bewildering lurch from, as it were, left brain to right brain, and back again.)

At school, the splitting of the sexes is intensified by subject specialization along the same numerical/verbal lines. The boys specialize in rational/logical serial relations between symbols and begin to develop special graphical skills; the girls begin to think systemically about people in networks or, as many men would have it, 'illogically' or 'emotionally'.

Anyway, playing with dolls demands a conceptualization not just of relations between dolls but also the relationship between all the dolls and the family or household they belong to. If little boys play with the idea of institution, the

[5] Quoted in Liam Hudson, *Human Beings*, St Albans, Paladin, 1978, p. 107; see also Lyn Carlsmith, 'Effect of Early Father Absence on Scholastic Aptitude', in Liam Hudson (ed.), *The Ecology of Human Intelligence*, Harmondsworth, Penguin, 1970.

institution will probably be the army, locked in mortal (and binary) combat with a detestable enemy.

It follows, of course, that more women ought to rise to high office. Unfortunately, the first to do so will, inevitably, rise via the virtual *absence* of the useful feminine logic so much needed in high places. It is very much in the interests of men (in their largely unconscious defence of male privilege) to ensure that those women who are permitted to rise will provide us with a chilling example of all the most disagreeable male traits.

THE BUILDER OR THREE-PART MAN

The 🔂 person, by contrast, is capable of absorption in some higher purpose and, for that purpose, able to lay on one side the business of direct human relationships. Therefore, the 🔂 type is capable of sacrifice and self-denial and able to lead others towards the goal via self-denial. Of course, history is littered with examples of charismatic leaders who pursued illusory goals. Arthur Koestler reminds us that throughout history, most human life has been laid down in religious zeal against one 'infidel' or another. We have therefore to examine goals closely and also to consider the 🔂 institutions you need to keep them under constant scrutiny.

The very best illustration of the difference between the o–o and 🔂 modes is to be found in relations between the sexes. It is the difference between two people shacked up together for as long as it suits them both (o–o) and another two people (or the same two) entering together into the institution of marriage (🔂). A lot of marriages are wrecked by one o–o partner not really entering into the spirit of the thing. A lot of men see all relationships as o–o power relationships, in some of which (e.g. marriage) you are automatically entitled to be top dog. In the efficient marriage, when things degenerate into 'I did not' 'Yes you did!' (o–o) the institution (or the 'third corner') is the place to which you retreat in order to reconsider the role of spouse. An argument about *that* may actually lead somewhere. The successful marriage is not fight-free (that would be unnatural) but simply contains *high-quality* fights.

THE GOOD LEADER

Over many years I have employed a simple stratagem to elicit the views of hundreds of people about successful formal leadership. I begin in the formal context of work by asking, 'How many bosses have you had in your working life?' Some people turn out to have had a great many. Then I ask, 'Which ones do you recall with gratitude and affection as really good?' Par for the course here is around one or two, at any rate a tiny minority of the whole. Most people, in other words, think most of their bosses are not particularly good at bossing. Last, I ask for a simple form of words to characterize the good ones.

When the questioning broadens, it turns out that the same words do for any authority figure and particularly for parents and teachers as well. By far the most common formulation is 'Tough (or firm) but fair'. This is not a particularly scientific formulation, but the important thing is that almost everybody seems to recognize it. Nobody says, 'Fair but tough' or even 'Tough *and* fair'. 'Tough' comes first, expressed as a necessity, then the modifier 'fair' – you *have* to be tough, but the toughness is OK if it is fair as well.

The interesting thing is that so many people then ascribe these qualities to people as though they were charismatic personal properties. So-and-so is a good boss because he is a 'tough but fair' sort of person. At any rate, that is the ०—० way of looking at it. My preferred interpretation is that people who are recalled in tranquility as 'good' in this way actually possess a certain kind of intelligence, a particular way of thinking that renders them memorable. Their great virtue is that they do not exercise charismatic influence at all; they simply keep their eye on the ball, with a certain humility, but nonetheless grow in the fulness of time and in the eyes of others into charismatic giants.

Where, then, does toughness and fairness come from? If we can answer the question, we have solved the problem 'What is a good boss?' and we will be some way towards ensuring that slots, when they fall vacant, are not filled from the shallow sea of ambitious, self-interested charismatics.

I go some way towards the 'contingency' view of leadership: that you need different types for different tasks in different circumstances.[6] But there comes a point where everybody (that is everybody who has ever experienced a good parent/teacher/boss – a lot of people never have!) recognizes a certain threshold beyond which certain universals obtain. At any rate, ⋈ people tend to know such things, and they are the most useful and important employees because they are capable of really caring about their work. On the other hand, if the work to be done is entirely shameful, I suppose, according to contingency theory a ∞ boss may be called for.

Tough

In the first place, ⋈ bosses are not tough on people but uncompromising in the pursuit of standards in relation to outputs. Much of the time they do not notice at all that achieving the output is tough on people. This is an unfortunate blind spot but not nearly so damaging as viewing people as objects to be manipulated in the interests of power. The ⋈ manager, at any rate, is tougher on himself than on anybody else, so at least it isn't unfair. Of course, one must recognize that this singleminded attachment to output can lead to problems (like poor delegation), but it is a more benign fault than the ∞ orientation, about which one can do very little.

In a famous speech, Prince Charles remarked that British industry lacked the 'human touch'. The statement was not

---

[6] American behavioural scientists call this 'situational leadership' and extract large sums of money from gullible industrial managers in exchange for teaching them how to behave differently with each subordinate. The subordinates see through it all, of course, though it doesn't seem to matter, provided the boss is good in the first place.

exactly wrong, simply misleading. One way of looking at British industry is that it is nearly all human touch and very little attachment to the object. It is better to have a minor Fascist in charge with a loving concern for, or even an obsession with, product quality than somebody indifferent to quality who has attended all the right 'human relations' courses. Then the tail wags the dog. It is better still to appoint ⟟ people and educate them in constitutional (⟟) human relations (see Chapter 8 below). Still, if you are going to have an important fallacy, it might as well be graced by royal assent.

So far, so good. But in the era of the huge corporation, a great many people, among them managers, become isolated from the essential purposes of the organization. Indeed, some corporate purposes are not exactly admirable. If we take two dietary staples of Englishmen through the centuries, bread and beer, we discover that both industries have recently had to be forced, by relentless consumer pressure, to reintroduce 'real' elements into their products. (Of course, quite a few of those same consumers were married to the producers of bread and beer.)

In the case of the British bread industry, new technology — the 'notorious' Chorleywood process – had enabled the cheap production of an extraordinary white factory loaf largely devoid of the value (e.g. that of wholemeal flour) traditionally associated with bread. One consultant surgeon went so far as to say: 'Not only does the white loaf do no good, it is actually harmful to the body. Every encouragement should be given to the abolition of this foul food . . . the white loaf is not even fit to be given away.'[7] The point was at that stage there were only three major bread combines in Britain (now two!), and they had contrived, through acquisition, to tie up most of the high street outlets. One, in its TV advertising, even presented the bread's primary virtue as its springiness to the touch or squeeze, as if the product were a foam-rubber toy.

What concerns us is the possibility for leadership in an

[7] Elizabeth David, *English Bread and Yeast Cookery*, Harmondsworth, Penguin, 1979, p. 37.

industry bent on prising maximum profit out of minimum product. How do the people feel when it comes to 'motivating' or being 'motivated' if you can't take the product seriously? You might, I suppose, be the head of a competent and dedicated sub-system in such an organization – for example, a service department – and thus buffer yourself from the pointlessness of the end product. In the end you are likely to be forced back to the o—o model; in fact, I have the impression that 'human relations' tend to be spectacularly good, as a compensation, in those big corporations where the true 'demand' for the product has a spurious feel to it.

For example, I overheard a conversation in one of the most successful and humanely managed international perfumery houses, which showed how different people cope with the problem. One brave soul said: 'Look, shampoo is just detergent with a bit of perfume in it. We've just found a clever way to charge three times as much as—for it!' A colleague, horrified, responded that their output was not clean hair at all, but a kind of well-being – a *sense* of beauty, enhanced by the price of the product. You feel better after an expensive shampoo, she seemed to be saying, and she gave every appearance of believing it. She had to, I suppose.

The consumer movement for 'real' British beer was also a spectacular success story. Traditional British beers are volatile, short-lived and very tasty. Over the years the big brewers (another near-monopoly – six firms) had weaned most of the consumers on to a bland, fizzy, easily stored, cheaply produced, lager-type beer. The minority of 'real' beer fanciers didn't mind, as long as there was a choice for the consumer. They turned nasty when the brewery companies began to withdraw even that. You might say there was an over-supply of o—o 'marketing' experts and too few people (e.g. brewers) who cared about or understood the loving, careful ⋈ process of making a traditional drink out of natural ingredients. (Here o—o = get people to buy it whatever it is and ⋈ = take care of the product and the 'marketing' will take care of itself.)

Secondly, there was nobody who foresaw the passion and

energy of the consumer revolt when it came to embarrass the big corporations. To foresee such things you need to think in a ⟁ fashion. At the same time, in an attempt to reduce landlords' perks, some of the firms started to replace licensed landlords with salaried managers and oak beams with plastic or, better still, simulated oak plastic. This move neglected the truth that the British pub is an institution, not simply a place to pass various liquids through the alimentary system and out again. In the rural pub the vicar and policeman and all they represent (virtue, sin and dependence) may well be present at the bar. Some even say that the pub has replaced the church as the nexus of rural life.

But to the o─o mind in search of promotion the pub was simply the fag-end of a linear managerial line, with a supply of cost and quality-controlled 'product', plus an electronic, pilfer-proof till for the *real* product. Such people gained, for a while, a young, plastic clientele and lost, perhaps for ever, a long and admirable tradition. Only those with a ⟁ orientation foresaw this, mourned the passing and, in the end, fought back. Once the fight started they quite understandably mobilized their own o─o (fight/survival) instincts by making ogres of the big brewers and by denying the existence of decent ⟁ minds within the industry, although of course they existed.

So the quality of leadership and the nature of respect for leaders must be viewed in the context of outputs and their true usefulness. There is an enormous worldwide industry, whose components are management training, education, consultancy, research, development, etc., etc., housed in prestigious universities and firms, which contrives, mostly, to forget that consumers and producers too know, in their heart of hearts, how pointless a lot of modern output really is. The hope is that 'management techniques' can be applied equally to organizations of wildly varying usefulness and morality. The o─o mind doesn't give a damn about output, provided there is a job to hand and, perhaps, the chance to 'get ahead'. The ⟁ mentality worries away at the illogic and immorality of it all. The ⟁ mind asks, 'What's it *for*?'

It may not be fanciful to divide societies into three camps, two fundamentally stable and benign and one, according to this analysis, volatile and malevolent:

(1)   the boys at the top: not necessarily very clever or very responsible but at least safe enough to think about alternatives; rather isolated from the consumers; ageing now so that ⊅ considerations are beginning to bear in from other existences (as parent, community member, etc.);

(3)   the people at the bottom of organizations, producers and consumers (who may be married to each other), many of whom care about standards, quality and the purpose of things (but maybe not obviously at work) and most of whom are resigned to staying at, or near, the bottom;

(2)   the risers in the middle, focused on competition and movement rather than the verities of life, and perpetually threatened by the possibility of 1 and 3 talking to each other. The risers are at an age when ∘–∘ considerations tend to crowd out morals; a few of them are *really* dangerous.

It is as if a significant number of the risers and strivers after advancement are locked awkwardly into a kind of grown-up spotty adolescence, halfway between the innocence and simplicity of childhood and the certainties of adulthood, neither one thing nor the other. Such restless ambition is dangerously malleable; Hitler was about 40 at the beginning of his final run for power. His most significant new party recruits were young, rising white-collar workers and a few members of the 'sinking middle class'. Goebbels became a *Gauleiter* at 28; Baldur von Schirach was 26 when he was appointed Reich Youth Leader; and Himmler was only two years older when he was promoted to Chief of the SS. This use of ambitious young men distinguished the Nazis from the competing and relatively ⊅ parties of the time.

The *Gauleiters*, the middle management of Nazism, were not all roughnecks, any more than middle managers in bread and beer. In fact, of Hitler's seventy-three *Gauleiters*, no fewer than twenty were drawn from the teaching profession! These were Adorno's 'pseudo-conservatives'[8] – the kind of people who never experienced a rigidly authoritarian school as a sinister institution. At the height of Germany's economic crisis, surrounded by despair, Hitler said: 'Never in my life have I been so well disposed and inwardly contented as in these days.'[9] He was about to get his chance, and so were his lads, and the devil take the country.

It is important to remember that at any given time a high proportion of 'managers' in commerce and industry have risen from non-managerial stock. Pyramids are broad at the base, and although it is true that most of the top jobs at the apex are reserved for sons of the Establishment, the gross proportion of climbers is high. One study in British retailing showed 55 per cent of all managers to have climbed from families in which the father's occupation was manual work.[10] If the sons of 'clerical and other non-manual' fathers were included as 'working-class', the proportion rose to a remarkable 92 per cent. This is not the classic picture of Oxbridge or Ivy League preponderance in the managerial ranks. But, of course, most of the climbers are clustered just above the bottom of the pyramid, and it is the ambitious and thwarted people, fated to stay there, who vent their frustrations on those below who have not managed to clamber aboard the (overcrowded) lifeboat. Often the climbers harbour a barely disguised contempt for those still, so to speak, in the water. Contrary to popular belief, it might work very well indeed to conscript the entire output of Eton College into first-line managerial jobs in British industry. They would know nothing about what you *don't* do and would be impervious to the usual jibes. Some of them might even be fascinated by all the machinery. However, it would be important to exclude from this

[8] Adorno *et al.*, *The Authoritarian Personality*.
[9] Joachim C. Fest, *Hitler*, Harmondsworth, Penguin, 1977, p. 410.
[10] S. G. Redding, *The Working Class Manager*, London, Saxon House, 1979.

scheme the sons of *nouveaux riches* parents, for the reasons given above.

The point is that if you are at the bottom, a manager is a manager is a manager – a paid-up member of 'them'. 'Them' is a club you can't get into, so the only alternative is to join a club yourself, another rigidly exclusive power network called a union. Meanwhile the climbers try to pretend that the distinctions between first-line management and the boardroom are of degree rather than of kind. If they got to spend any time in boardrooms, they would know better.

The disposition of upwardly mobile people showed up with astonishing clarity in the USA in the late 1960s, as opposition to the Vietnam war gradually hardened. The mythology was that 'youth' was against the war, an impression nightly reinforced by TV pictures of disaffected students protesting at up-market universities – Berkeley, Michigan, Columbia and so on. The truth was that the vast mass of college students at less fashionable institutions was markedly more hawkish than the population at large. In general, it was the least well educated of the population who tended to oppose American involvement in Vietnam most strongly of all – after all, they it was who had to go away and fight the bloody war.

Only the Establishment students worried about Vietnamese casualties (as well as the American) in particular and the morality of the war in general. The down-market students

appear like so many poor souls in limbo trying to scramble out of the harsh realities and stern beliefs of the American working class into the loose, cool freedom of that upper-middle-class culture in which, not needing to 'make out', a fellow could afford to think, with an idealism perhaps tinged with condescension, about the opportunity to change things.[11]

But then again (this will sound like a Platonic argument in favour of aristocracy), America was led at the time by anti-Establishment, newly risen businessmen, advertising

---

[11] Godfrey Hodgson, *In Our Time*, London, Macmillan, 1976, p. 390.

agency hacks and so on. As Father Andrew Greeley of the National Opinion Research Centre commented:

If the white ethnic is told in effect that to support peace he must also support the Black Panthers, Women's Liberation, widespread use of drugs, free love, campus radicals, Doctor Spock, long hair and picketing clergymen, he may find it very difficult to put himself on the side of peace.[12]

The protesters who took a ⟐ or 'What's it for?/is it right?' line were of true-blue Establishment stock. That is partly why Nixon, Agnew *et al.* hated them so. By the end the great mass of protest came from ambitious and hawkish risers whose self-interest was finally beginning to be jeopardized.

Competing aggressively and climbing the ladder of 'success' are normal processes, as Daniel J. Levinson reminds us. After his twenties a typical man enters a 'settling down' phase.

At the start of this period, a man is on the bottom rung of his ladder and is entering a world in which he is a *junior member*. His aims are to advance in the enterprise, to climb the ladder and to become a *senior member* in that world. His sense of well-being during this period depends strongly on his own and *others' evaluation of his progress* towards these goals. [my italics][13]

Looked at another way, this period is startlingly like adolescence – transitional, awkward, self-conscious and self-obsessed. Of course, as with adolescence, a few people sail through without apparent embarrassment, presumably those who feel able in some way to take the next phase, whatever it is, for granted. For Levinson the next phase, after about 35, is 'becoming one's own man', closely followed by the fabled 'mid-life transition' after about 40. The inveterate climber, it seems, gets stuck with 'settling down' so he never 'becomes his own man' at all. Perhaps (see Chapter 2) he got stuck earlier still.

---

[12] ibid., p. 394.
[13] Daniel J. Levinson, *The Season of a Man's Life*, New York, Ballantine, 1978, p. 60.

Our 'tough' boss is, therefore, someone who is adequately attached to the output of the system. He is not in conflict with it or ashamed of it, and most of the people who work with him are aware that his toughness relates to that fact and not to a need to bully people. The father who has a hunch about what families are for and institutes discipline accordingly is a world removed from the father who wants to preserve his creature comforts via an autocratic regime. From the outside they look rather similar – 'strict' – but only one is manufacturing authoritarian/anti-authoritarian ○—○ children.

The really sensible father (or boss) not only thinks about what the institution is for, but also institutionalizes time to talk or argue about it with all the members of the system. They don't have to like the institution, but they should know it exists, that there is 'nothing personal' in the discipline. As a matter of fact, it isn't entirely clear these days what the family is for. Operating definitions (usually unconscious) clearly differ from family to family, and since so many people stopped going to church (except to get married), the linking institution (marriage) has become less useful for explaining things. Unfortunately (as marriages concern men and women), the linking institution and its foundation (the Church) are starting to seem a little sexist to some people (mostly women).

'Fair'

'Tough', as we saw above, properly relates to output, so toughness is ultimately impersonal. Fairness is more complicated because it pertains primarily to human relationships, but the rule is similar: we ought to achieve it by distancing ourselves from people via the use of institutions. Herein lies a paradox. The kindest and most empathetic people (in interpersonal relations) achieve institutional fairness through distancing, but those who use interpersonal contact to regulate fairness in the system tend to manipulate people as objects.

This paradox can be expressed in another way. In order to be optimistic about people at all, you need to have passed through the trough of absolute pessimism about man's inhumanity. Once you've seen the worst in man (and especially in upwardly mobile man) you will leave nothing to personal relations, because if you do, the ∘–∘ aggressors will prevail and the meek will definitely not inherit anything, let alone the earth. Instead you will create rules (or, if you like, institutions) which, once established, free people to be creative and lovable again. The point is that the intelligent boss does not depend on the love or respect of each of his people. If he does, he rides a frisky steed. Instead, he earns collective respect by establishing a system which is fair – i.e. the same for everybody.

My sister was once involved in a strike call. It was the classic dilemma: she didn't want to offend her work colleagues in a closed-shop firm but, being a widow, she needed the money, and anyway the union was behaving irresponsibly. In the end nobody came out because Mr X (the boss) was 'such a nice man'. Admirable as the sentiment was, I quibbled in what seemed to be a churlish way with the logic. I argued that there were, in fact, three possibilities to consider:

(1)   everybody strikes, which means Mr X has gone wrong somewhere (worst case);
(2)   everybody wavers and then decides to stay because they like X (better);
(3)   nobody contemplates strike action because X's system somehow makes the union irrelevant (best of all).

Anyone who has observed such situations, repeated endlessly (and especially in the Anglo-Saxon cultures), is inclined to believe in rules, rule books, formal institutions and carefully elaborated role relationships. Possibly the biggest obstacle to organizational harmony in the USA, Britain and Australia is a deep-seated distrust of formality, based on a confusion of authority with rigidity. Originally, this distrust was an habitual British working-class reaction to rules bent for Establishment greed, especially among the Irish. Inevitably, this world view migrated to the old colonies via convicts and a host of disenchanted others. From

the eighteenth century on, other European emigrants
swelled the numbers in the USA, most of them with very
good reasons for distrusting big bureaucratic organizations.

It is only a short step to confusing formal institutions
(which are neutral) with the ∘–∘ types who sometimes bend
them to their personal whim. I find when I talk in public of
such matters as form, structure and institution that I am
often accused of espousing discipline, control and authoritarianism because many people *hear* them as just the same.
Our collective problem is that so few people have seen a
proper flexible institution at work in their homes, their
schools, their work or their communities that they are
incapable of distinguishing between an organization in the
grip of ∘–∘ exploitation (all are assumed to be this) and an
organization in which personal hegemony really has been
surrendered to the rule book.

Our present corps of workers and managers is the first in
recent history to have had no collective experience of the
verities. To have seen active service in the Second World
War, you need to have been born by about 1925. Some
American, British and Australian youngsters have, it is
true, shouldered the burden of domino theory in Korea and
Vietnam, but they can hardly be said to have experienced
authority as a 'good object' as a result. For that you need to
have a deep conviction about the value of your output (see
above, p. 22). The young British National Servicemen who
went to Suez had the feeling of participating in a post-
colonial pantomime, as though the small quantity of
(mostly Egyptian) blood spilled was really ketchup.

The bestselling novelist James Clavell, born in 1924,
captures the experience of his generation. Clavell, a mil-
lionaire many times over, doesn't try to write bestsellers: 'I
find it awesome that I've got this multi-million audience
out there. I don't write for a million people. How can I? I
simply write to try and satisfy myself.' But Clavell was one
of the one in fifteen people to survive Changi, the notorious
Japanese prisoner-of-war camp. There he learned 'how to
live one day at a time, how to endure . . . . People suppose
that being wealthy means having assets . . . but, honestly, I
don't feel that way. . . . Since the day I got out of Changi,

being wealthy means being alive.'[14] Anthony Burgess, another enormously successful writer, was born in 1917. He had to endure the death of his first wife and the diagnosis (at the age of 42) of an incurable brain tumour. He was given a year to live; he wrote five novels in the space of the next twelve months. A lesser novelist but a richer one, Paul Erdman, had the good fortune to spend ten months in jail as a result of currency irregularities revealed by the failure of the Swiss-based bank he managed. Like Hitler, Erdman spent his jail sentence in reasonably pleasant surroundings (a room in a Basle monastery converted for use as a prison). He was allowed a typewriter, and he had the intelligence to seize on the fortuitous 'space' created by his misfortune.[15] These three successful writers (I exclude *Mein Kampf* as a work of literature, though it emerged from the same kind of 'space') found their vocation late in life, as a result of the experience of being constrained, even trapped, in one way or another.

Yet in the new generation we find, ironically enough, a great yearning to be 'free', and especially to be free from 'authority' – viewed as a bad object and confused with power. And why not, if parents are crudely materialist or self-seeking and schools bureaucratized and uninterested? The trouble is that the pursuit of freedom for its own sake leads almost inevitably to the chains of aimlessness and boredom, just as the pursuit of bestsellers as a primary aim is doomed to failure. In the long run, bestsellers, freedom, profit, and, ultimately, happiness are by-products of other, worthy, pursuits.

Therefore to make sense of the idea 'fair', rather than use words such as 'rule', 'authority' or 'institution' – all tainted by our experiences of parents, teachers and bad bosses – let us use, running the same risk, the word 'constitution'. I take a constitution, formal or otherwise, to be an agreed arrangement about how people will relate to one another. The more formal it is, the clearer it can be and, again somewhat paradoxically, the easier it will be to change. If

[14] James Clavell, interview with Philip Oakes, *Sunday Times*, 31 May 1981.
[15] Daniel Seligman, 'Luck and Careers', *Fortune*, 16 November 1981.

you are clear about something in the first place, it is possible to know which bits to change. If you are unclear, you don't know where to start or, indeed, what the people think the existing arrangements are.

To be free, paradoxically, you must be bounded. To attempt to do without boundaries is to become entrapped in a power web of covert and subtle accommodations. For change you need stability; without stability people pursue survival and, after ructions, return to square one or worse. Anyone who has watched children grow up, suffering under varieties of parental 'theory', knows that they need boundaries in order to grow towards true autonomy. If you, so to speak, push them in the deep end in order to toughen them up for their encounter with a naughty o—o world, they *do* learn to swim, and fast, but the legacy is a lifetime of drowning nightmares. If you over-protect, they push clumsily to find their proper limits and end up hating you in the end. The right balance is a boundary like a chalk line on the ground rather than a stone wall. You are free to cross it, but you are also very clear where it is and what the consequences of trespass will be. A constitution is such a chalk line. Bad parents, of the one persuasion or the other, make us reject formality, and we usually pay a heavy cost for it. The problem with such statements, essentially neutral, is that they sound Fascist, conservative, authoritarian to many people, as I have discovered to my cost.

So, returning to the good boss (see Figure 4), he achieves two things.

(1) By focusing on output (having associated himself with work he can live with), he reassures subordinates that his picture of the institution (⌂) is output-led. The output justifies the institution and him. He is not boss of the people so much as slave of the purpose. The people can live with this, no matter how 'tough' he is.

(2) By creating 'fair' constitutional structures, he ensures that most situations have a common rule to deal with them (cheers from Conservatives, cries of 'Fascism' from the 'left') and, furthermore, he institutionalizes some way for the people to have a stake in constitu-

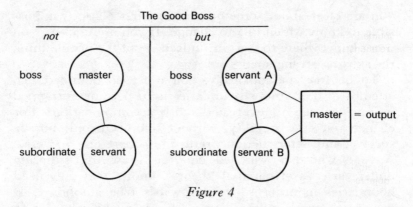

Figure 4

tional change (cheers from the 'left', cries of 'Social-ism' from Conservatives).

Up to a certain size of organization,[16] it may be suffi-cient to achieve (1) above alone. Beyond that size the good boss must take care of (2) as well. It doesn't follow that the good boss would describe his work thus or be conscious of these aspects. It is, however, a formulation based on many years of boss-watching. It is a description of what ensues when people who quite naturally think in a ⌐ way rise to positions of authority and achieve great success. It will be quite obvious that other sorts of people achieve success as well; later I shall argue that their success is always pre-carious and achieved at great cost.

To represent the twin requirements of output orientation and constitution, we need a three-dimensional model (see Figure 5). Gregory Bateson argued that the two areas of human endeavour which bridge the worlds of conscious and subconscious are religion and art. We see here a rough

[16] The essential building-blocks of large organizations are the 'stratum 3' sub-systems at their base – that is, those three-tier units within which it is still possible for everybody more or less to know everybody else. At stratum 4 the game changes, as Jaques points out in *A General Theory of Bureaucracy* (London, Heinemann, 1976); you begin to need constitutional structure as well as a sense of clear and unconflicted purpose. Big stratum 3 units (say, 300 people) are difficult to manage, but the work still has a concrete quality. At stratum 4, you have to abstract the system. It calls for a different type, and level, of brain.

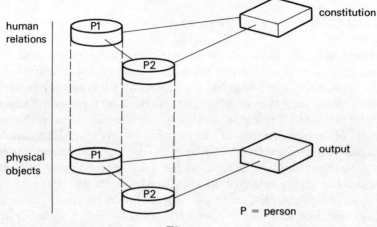

Figure 5

approximation, with output representing the artefact (the epicentre of the artist's field) and the constitution representing the rules and rituals that govern relationships between people and with authority. As drawn, P1 and P2 are two people who relate to one another *in the context of* an institution (suitably constitutionalized) which produces an output.

At first glance, the boss (e.g., P1) who insists upon dealing with an employee (P2) at work, in the context of constitution and task, may seem to be a cold fish, seeking a distance from the warmth of interpersonal relations. Yet this is the boss who is 'always the same' wherever you meet him, who embodies stability and continuity. This is the kind of person who is perceived as grafting on to the humdrum management task the vision and trustworthiness of a 'leader'.

To summarize, the $\triangleright$ mentality, conscious or otherwise, is appropriate for leadership roles. That is to say that those who achieve *durable* success are *capable* of operating within the $\triangleright$ mode, even if, under pressure, they spend substantial periods in $\circ\!\!-\!\!\circ$ aggressive/survival activity. They are, to put it simply, interested in their work for its own sake and anxious to be fair to people – employees, customers and others.

BIPODS VERSUS TRIPODS: REGULATING RAIDERS

There are, of course, a great many people who succeed in material terms by virtue of their opposite ∘–∘ orientation. That is, they are badgered by insistent survival needs and are anxious, above all, to exert control over their environment. Trying to get very rich is the most obvious way of achieving this. The institutions created by such people are fuelled by the unpredictabilities and excitements of interpersonal relations. They are rarely boring but always unstable because, as they are built on a ∘–∘ base, they have a bi-podal character. A tripod stands by itself; boring perhaps, but you can go away for a while and it will still be there. A bipod requires a constant steadying hand, and the ∘–∘ type of person needs to be the one doing the steadying or shaking, or whatever is in his whim. He needs a bi-podal system, because it needs him.

The costs of too many ∘–∘ types in high places are difficult to discern and impossible to quantify. In simple terms, such people tend unknowingly to export their internal anxieties to their colleagues, employees, families and surrounding communities in the form of fear, uncertainty and immature dependence. Also, because it is largely immaterial to the obsessive climber what his product or output is to be (provided it makes money or ensures control), he may well contribute hidden costs in pollution and economic irrelevance.

When Jim Slater[17] took over Crittall-Hope, a major international metal window manufacturer, he announced at his first board meeting, 'The product we are going to make is *money*!' When Slater-Walker finally unloaded Crittall-Hope to yet another conglomerate, the new owners announced that, for the first time since the 1930s slump, the window business was running at a loss. When the Bank

---

[17] Slater, one-time chairman of the spectacularly bankrupt conglomerate Slater-Walter, remarked when asked by a journalist about the company's South African interests that he had never noticed any particular injustice there. The point is, we have no reason at all to doubt his word. See Charles Raw's important book, *Slater-Walker*, London, André Deutsch, 1977.

of England bailed out Slater-Walker itself, the rescue cost the British taxpayer millions. In the meantime, while a few people had made a great deal of money, a large number of people were left reflecting that they had just spent a lot of years (and in some cases money) engaging in activities with no real point at all.

It would be going too far to argue that we should try to do away with the ∘–∘ type of leader or to exclude him from high office completely. In the first place, it is not realistic because ∘–∘ people have the strength and guile of ten men, just as a cornered animal fights as fiercely as ten. They cannot be controlled, any more than the tides. Secondly, they do inject and release energy. Most organizations need more of this commodity, even if some of it is aimless. However, the day is fast approaching when too many of the ∘–∘ 'squeaky wheels' (people who get promotion by asking for it – endlessly) will be seen as a luxury we cannot afford. ∘–∘ people ought to be seeded in critical and moribund loca- tions in organizations, like selective week-killer, rather than simply given way to meekly. Too many of them, and the entire eco-system goes haywire. We should, however, think very hard indeed about political processes which throw up ∘–∘ national leaders (cf. Reagan, Thatcher, Fraser above). These, in the long run, may be a very expensive luxury because they lead to such events as Vietnam, the Second World War, etc., etc. The two-party system has a lot to answer for.

We face a number of problems in regulating the relation- ships between ∘–∘ and ⊱⊐ elements within organizations.

(1) Many existing office holders are quite bad at dis- tinguishing between ∘–∘ and ⊱⊐ orientations or even recog- nizing the importance of doing so. ∘–∘ office holders are hopeless at it, because their brains don't work that way.
(2) The nicest and gentlest office holders tend to harbour a sneaking admiration for the 'cowboys'. Sometimes quite nice people will promote those they not only don't like but don't trust either, on the assumption that a little brutality will move things along a bit. General Amin of Uganda got his start this way, by courtesy of senior British military

personnel impressed by his combination of unquestioning loyalty and general thuggishness.

(3)   Office holders like to subvert formal systems in the interests of personal patronage. The one near-certain route to the top for a young man is to find a patron, fifteen to thirty years his senior, who happens to have a lot of daughters and no sons at all. It is a natural human urge to 'bring on' a young man in one's wake, thus satisfying the impulse to 'generativity' referred to by Erikson in the ageing male.[18] Whether as powerful an instinct obtains among women, or between men and women, we are not yet in a position to say. On slim evidence, it appears so.

(4)   Office holders are almost invariably uncertain about their capacity to judge character. It is a fiendishly difficult thing to imagine how a particular human being will behave five years hence, and five years older, in a new setting. Most top people are easy prey to any reasonably plausible and confident 'expert', or quack, on selection. Most senior office holders studiously avoid arguing formally and at length about their personal and probably implicit definitions of a 'good bloke'. Instead, 'bizarre' names pop up at selection panels, prejudices are aired and ill-considered and probably expensive promotional decisions are taken on skimpy or biased evidence.

It doesn't help either to aim at 'objectivity' because that way you simply leave out all the subjectively knowable elements that really matter. To leave out contemplation of the o—o/⟨⟩ dimension, which nearly everybody knows about intuitively, is to court disaster. Nearly every selection process leaves it out, with the result that very considerable numbers of sensible, honest, dedicated ⟨⟩ people languish, unrecognized, until it is too late.

A few years back, when I was teaching at the Manchester Business School, the managing director of one of the big oil companies came to the school. He had a reputation for brilliance, but he didn't look particularly charismatic. At the bar, late in the evening, he overheard somebody refer to

[18] E. Erikson, 'Identity and the Life Cycle', *Psychological Issues*, vol. 1, 1959.

an obscure village pub in Devon. It turned out that he knew that pub, and all the other pubs in the area, plus the proprietors' names. When quizzed about this unlikely erudition, he revealed his party trick: 'I know every pub in Britain!' he announced. He did too. Armed only with a photographic memory, he had spent fifteen years on the road looking for service station sites, which means *corner* sites.

The assembled managers tested the claim but had to admit defeat. The point is he had been a late-comer, and somewhere out there on the trail a modicum of humility had set in. In the end he was one of the most successful and respected executives in Britain, yet nobody had spotted him for the fast track. He had the combination of perseverence and luck to win through in the end. Most don't.

We can't outrun the survivors, but we can, if we try, ensure that the slow-flowering genius of the ⌐ mind gets its chance. Anyone who has seen a large organization 'turned round' by a new man at the top cannot fail to be impressed by the incredible speed of the process. Commercial organizations deep in the red sweep to profit in two or three years, against all the odds. Moribund schools suddenly take on a new lease on life. Demoralized armies spring to new determination and physical courage. Even countries not at war 'turn round' under the influence of a great leader.

We can call it 'charisma' if we want, but the speed of the process suggests that everybody, or almost everybody, in the organization has 'known' all along, in a semi-conscious way, what had to be done. Suddenly this mass intelligence is mobilized in a collective way by a sense of 'rightness' and relief. The surge of energy accounts for the extraordinary change, and the energy pours into the 'third corner' (⌐), now clarified via the leader.

In the UK, Australia and the USA there is an adequate supply of such thoughtful, late-flowering but potentially energetic leaders, but we have failed dismally to recognize the ⌐ nature of their worth and to make space for them among the self-interested survivors. It has cost us dear in commercial competition with the likes of Japan, where management and leadership is very old-fashioned, uncharismatic and output-centred. It may yet cost us dear in the political sphere, in which the o—o mentality has its hands on several billion dollars' worth of lethal weaponry.

2
The Leader in the Nest

Although both the binary and ternary modes of thought are quite normal (and we tend to oscillate between them), some people seem to 'fix' in one mode rather than the other. How they get this way in the first place is the subject of this chapter. The principal components are breasts (the ⌐○ mode) and birth/ pecking order (a strictly ○—○ consideration). The reader who finds neo-Freudian speculation a bit sickly, or simply unconvincing, may pass straight on here. However, the very laid-back (⌐○) reader may wish to linger a while. The point is that patterns of thought seem to be 'soldered in' very early in life, and so, tactically speaking, we may be wasting our energies on trying to reform or otherwise control raiders.

One of the nice things about speculation about very young infants is that, while you can never prove anything, no one can prove you wrong either. The psychiatrist R. D. Laing claims that almost anyone can relive the experience of being born if he is prepared to concentrate hard enough. But until we can teach language in the womb, we are left with speculation. What you speculate may well depend on your own experience in the womb; if you 'remember' it as a hospitable place, then you may be inclined to acknowledge the importance of pre-natal life for ultimate personality.

I find it convincing that later character will somehow be affected by, for example, the experience of swimming for nine months in diluted gin, sustained by an oxygen/ cigarette-smoke mix. Or, if a mother is an international (gin-drinking) gymnast who takes the view that it is cissy to be too inactive during pregnancy, then I give you a baby with a special, and slightly giddy, perspective on life. Furthermore, Frédéric Leboyer's approach to childbirth seems to me eminently sensible, mainly because it accords with most mothers' common sense. His babies arrive in a warm, quiet, dimly lit, undrugged world and are not suspended upside-down and slapped on the bottom; they spend the first few moments in the outside world either crawling on mum or floating in a warm bath not unlike the recently vacated, but latterly rather cramped, quarters.

During this period the Leboyer baby may be seen not to cry in terror but to peer about knowingly and calmly, as if surveying a scene imagined and speculated upon but, till now, hidden. In the event of a Caesarean birth, Leboyer is not above chatting to the new-born infant about the misfortune and explaining its necessity. Baby, no doubt, does not understand a word, but the music comes through. The essential element is the calm; if the new-born baby can introject a sense of calm, then perhaps his perspective ever afterwards will be suffused with calm. On the other hand, if the womb was a bilious prison and the birth a frenzied nightmare, it will probably not be calm that the infant projects on to his environment later on. Also there is a suggestion, difficult to put to proof, that Leboyer babies end up cleverer – difficult to prove because they are bound to have clever mums anyway.

Let us be clear: I am not suggesting we choose our leaders by reference to a sort of pre-natal curriculum vitae, simply that calm is an important quality of successful leadership, and a bad birth represents a bad start for an unflappable leader of men.

Breasts

Be warned, dear reader, what follows is unashamedly Freudian, Kleinian and so on because, whatever one thinks of Freud and his disciples, it goes against logic to deny the importance of the mother's breast. It is important because when we consider the leader we have also to consider the relationship between people and objects. Bad leaders treat people as if they were mere objects, and dangerous bad leaders objectify complex circumstances, converting them into a focus on simple-minded, easily hateable bogeys. Hitler did both, on a colossal scale.

The new-born infant encounters the breast or its pale surrogate (a bottle) in a number of guises:

(1) a visible, touchable object;
(2) a mysterious device capable magically of converting inner feelings of emptiness and discomfort into a sense of supreme well-being;
(3) an idea about an object.

Some have gone so far as to argue that the primeval circuitry of the brain is programmed with a preconception – a kind of 'breast-shaped blank' – and that the circuits in the developing brain will not forge correctly until the preconception merges with the physical object to form the idea 'breast' (see Figure 6). To be more precise, the argument runs like this. The realistic conception 'breast' really comes from putting together the idea of the presence of the breast with the sensation of its absence, which feels just as real or present to a baby. This realness of absence is echoed, in adulthood, by the words of C. S. Lewis after the death of

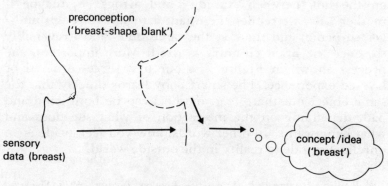

Figure 6

his wife: 'Her absence is like the sky, spread over everything.' Milton wrote in the same vein about his blindness, experienced as an ever-present non-sight. The unfed baby incorporates the non-breast, just as he does the breast, and experiences pain, frustration and terror, which he attributes to the bad non-breast that has taken possession of him.

The capable mother helps the baby to begin to think constructively by containing these dreads after the baby projects them on to her (in the role of bad object). As Bion says, the good mother feeds back the fear 'in a manner which makes the infant feel it is receiving its frightened personality back again, but in a form it can tolerate – the fears are manageable by the infant personality'.[1] This is the primitive beginning of abstraction. It is also very like what a successful consultant does with a worried or confused client. He may not 'solve' the client's problem but, by simply listening and then feeding back, he converts an indigestible mass of confused anxiety into some kind of shape or outline. At that stage the client may be able to think constructively again, to take charge of the work of problem-solving for himself.

It is an alarming thought that maternal failures at this stage lead not simply to emotional disturbance but to intellectual dimness as well. We know that after a certain time simple defects in the human eye become irreversible, not because of anything to do with the eye itself but because the eye–brain paths atrophy. Freud wrote a famous paper on the link between stupidity and arrogance; maybe if mother fails, we render the infant arrogant (through undigested panic) and thick at the same time, and irreversibly so, once the brain circuitry is fixed. More important, the process shown in Figure 7 is our first three-cornered or layered experience. The smart baby learns quickly that the same object out there (e.g. mother) can be both good and bad, depending on the interaction of what she does and what baby wants. In other words, how you feel inside is an unreliable guide to reality in the outside world.

---

[1] W. R. Bion, *Attention and Interpretation*, London, Tavistock, 1970. The argument about non-things is contained in pp. 16–17.

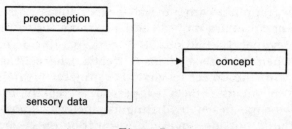

Figure 7

There is a lot to be said for precocity; the infant who gets such ideas early and goes on building new ideas into the quickly growing store of perceptions has an important head start. Where do the Einsteins and Newtons come from? How is it that they utilize so much more of the brain's vast capability? How is it that child prodigies like J. S. Mill or W. A. Mozart can achieve by four years of age what it takes most of us a lifetime to do, if at all? We have to remember that each new conception is not simply an addition to a crude store but also, from time to time, an idea *about* an idea and so on, at increasing levels of abstraction.

We can speculate that there is probably a link between mother's skill as container, the calmness of the first few weeks of life outside the womb, and the capacity of the child, later on, to distinguish objects from people and vice versa. The good boss, as I suggested in chapter 1, does not perceive himself to be engaged primarily in human relationships at work. He is clear that how he relates to his people is a function of the primary output. In the case of manufacturing industry the output is an object, and the best manufacturers fondle the thing, croon over it and bore you to tears recounting its virtues almost as if it *were* a new-born infant or (from the baby's perspective) a nice and useful breast.

The great thing about objects is that they are outside you and can't usually get inside you the way people can, though very disturbed people may need to stab or rape you or otherwise invade or pollute your territory. The new-born infant is grappling with a massive experience of insideness-/outsideness; he has moved suddenly from one to the other but, presumably, without the concept 'inside/outside'. Thus, when he feels bad inside (colic?) he confuses that feeling with the object in view. He projects badness on to whichever outside object or person is readily available. Healthy people learn to distinguish between inner states and genuine outside bogeys. As someone once said, 'Just because you're paranoid doesn't mean they're not out to get you!'

But many adults, and a horrifying number of those who rise to high position, are very bad indeed at distinguishing accurately between inside and outside. Some people have even attempted to alleviate their internal persecutory tensions by projecting all evil on to Jews, communists, Catholics/Protestants, etc., etc. If enough other people suffer the same internal tensions, then the 'natural leader' is he who suffers most and believes with the greatest conviction in the evil of the 'bad' object. He then becomes a kind of sluice for mass looniness – a means of simplifying the complicated and relieving, for a time, an unbearable inner pain. A colleague of mine, working in Northern Ireland at the height of the recent troubles, commented: 'The madness is projected on to a few people, and the only way they can release their tensions for a while is by killing somebody.' Projection *does* relieve inner tension, but it is rather bad news for Jews, Vietnamese, Catholics, etc., etc.

All of this may seem at one remove from the competitive executive who has never killed off anything more than a few careers and, perhaps, the careers of a few furry animals. None the less, we deal in the same phenomena. Some people, the lucky ones, have a beneficent passage through the absolute dependence of infancy; they have the experience of being 'held' safely and of their infantile dread being ameliorated by sensitive maternal responses. The competent mother can take in and feel the panic and dread and feed it back, modified and softened, like a psychic shock-absorber. The child can then synthesize 'good' and 'bad' objects and grow to acquire a realistic hope in the world outside.

The mother is managing an interpersonal relationship with the baby, and they are both managing a relationship with a magical intervening object which connects them at peculiarly poignant times. We must remember, mothers get a variety of sensations from suckling, just as babies do. This dual quality of the communion resurfaces later in life and provides a model for the relationship between people and objects. As I noted in Chapter 1, employers and employees also have to manage interpersonal human relationships, and their communication is also mediated by an object, in this case the 'objective' or product of their institutional relationship.

Clearly, the object comes first and the ideas about human relations dawn later on. The kind of ideas the individual will have about human relations will by then have been 'soldered in' by relations with that primal object. If the baby feels good inside, he will at least be capable of a range of behaviours in adulthood, even if family life inculcates a host of other unrelated bad habits in behaviour and thought.

But, as Bion remarked, 'The infant who started with a fear that he was dying ends up by containing a nameless dread.'[2] What makes Sammy run?[3] Why, it is the nameless dread that can never be discovered but only projected outwards on to a world perceived as hostile. Sammy's mother is not wholly responsible for his psychopathology or even for his great success, but she can't be ignored either. Sammy's view of the world, of course, is locked in the binary mode. Everybody is a potential adversary, and *nobody* is going to out-survive Sammy. Although Sammy Glick is by way of being a caricature, there is a lot of him in a great many otherwise presentable, conservative, decent Christian folk when it comes down to competition for preferment, professional opportunity and political clout – that is, at those times when primitive dread tends to resurface.

---

[2] ibid.

[3] Sammy Glick, the anti-hero of Bud Schulberg's famous novel (*What Makes Sammy Run?*, Harmondsworth, Penguin, 1941; repr. 1978), was the archetypal entrepreneur who could never stop, even after his fortune was made, and who was driven to exert power over people.

In all these matters we can but speculate. Melanie Klein[4] suggested that some babies simply are, constitutionally, more envious than others and therefore less capable of taking in nourishment, of synthesizing 'good' and 'bad' and, ultimately, less capable of generosity. Whether this is the genetic endowment, the result of existence in the womb or both we shall probably never be sure.

INTO THE FRAY

A disproportionate number of first-born people rise to high office in politics, business, the professions and so on. It is a standard trick in business schools to demonstrate to senior businessmen how many of their number are first-born sons. (Maybe in fifty to a hundred years' time we shall be talking about first-born daughters, but at the moment most of those few women who do succeed at the highest levels are associated in some way with celebrated men and are often their daughters.) The problem is to interpret the meaning of this phenomenon. Are first-borns more able or more energetic, or are they simply sufficiently neurotic to succeed in a neurotic world? Do they make good leaders?

The evidence for the general phenomenon is unarguable. Perhaps the best-known example is that of the National. Merit Scholarship competition in the USA, where of the 1,618 finalists an overwhelming proportion were first-born. Of the 568 from two-child families (random probabilities in brackets) 66 per cent were first-born (50 per cent); in three-child families 52 per cent (33 per cent); in four-child families 59 per cent (25 per cent). Of the 85 children from five-child families, 52 per cent were first-born, against a statistical likelihood of 20 per cent. These statistics held good only for the finalists; in other words, the more highly selected on intellectual grounds a population is, the more marked is the birth-order effect. Also, as can be seen, the bigger the family, the greater the advantage of the first-

---

[4] Melanie Klein, 'Envy and Gratitude', in *Collected Writings*, London, Hogarth Press, 1975.

born. The psychoanalyst Alfred Adler referred to the first-born as a 'power-hungry conservative'.[5] The oldest son is usually more conscientious and more carefully attuned to the requirements of adult society. He also, clearly, gets into the habit of bossing groups about. In multiple births, interestingly, it isn't always the first out who is at the top of the subsequent pecking order, nor is it necessarily the strongest or the brightest. In other words, dominance as a social phenomenon is a subtle matter. However, we know it when we see it.

There are two generalizations in particular that we can make about the first-born:

(1)   he is nurtured by first-time parents;
(2)   he is dispossessed (assuming he is not an only child).

There is a qualitative difference between something done for the first time, and all subsequent repetitions. (Dr Johnson, in an essay entitled 'Horrour of the Last', which appeared in *The Idler* (no. 103), pointed out that things done for the *last* time have the same, special, quality.) There can be very few people who cannot recall, in fine grain, a first love-making experience – or, to borrow Bateson's paraphrasis of Heraclitus: 'No man can go to bed with the same girl for the first time twice.' All subsequent experiences differ from one another in degree, not kind. Watch a midwife seem to hurl a baby about like a small sack of potatoes and you will note that the baby *knows*, somehow, he is in safe hands. Handle the infant gently and gingerly, like a Ming vase, and it will probably cry.

First-borns, except perhaps for the offspring of midwives, are held, physically and spiritually, in an inexpert and hesitant grip. Such a baby has, at the same time, an experience of insecurity and of eerie power, like a tiny unexploded thermonuclear device; they come running all right, and in a panic as like as not, yet their ministrations

[5] A. Adler, 'Characteristics of the First, Second and Third Child', *Children,* vol. 3, 1956.

never quite quell the nameless dread within. For the baby to trust in the world, the parents have to express absolute calm. Young newlyweds hardly ever do. Most parents know there is a special endearing neuroticism in the first-born.

After a while, as the parents gain confidence, the first-born settles down in a cosy *menage à trois*, the absolute possessor of two slaves. Of course, not all parents buckle under in this way, but most mothers at least do. Then disaster strikes. The party is broken up by a small object, hardly a person but a threat to the old order, like a tiny revolutionary. Indeed, the first-born sometimes allays his sense of fear and envy by objectifying the newcomer – by pretending it really is a doll. The difference is that you hope a doll will speak (if it is expensive enough) and you hope, deep down, the baby won't, ever again.

The truth is the newly born first child enters into an chummy interpersonal ∘–∘ relationship with two friends; the second-born enters an institution, ( ), a family, with differentiated roles, structure, hierarchy and a nascent sense of task. The second-born (and every successive child) is a democrat with a passionate interest that family life, whatever else it affords, ought to be fair. In contrast stands Adler's 'power-hungry conservative'. The first-born has had a special relationship of the 'you scratch my back . . .' variety. Suddenly he has not only lost influence but is saddled with a kind of familial Weimar Constitution, an unwieldy obligation to internalize a set of rules that actually operate to his disadvantage.

The first-born usually takes to it with all the enthusiasm of the German nobility in the 1920s. They felt that Weimar wasn't really a part of history at all and that somehow true life would soon reassert itself in the form of their special relationship with the *real* power. Even Hitler and the Nazis were better, for a while (so they thought), than this monstrous democratic regime. The first-born orients himself towards adults (or seniors) in the hope of re-entering the lost Valhalla. He is a sucker for delayed gratification, like an infantile Siegfried; one day, after suffering and struggle, he will inherit. (In primogenitary legal systems, he really *will*, of course.) He will study for exams, do as he is told and enter career systems more or less patiently, denying the while his impulsive, existential and feminine instincts in the pursuit of 'home' and a regained omnipotence. Francis Galton argued that the pre-eminence of first-born scientists actually owed something to their independent means and thus the luxury to pursue their particular hobby-horses.

The younger siblings tend to orient themselves towards each other in a kind of primitive worker's solidarity. Parents cannot be possessed, or if they can, somebody else has prior claim, so you must make the best of the awful reality here and now. You may succeed in arrogating to yourself some power in the pecking order, but you do not hanker after absolute, parental power. Even in adult life, exhortations to delay gratification may fall on deaf ears because the second-born does not really believe, as the first-born does, that there is an inheritance at the end of the tunnel.

If we project, we will find a good many first-born bosses attempting to regulate the present working behaviour of grown-up younger siblings by promising jam 'later'. It is not done cynically; the first-born believes in jam for every-body later, provided they are suitably grateful now and delay gratification for long enough. They are talking differ-ent languages, using the same words. The younger sibling is not grateful to any *one* in particular and is even less inclined to place unquestioning trust in anyone in particu-lar. His infancy taught him otherwise. He will relax only when the *system* is fair, a topic covered more fully in Chapter 3.

Perhaps the most important outcome of the birth-order accident is the mode of thought of the infant, the filter through which he views, and makes sense of, the surround-ing world. If the younger sibling really is a natural demo-crat, then he internalizes the ⊶ idea at a very young age, at about the time that the notion 'fair' first occurs to him or even sooner. In effect, he is asking: 'What exactly is a family? What is it for? What are the rules around here and, more particularly, what are the institutional arrangements to protect me in my helplessness and lowliness in the power structure?' The second child in a big family may have to

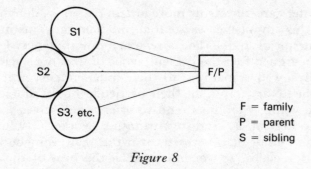

F = family
P = parent
S = sibling

Figure 8

consider such questions on behalf of his followers, at which point he assumes leadership, no doubt for the first time. Figure 8 illustrates the younger sibling's family view. When he grows up, his view may be like that shown in Figure 9.

The position, and the world view, of the first-born is different. He is not properly differentiated from the parent/family nexus. In fact, he is inclined to locate the idea 'family' in the parents and to try to incorporate himself within the same all-enveloping notion. It is as if he wanted to get back inside the womb, or to incorporate the 'good breast' permanently, so that he needn't share or tolerate deprivation at all. His family view is thus a bi-polar one (see Figure 10).

As usual, Hitler provides the grotesque example of the bi-polar mode taken to the extreme. When so many Germans sold their souls to Hitler, the deal was that the 'Führer' was Germany and Germany was the 'Führer'.

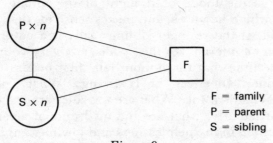

F = family
P = parent
S = sibling

Figure 9

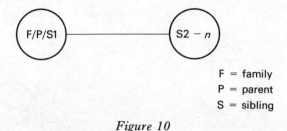

F = family
P = parent
S = sibling

Figure 10

That is why, as the writer René Schickele observed, Hitler's speeches seemed like 'sex murders' and the mass rallies like obscene mindless couplings between two beasts in a transport.[6] Hitler frequently referred to the masses as 'woman' and usually ended his orations 'soaking wet and having lost four to six pounds'. But it was incest; mixed in with the baying, quasi-religious responses were the family homilies:

Not every one of you can see me and I do not see each one of you. But I feel you, and you feel me! . . . You come out of the little world of your daily struggle for life, and of your struggle for Germany and for our nation, to experience this feeling for once: now we are together, we are with him [Hitler] and he is with us, and now we are Germany![7]

PECKING ORDER IN FAMILY AND FIRM

The bi-polar world view resurfaces less dramatically in junior management in industry. The upward-looking junior manager is inclined to resist the idea that he really has much more in common with his immediate subordinates, or even his peers, than with the corporation president, six hierarchical levels up. We should mount a large research programme to discover if those members of supervision and junior management who are now at last unionizing themselves (even in the USA) are predominantly the

[6] Joachim C. Fest, *Hitler*, Harmondsworth, Penguin, 1977, p. 481.
[7] J. P. Stern, *Hitler : The Führer and the People*, London, Fontana, 1977, p. 90.

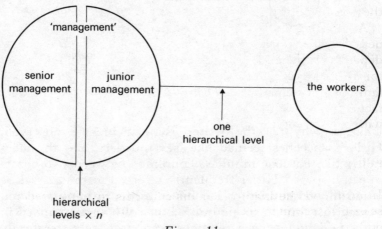

Figure 11

younger siblings among their number. Certainly, the creation of a brotherhood of 'management' has served to mask inequities between the novitiates (junior management) and the true Establishment.

The Germans, sensibly enough, have done without the word 'management' or anything like it, for a very long time. Instead, very senior managerial staff (just below the board of directors) are titled *lietende Angestellten* ('leading *employees*'). Of course, anybody in between the factory floor and the boardroom is both employee *and* employer. As Elliot Jaques points out, in a firm of 1,000 people there are 999 employees, no matter how many of them, in the English-speaking countries, insist they are really managers.[8]

The Germans, therefore, have a clear ▷ notion of institution in the firm, as evidenced by their very elaborate constitutional and participatory arrangements. Yet they seem to have no word for 'unfair', at least not in the precise English sense. *Unehrlich*, for example, means underhand; if a footballer kicks an opposing player in order to prevent

---

[8] Elliott Jaques, *A General Theory of Bureaucracy*, London, Heinemann, 1976.

him from scoring, the victim's team-mates may well shout 'Nicht fair'. There again, the English language contributed the word 'sport' to German as well.

At first sight, this loop through the etymology of 'fairness' weakens my case that ⚲ thinking in the infant depends on the experience of unfair treatment and the need for proper rules. Yet there are other factors at work in families, principally to do with class, and very special factors at work in the German family, principally to do with sex stereotyping.

PECKING ORDER AND MANAGERIAL TYPES

In adulthood the birth-order effect seems to be related to scientific creativity, as Hudson and others have pointed out. Scientific revolutionaries like Newton and Einstein tend to be first-born, except that where the scientific revolution is somewhat less mathematical and really does overturn our conception of man's place in nature, as with Darwin, Copernicus or Freud, the protagonists are younger siblings. In fact, virtually *all* the evolutionists, those quickly converted to the new ideas, were, like Darwin himself, younger brothers. Almost all the eminent men who opposed evolutionary doctrine were first-born or only sons. Sulloway argues that these 'emotional' revolutions in science are almost invariably instigated, if not by younger sons, by first-borns brought up to reject their fathers or *sons* of revolutionaries.[9]

Let us now pull together some of the implications for the leaders of tomorrow of these two primitive and speculative subjects. The argument so far is that mothering (or nurturance) and birth order together provide the bedrock upon which personality is built. The foundation cannot specify the edifice that will grow on its site, but it *limits* the kind of structure that is possible. It characterizes the quality of leading and of following that an individual will be capable of and impelled towards.

[9] F. Sulloway, 'The Role of Cognitive Flexibility in Science', in Liam Hudson (ed.), *The Ecology of Human Intelligence,* Harmondsworth, Penguin, 1970.

	first-born	second- to *n*th-born
competent nurturance	sense of abundance subtlety conformist power drive ('authoritarian') A	sense of abundance subtlety nonconformist authority orientation B
incompetent nurturance	C conformist power drive ('authoritarian') inner dread rigidity	D nonconformist authority orientation inner dread rigidity

Figure 12

Provided that there is more than one child in the family, the mothering/birth-order variables suggest four dispositions, arranged as a matrix (Figure 12). Now, if we were to label the dispositions, we would have something like: A = benign autocrat; B = creative democrat; C = bad boss; D = confused revolutionary. In the case of an only child, we must add: E = non/malignant narcissist (dependent on the quality of the mothering).

For the birth-order aspect I have taken Adler's idea of the 'power-hungry conservative', and for the mothering variable I have assumed an impact on security and thought process (see above). This is not, of course, 'serious' social science but rather a way of thinking out loud about the ways that people of different character come to be the way they are. It is, however, the kind of speculation which tends to drive a certain kind of psychologist to apoplexy; which kind of psychologist may be discerned in what follows.

The benign autocrat (BA) : first-born and competently mothered

A parent-orientated and rather bossy person, strongly ambitious and demanding of loyalty but capable of generosity and perseverant thought. Able to cope with reverses because of built-in security; energetic and single-minded. Inclined to crush subordinates thoughtlessly, though without malice. Uses good intellect best in familiar settings. Not particularly self-aware and rather old-fashioned. Chooses obedient spouse to fit, and tends to create a secure and uneventful family life (if married). Most successful professionals and bosses in traditional callings are a bit like this.

The creative democrat (CD) : second- to nth-born and competently mothered

Warm-hearted, unpredictable, but serious. Inclined to take greater personal risks than the BA and to spread interests wider. A leader of causes, sometimes unpopular ones, with a strong sense of justice. Likely to choose relatively androgynous/liberated wife (if male) and to have a somewhat eventful marriage, yet loving and needing love. Career success much more subject to circumstance than the BA's. A counter-puncher, occasionally very successful indeed when turned on by creative energy; often found in the creative arts and in the farther reaches of science and manufacture.

The bad boss (BB) : first-born and incompetently mothered

If we examine the traits of the first-born and incompetently mothered person – conformism, power drive, rigidity and inner dread – we see a person uncomfortably like many bosses. When people are questioned about bosses (see p. 20) this is the person they recall with disquieting regularity. He is exactly the kind of person who is, unless we are very careful, bound to rise through the ranks precisely because he is fearful, rigid and very, very determined. He is not determined upon doing or creating anything in particular because he cannot really understand the ⌐ principle. Rather, he is determined not to be bottom man in the great ∘−∘ totem pole of life. Inner dread starts him running in the first place; power-drive keeps him going; conformity draws him into conventional institutions and into obedience; and rigidity stops him from understanding the trajectory of his own life or the effect he is having on those all about him. He is like an aimless robot nobody can turn off. He is a terrible boss.

The confused revolutionary (CR) : second- to nth-born and incompetently mothered

This person has that low-status, powerless feeling but few resources with which to think straight or to do anything constructive about it. His orientation to authority is not hopeful, like the CD's. Instead he gloomily and fatalistically equates 'authority' with authoritarianism and autocracy. He finds a great deal to complain of and has little difficulty in identifying culprits. Still he *is* capable of understanding injustice and empathizing with underdogs; the trouble is, his response is rather rigid and he is easy prey for any nonconformist dogma. He feels the same way about (e.g.) BB as BB feels about 'ungrateful' workers and 'communist' union bosses. They make a great pair in one way. As a boss, although he is much less likely to make it, CR is as terrible as BB and more boring.

The only child

The only child is a special case. His mothering or nurturance may be more or less competent, but the central aspect is the absence of competition in infancy. It is potentially a narcissistic life, and there is the chance that self-absorption, together with the sheer capacity to be alone for lengthy periods, may lead on to high creativity. Most great philosophers have had this sort of childhood, whether or not they were only children. It seems that the only child becomes fascinated by himself as a phenomenon, or by the phenomena all around or, in the case of the highest intellects, by the relationship of self to the world. It is not a promising start for a leadership role except perhaps in the other-wordly realms of philosophy. Leadership is mostly about *purpose*, but it is also a social phenomenon. The novelist Ian McEwan comments:

Recently I carried out a little survey among friends. I asked them which words best described the adults they knew to have been only children. Some key words from my respondents were *selfish, self-absorbed, spoiled, over-ambitious, demanding* and even *emotionally dishonest*. On behalf of only children everywhere, I would like to submit my own list: *sensitive and secure* (a rare combination, that), *a great capacity for love* (giving as well as accepting it), *a deep sense of responsibility* (almost to a fault), *a rich imagination* . . . and, most important, a lack of fear or even a taste for, *solitude*. I know of people who grew up in large families who cannot keep their own company for more than an hour or two, after which they begin to wonder if they exist. . . .

What is distinctive about the only child's lot is his or her relationship with its parents. The only child stands at the apex of a tight little triangle, the focus of love, expectation, indifference, even cruelty – whatever is on offer, the only child gets it all. Probably, in most cases, it is love, and then the question is whether the child is sustained or stifled by being the sole recipient of parental love.[10]

All of these musings on the relationship of birth order to mothering find a metaphorical echo in the class system. The point about birth order, psychologically, is its bearing on inheritance. In a sense, all the offspring of prosperous families are bound for inheritance, just as all working-class kids have to fight up from the bottom of the big pecking-order.

[10] Ian McEwan, *Observer*, 31 January 1982.

Perhaps the other great variable of childhood, apart from birth order, is the mortality of parents. It is less a factor now than it used to be, though the new legions of the 'one-parent family' suffer a kind of half-death. Rather inconclusively, R. S. and C. M. Illingworth assembled a table of parental mortality among eminent-to-be children, from Ivan the Terrible and Cesare Borgia to Abraham Lincoln.[11] In particular, they sought out parental loss among 'evil men' – a blood-curdling roll of mass-murderers, most of whom seem to have been lazy and self-obsessed in childhood and all of whom seem to have developed a kind of interpersonal power early on. In the end, the Illingworths found little of statistical significance.

The one-parent child probably has the worst of both worlds – the opposite, in fact, of the experience of Lyn Carlsmith's Harvard alumni (see p. 17). Instead of an absent father restored (after a beneficent maternal grounding), there is an irritated father expunged – an unsatisfactory role model replaced by an incomprehensible vacuum. We shall know soon enough the effects of all this as the divorce rate climbs.

---

[11] R. S. Illingworth and C. M. Illingworth, *Lessons from Childhood: Some Aspects of the Early Life of Unusual Men and Women,* Edinburgh, Livingston, 1966.

3
The Tender Trap

Leaving aside the institutionalized breast, the family is the first institutional experience of the young child. Families differ in their shape and size, in their economic settings, in their class assumptions, in their activity patterns but, most of all, in their explicit and implicit assumptions about what families are for. The more clearly elaborated that notion is, the more surely the children are set upon the $\square$ path in their thinking, even if the family in question leaves much else to be desired. The family is a kind of trap but it can, sometimes, be a high-quality *trap.*

Powerful as the impact of birth and birth order may be, the forcing-house of character is the family and, in our sort of culture, the nuclear family. It will not have escaped the reader that families differ, and differ most markedly along class lines. It matters not that the USA and Australia lay some claim to classlessness – their classes are simply more elusive than those in Europe and harder in some ways, because denied, to cope with. If experience in infancy predisposes a child towards a 'survival' (o–o) or 'work' ($\square$) orientation, how does family life fit in? What are the o–o and $\square$ properties of families, and how do they reinforce the life trajectories of little leaders and followers-to-be?

The plot thickens at this point because, as I have noted, nobody thinks exclusively in the o–o or $\square$ mode. We may be entirely secure and able to work effectively at one time or in one place, yet at others be consumed by anxiety and dread (at which point the o–o mode of thought is quite logical). Even Sammy Glick has his moments of repose and absorption in something other than his own demons. The question really is: what parts of our experience allow us repose (and therefore the opportunity to think straight) and what parts drag us back, screaming inside, to the helplessness and nameless dreads of infancy? As Vice-President, Lyndon B. Johnson homed in with enormous assurance on the 'Great Society' (⚬⚬); as President he was reduced to nightmares of impotence, a yearning for boyhood and the reality of psychological breakdown (see p. 138).

(see p. 138)

THE FAMILY/FIRM ANALOGY

An illustration of how the ⚬⚬ and ⧖ modes can coexist in families may be found on a bigger scale in a comparison of German and British company structures. The notable thing about the German board of directors in a manufacturing firm, compared with the British, is the presence of engineers and bankers and their obligation to work in a constitutional ⧖ fashion inside the firm. But in external competition the firm fights like a cornered tiger and, as opposing salesmen from gentler cultures frequently complain, often fights dirty. It looks a bit like Figure 13.

The parody British firm looks more like Figure 14. (This applies to big firms; the small British firm is a match for anybody.) First, the board of directors includes an uncon-

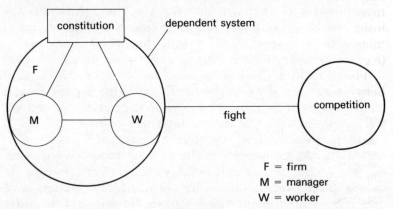

Figure 13

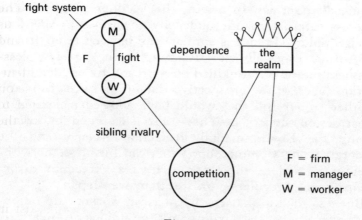

Figure 14

scionable number of peers of the realm (to connect the firm with the Queen so as to deny any distasteful 'trade' associations). Others on the board spend almost as much time on good works in the community as in the firm, in the hope of a knighthood or some lesser gong in due course. There are hardly any engineers who actually know about *making* the thing, whatever it is, and lots of accountants to launder the money.[1] Second, the salesmen expose the jugular vein (even in competition with French and German salesmen) in the submissive hope that international trade may be conducted on the same gentlemanly lines as diplomatic relations used to be. Third, and most important, inside the firm there is a ritualized binary warfare between 'management' and 'workers' and no constitutional forms (e.g. works councils) at all.

The American firm, incidentally, falls somewhere in between. Because American business blood lines are pro-

---

[1] A few years ago, there were 3,000 qualified accountants in all Germany as against 140,000 in Britain! Is this paradoxical or causal? How can we need nearly fifty times as many accountants to launder so much less money? At the same time Sweden, with one of the highest standards of living of all, was getting by on 800! Perhaps there is a Parkinsonian principle at work here, as with the inverse relation between numbers of capital ships and numbers of admirals. Maybe we should weaken our competitors by strengthening their corps of accountants, like controlling an agricultural pest by introducing its predator.

nouncedly German in origin, the leaning is towards the ruthless external posture, aided by government. American foreign policy (France is similar) can be seen as an arm of USA Inc., especially post-Reagan. In the last few years business interests have killed off a prospective Federal protection agency, a prospective labour reform Bill and another labour Bill that would have allowed picketing on construction sites. They have also succeeded in intimidating the Environmental Protection Agency and the Federal Trade Commission. American business, notwithstanding Nader, operates with a freedom from environmental regulation greater than even Japan's.

But less than a quarter of American workers are unionized; the numbers are falling and the unions are relatively tame. In place of German company institutions, the American worker relies, on the whole, on the vague promise of the American Dream, and the good sense of many employers in introducing stock-option schemes and the like. The economy (please God) will always grow (it always has), even if it depends on the manufacture of armaments, and *everybody has a share*. Europeans, with good reason, have a more sceptical approach. Their history teaches them that you need institutions to control ∘–∘ men, just as you need central government hand-gun control. The English, of course, do not trust in the economy at all but, then again, God looks after them.

In Britain, things were different in wartime, when the whole island required defending. Then there was a very clear-cut external fight; the British were in the right, and the devil take the French. What's more, people did as they were told, because authority seemed to be justified; nowadays, the German worker who actually does as he is told is regarded (illogically) by Britons as a brain-washed automaton and probably (still) dangerous for that.

However, war is a costly and elaborate way of relocating the ∘–∘ and ⊐ redoubts. It may be simpler to constitutionalize organizations internally (see Chapter 7). Anyway, in their far-sighted, unconscious way, the British may be indicating a future in which international trade really will have to be regulated so as to be gentlemanly.

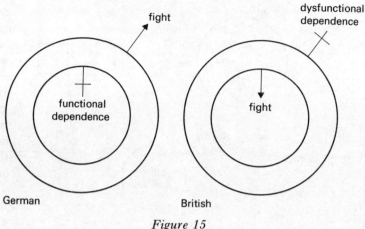

Figure 15

If we crudely associate the ∘—∘ and ⊳∘ modes with gender, with men carrying the fight and women the dependence, the two manufacturing companies look like Figure 15. Here the word 'dependence' doesn't necessarily imply helplessness or childishness. There is such a phenomenon as *mature* dependence, because there are times when we must realistically depend on others. The Britons' dependence on Churchill was as rational and mature as dependence on Hitler was irrational and regressive.

Back in the nuclear family, we find a startlingly similar juxtaposition between (for want of better terms) middle-class and working-class families. Remember, this is where our infant is going to reinforce his crude, half-formed world view. Once again, we must work with a parody to make a general point; there is no such thing as a family exactly like either of the following ones. However, we can say two general things about the stereotypical working-class family:

(1)   Internally, there is likely to be a 'conventional' power structure built around a male breadwinner. Although the mother will exercise leadership in many respects, her public role is submissive. The power disposition within the family has an unquestioned, taken-for-granted quality. Children do as they are told *or else*. However, there may be

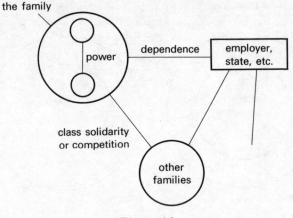

Figure 16

sporadic and lavish expenditure on gifts, dependent on parental indulgence.

(2) The family as a whole will have a relatively dependent relationship externally. The breadwinner will be an employee with a stark choice between obeying orders at work or a deeper dependence, via unemployment, on the state. The family is unlikely to own its living space or to be truly independent or self-sufficient as a system. It looks something like Figure 16.

The middle-class ethos is dissimilar.

(1) Internally, there is likely to be an elaboration of the idea 'family'. Rules will be justified ('Why do I have to ——, Mummy?' 'Because, darling, if you don't, then ——, and we wouldn't want that, would we?'). Mother and Father are likely to interchange roles (the trendier, the more likely) and children to be permitted the exhibitionist role in the interests of their development. Parents may well have read books which counsel an organized, time-bounded messiness, again in the interests of creative development. There will be an absence of short, sharp discipline and an abundance of (frequently rather boring) justification for everything. Parental behaviour will be relatively controlled. Pocket-money will be regular, organized and sparing (and

probably rather less than that of the working-class peer, and spent differently too), but there is, nonetheless, an awareness of ever-present financial reserves.

(2) Externally, the breadwinner, secure (even smug) in the rightness of his cause, competes successfully each day with a ferocity and guile which confounds the gentle paterfamilias he left behind at the front gate. After a long period of delayed gratification (study, working his way up, etc.), he owns most of the house (or two), has a healthy stock of insurances and something to inherit and controls his work destiny with reasonable certainty (at least he is in a position to sack others before resigning or being sacked himself). It is, in some ways, a Jekyll and Hyde existence, the morality of which is governed to a large extent by whether he is supplying an urgently requested professional service or simply helping a big corporation to foist shoddy and unnecessary goods and services on an unsuspecting working class. At the farthest reaches there may be a complete dual career structure or parental role reversal, at which point 'professionals' take over child care. This reinforces the children's delayed-gratification assumption about life. The 'middle-class' disposition is illustrated by Figure 17.

If we track the middle-class infant through, he is more likely to have had a gin- and smoke-free time in the womb and an up-market, hence calm, Leboyer-*ish* delivery; to have been breast-fed by somebody with substantial technical and spiritual support and some time to spare; and to have been *talked to* endlessly in infancy. When he begins to gain a sense of this institution he has entered, it has a ⊐ feel about it (though the first-born's ∘–∘ instincts may be aroused by the arrival of a second child). All this may obtain for the child of poor parents too, but it is less likely; for him, the air of all-pervading calm may well be lacking – and we all slip backwards to the ∘–∘ or survival position when calm deserts us.

Before the child enters the next institution, school, let us consider a few other variables in family life, not necessarily linked with class.

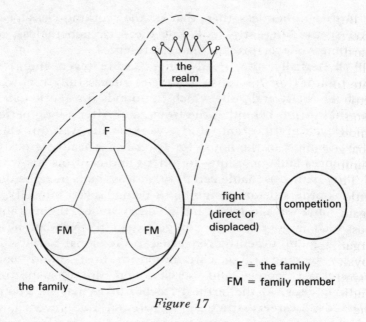

Figure 17

MESS AND GUILT

One aspect of the middle-class regime is that, while external appearances are kept up some of the time, there tends to be a notion of a safe place (or, if you like, a sub-institution) where mess is indulged. There will probably be physical space for gloriously uninhibited free associational play, and here, Bateson argued, the healthy intellect really develops; indeed, our communicational skills would not develop at all without the use of paradox, metaphor, fantasy and humour. (Einstein, on being asked by an anxious mother the best starting-out literature for a budding physicist, replied 'Fairy stories!' 'And after that?' she asked. '*More* fairy stories!' roared Einstein.) The projection of inner feelings on to a finger painting may well serve to process internal tensions and help the infant to manage the concepts of goodness and badness. As Freud said, 'Write it, write it, put it down in black and white. . . . Get it out, produce it, make something of it – *outside you*, that is, give it an existence independently of you.'

But while the middle-class child is encouraged thus to exorcise its demons through messy art, it may well receive hardly any firm discipline at all and, in the USA, none at all. (It was nice of Dr Spock to apologize, but it was a bit late for a whole generation which might have appreciated a little discipline.) Nothing is really *verboten*, and all is sweet (and largely incomprehensible) reason. This leaves the middle-class child, I suspect, with a residue of undischarged guilt, a guilt which plays an important part in sustaining the long delay of gratification to come.

The working-class child is left with his demons but very little sense of guilt at all. All this resurfaces when they meet again, years later, in the boss–worker relationship. The boss cannot conceive how the worker can subvert the organization's aims without feeling any guilt. For the boss, loyalty to the dependent, ⋈-employing institution (his 'family' now) is everything. But the worker's inner dread, undischarged in infancy, has to be projected somewhere. In the o–o mode of thought it will light on bosses, close to hand and not unlike dad, rather than on the bosses' idea of the 'real enemy' – fantasied competitors, probably with slanted oriental eyes.

INTELLIGENCE, IDENTITY AND WIT

The foregoing distinction between o–o and ⋈ modes of thought comes dangerously close to the suggestion that ⋈ people are cleverer, partly because they have more repose (during which thinking can take place) and partly because of a capacity to abstract – that is, to retreat to the 'third corner' in order to consider what is happening in the o–o mode. A ⋈ person in an argument will probably not get stuck in the binary mode ('Yes you did', 'No I didn't') but, after a while, will say something like, 'Look, why don't we approach it from *this* angle?' The crucial word is 'it'; he has seen that there is a 'third corner', the argument itself as an event or institution which one can get outside – not Figure 18 (a) but (b).

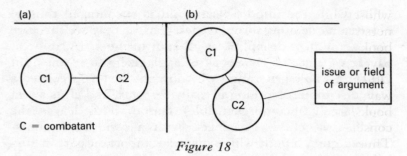

Figure 18

However, the capacity to perform this trick (abstraction) is only loosely related to IQ scores. In fact, very few people can agree on what constitutes intelligence. Sir Harold Wilson, the ex-Prime Minister of Britain, used to split opinion on this matter. There were those who argued that because he had a first-class degree in economics and a photographic memory for minutiae, he was, necessarily, very bright. The counter-argument was that people who devote part of their lives to that sort of pursuit are usually rather silly about important things – for example, the choice of associates and advisers.

Within a few years of Sir Harold's retirement from politics, a quite extraordinary number of his associates, and especially those he elevated to knighthood or peerage, were in some sort of trouble with the police. Some of them made Bebe Robozo look like a Sunday-school teacher. More to the point, Sir Harold had dedicated a large part of his considerable energies to 'holding the Labour Party together'. Considering the factions within, it was quite a feat, but to what end? The answer is simple: nothing was more important than prevailing over the enemy – the Conservative Party – in the age-old ∘–∘ struggle for supremacy. Labour needed the Tories in order to paper over its internal cracks, just as the USA needs the cold war. In the end, and inevitably, the moderate Social Democrat element split off anyway. Back in the 1960s it might have been cleverer to retreat to the 'third corner' (⊳⊐) to check what the party was *for*.

IQ tests stand revealed as culture-bound tests of 'convergence'. In 1976 it was revealed that Sir Cyril Burt, whose work on separated identical twins formed the cornerstone of the inherited IQ argument, had cooked his books. This news affected people in different ways. The psychological Establishment was scandalized, of course. Others felt that the event revealed, in a rather engaging way, the essential whimsy of science. Scientists cook their books all the time; Burt's overarching sin was to do it consciously. He must have said to himself, 'Why not?' Thus he exhibited mischief, a topic discussed more fully below.

Convergent intelligence is the kind that excels in forced choice IQ tests – that is, the sort of test in which you must choose the one correct answer out of five. The answer is deduced by riffling through a limited range of alternatives and homing in on the prey. But put a high IQ converger in front of a 'uses of objects' test and he may dry up very quickly indeed. The 'uses of objects' test may ask you to think of as many uses as possible for a brick, a blanket, a barrel, a paper clip, a shoe, a milk bottle, a car tyre, a suitcase, etc., etc. Divergers can keep it up all day (brick = tombstone for a mouse), sometimes lighting on quite astonishingly obscene or sadistic uses, and this skill in inventing endless variations on a theme is only loosely related to classical IQ. Some people are good at converging *and* diverging. The point is, how are these skills useful?

'Brain-storming' and 'lateral thinking' are examples of divergence. Many leaders pay lip-service to their importance (because they can lead on to useful innovation) while creating administrative systems which limit top-level decisions to simple convergence. When top people talk about 'effective staff work', what they are usually concerned with is the question: 'How can I get my underlings to pre-digest and filter all the ambiguous data so that I am left with the choice of simple, clearly argued alternatives?' This, believe it or not, was how successive decisions to escalate the war in Vietnam were taken. That is a cost of the ∘–∘ mentality in high places.

But then psychologists like David McClelland argue that the technical types who get to massage the data for such decisions are themselves working out psychological problems.[2] His conclusion was that most physical scientists have unusual difficulties in coping with aggression. Their work, subject to impersonal, external laws, redirects a destructiveness that might otherwise be vented uncontrollably on people. American physical scientists, on the whole:

(1) spring from Puritan families;
(2) are aggressively masculine;
(3) avoid intimate personal contact;
(4) like music and photography (impersonal representation) but not painting and poetry;
(5) are already identifiable, between the ages of 5 and 10, as focused on the material world;
(6) work hard to the point of obsession.

We must ask where all this aggression comes from in the first place.

Here we see an association of the ∘–∘ mode of thought with a psychological hang-up or, as McLelland implied, a way of thinking caused by the hang-up. To grapple with the physics of the atom bomb called forth a gladiatorial energy, making hermits of its creators. Only J. Robert Oppenheimer saw it from the 'third', abstracted corner, when he remarked that now the physicists had come to 'know sin'. While Oppenheimer was reminded of the Hindu god Vishnu's saying, 'Now I am become death, the destroyer of worlds', his leader, President Truman (whose decision to drop the bomb constituted a decision not to countermand 'staff work' – the existing order to drop it) remarked, 'If it explodes, as I think it will, I'll certainly have a hammer on those boys!'

That unusual physicist and musician Albert Einstein never stopped searching for the unifying laws of his field. Yet Einstein, more than anyone, overturned the old order, in which matter was distinct from energy and causes produced reliable, consistent effects. For all his 'serene

[2] D. C. McClelland, 'On the Psychodynamics of Creative Physical Scientists', in Liam Hudson (ed.), *The Ecology of Human Intelligence*, Harmondsworth, Penguin, 1970.

daring', Einstein insisted, 'God does not play dice with the world.' But then Einstein was the classic converger/diverger who knew that nature's secrets are discovered through the 'free play of the intellect' – through that inductive and unprogrammable thought which is most like the play of children.[3]

For our simple purposes, ○–○ thinking and convergence are closely linked, if not identical; likewise, ⌐⌐ thinking and divergence. It may even be that the capacity to think divergently at all depends on the ⌐⌐ mode of thought and that that mode of thought is 'soldered in' to the circuitry of the brain by primal experience in very early infancy. Vietnam, in other words, was an intellectual blunder, based on oversimple premises and perpetrated by people about whose mothering and nurturance we ought to learn more.

The most important contributor to this important field is the psychologist Liam Hudson, one of the surprisingly few of his discipline to evince real curiosity about the way in which people's lives shape themselves. He has put forward a theory of startling force to explain the way that the personality (or, as I would say, mode of thought) emerges.[4] Its importance for us here is its emphasis on the organization and culture of the family. Hudson argues that personality 'fixates' at one of three stages of development:

(1) infancy (approximately 0 to 5–7);
(2) latency (5–7 to 12–13);
(3) adolescence (12–13 to ∞).

'A person's frame of mind takes on its enduring shape during one of these three stages and . . . each stage of fixation is associated with its own characteristic way of life.'[5]

It is as if we each travel along a road of life lined with stalls offering a range of alternative life-styles. A few of us, fearful, like panic-buyers in a shortage, that stocks will not last, plunge instantly into the nearest stall; others travel a

---

[3] Newton too characterized himself at work as a child playing with seashore pebbles.

[4] Liam Hudson, *Human Beings*, St Albans, Paladin, 1978.

[5] ibid., pp. 121–3.

little further in search of a neater and better-finished product; others still resist the temptation to buy at all. Most of us can remember contemporaries who became, as it were, middle-aged at around 10 years of age and whose only significant subsequent developments have been physical and material – more weight and money, less hair, etc. These are the denizens of government departments and big corporation 'career development' schemes, fixed for the duration into an orderly, convergent and unimaginative life-style:

The individual who fixates in infancy is someone whom the incest taboo has failed to expel. Psychically, he remains trapped within the family. He will think intuitively. Also, because he fixates before he has any objectifying skills – before he can read and write – he is someone, we predict, who will prove incapable of crisp discriminations between facts and wishes, between the rational and non-rational, between the 'I' and the 'not-I', between people and things. His fortifications are permeable. In the jargon, he has weak 'ego-boundaries' and, hence, good access to his own 'primary process' thought.

The person who fixates during the latency period offers a total contrast. For whatever reason, he has been vigorously expelled from the Oedipal nexus, and feels an unusually pressing need to establish for himself a secure position outside it. He thinks in an orderly, analytic way; he likes to be rule-bound, and is happiest dealing with the world of things. His ego boundaries will be rigidly defined; and he will distinguish sharply between the objective truth and his own wishes. And – a delicate point – whereas the fixator-in-infancy will see as real only his own inner life, the fixator-in-latency will see as real only what is external. His sense of reality is based squarely on the concrete world outside. He needs to be in the right; and his equilibrium, his sanity even, depends on a sense of order.

The life of the fixator-in-adolescence is a more complicated affair. For, when he comes to fixate, he already possesses quite high levels of conceptual skill. In returning to the world of emotion, he cannot plunge back, neck and crop, as though he were an infant, into the world of intimate relations. Instead, he must achieve a compromise; and the compromise lies in the use of rational systems of thought upon subject matter that is inherently personal. He tries to be objective about the subjective, to treat the personal impersonally. Expelled from the nuclear family, he is held to it by a long, elastic thread. And although his ego-boundaries are strong, as with the fixator-in-latency, he is compelled continually to reach across these boundaries, and attempt to colonize the irrational world outside. His mode of address is that of symbolic exploration. He needs to tempt danger, to prise up the lid of Pandora's Box – to tease out and objectify human feelings, and the potentialities of human relationships.[6]

The fixator-in-adolescence is therefore, potentially at least, an artist. Anton Ehrenzweig suggested that artistic creativity proceeds in three phases: first, the (schizoid) scattering of partly conscious fragments on to the canvas or whatever – a phase characterized by fortuitous but ultimately meaningful 'accidents'; secondly, a manic phase of unconscious scanning, when a certain glazed look typically overtakes the artist; and finally the sober (depressive) re-introjection of the work back into consciousness, when the artist's limitations of technique once again become inescapable.[7] The object never quite matches the ideal in the mind but takes on at least a new identity of its own. In my terms, the artist has moved from a paranoid-schizoid trough (loosely speaking the ∞ survival position) to a mature, and perhaps rueful, appreciation of his *output* (⊡).

At this stage, 'It is astonishing to see how artists after finishing their work may begin to study it in great detail as though it were the work of somebody else. . . . The work of art acts like another living person with whom we are conversing.'[8] The link with Bion (see p. 44) is precise.\ The canvas acts as 'mother' to the artist, receiving the projected fragments, 'nursing' them (Klein referred to this dreamy state in the nursing mother as 'reverie') and then preserving them for re-introjection in a more manageable and conscious form. This is the 'compromise' between conscious and unconscious to which Hudson alludes. It is a demanding activity but a satisfying and edifying one, as

[6] ibid.
[7] A. Ehrenzweig, *The Hidden Order of Art*, London, Weidenfeld & Nicolson, 1967.
[8] ibid., p. 103.

with any form of creativity, however simple. It applies as well to bits of completed 'staff work' in offices, to manufactured objects in factories and, quintessentially, to meals created with love and skill – in fact, to any valued creation which carries in it something of its author. To that extent, we are all artists; the problem for most of us is to press on, to create a quantity of 'good enough' work in a 'good enough' field.

The fixation theory of personality has its pitfalls, however, as Hudson cautions us, it may lead on to somewhat unreal stereotypes. Excluding the virtues for a moment, we are left with nutters, boring conservatives and unreliable charmers. None the less, at an intuitive level it is a powerful idea and, of course, a three-cornered one (with the 'fix' in adolescence held in reserve as the 'third', abstracted corner).

Why we should, as it were, decide who we are to be at different stages of life remains a puzzle. Hudson says that probably the 'sexual politics of the family' determines such things, but we have no detailed research on this and are left with speculation. Mine, for what it is worth, is that the behaviour of the mother with the infant, the 'sexual politics' as a whole and the ○-○ or ▷□-ness of the 'family idea' are closely linked. By 'family idea' I mean the largely unconscious notion about the institution held individually and collectively by members. At any rate, it seems that it takes a certain amount of raw confidence to postpone the 'decision' about identity. The diverger preserves his vulnerability to ideas and to emotion. He ends up, demonstrably, more vulnerable, which must mean stronger.

The infant who experiences the family as an institutional vacuum – that is, simply as a series of interpersonal relations – is launched on a ○-○, convergent pathway. If, worse still, he gained no succour at his mother's or surrogate's bosom, then the ○-○ mode will have been 'soldered in' even earlier and in a more rigid and potentially more destructive way. On the other hand, to diverge – to resist the temptation to plunge into one of those life-style stalls – speaks for a deep, Micawberish inner confidence that 'something will turn up'. This is the dependent position *par excellence* and runs very close, especially in atheists, to spiritual belief in *something* or other. Where that belief comes from must be buried very deep in our primal experience.[9]

Leaving aside the 'sexual politics' of the family, there is also, of course, the simple knock-on effect of ⌂-minded parents. The family that elevates silliness to a kind of art form grasps the reality of paradox. A great deal of life is uncontrollable and somewhat paradoxical; institutions perform functions which are the precise opposite of formal intention; individuals, in the attempt to survive, destroy themselves; people continually find themselves in situations in which they are expected to obey contradictory imperatives. It all leads on to madness, unless you have a sense of humour or, more precisely, of the ridiculous.

Consider the difference between a family in which the simple pun is *verboten* and another which gives prizes for the best bad puns. I know of one family in which a favourite game (or, if you like, institution) is the awarding of points for the achievement of having never done something or other, like watching *Dallas* on the TV. If there is a Catch 22 in such a family, it will probably be identified as such and even rated on a scale of triumphant silliness. It will certainly not entrap the children in a web of incomprehensible and contradictory rules.

Bateson's famous 'double-bind' theory of schizophrenia[10] rests on just this kind of trap. He was writing before the latest evidence on the illness, and anyway the tag 'schizophrenia' covers a great many infirmities. The essence of the argument is that the apparently irrational behaviour of a 'mad' person is often, in fact, the only rational response to an entirely paradoxical situation created by the surrounding family.

In modern 'brief' family therapy, paradoxical interpretations are thrown into the family ring – for example, an interpretation of why the diagnosed schizophrenic, or autistic, or anorexic member is behaving as he is. What is

---

[9] The matter of religion and religious leadership is taken up in Chapter 6.
[10] Gregory Bateson, 'Double Bind', in *Steps to an Ecology of Mind*, St Albans, Paladin, 1978.

its internal logic? Sometimes this frees the 'patient' to change, in which case another member of the family promptly goes sick. The real problem is to change the whole unconscious family game so nobody has to sacrifice himself in order to obey the unspoken 'rules'.[11]

To be comfortable with paradox is to escape the most numbing neuroses and obsessions. It is hardly a diversion to talk here of craziness in the family, when around one in nine of us will spend some time under treatment for mental disturbance, and practically nobody has never experienced a crazy boss, schoolteacher or parent. An essential component of the ⋈ mentality is its capacity to handle paradox without feeling threatened or debilitatingly confused. The classic schizophrenic is not supposed to see the joke below (as a joke). Like all jokes, there is a horizontal association

"Poor chap thinks he's suffering from delusions. . . "

involved but also, in this particular case, a *vertical* abstractional jump. Koestler recounts an even better example of the same kind of thing in the story of the Austro-Hungarian invasion of Bosnia in 1878. The apocryphal version relates that the Bosnians, justifiably incensed, began to take pot-shots at Austrian officials. The situation grew so serious that a Draconian law was drafted in Vienna

[11] Mara S. Palazolli, *Paradox and Counter-Paradox*, New York, Aronson, 1958.

to this effect: 'For shooting at the Minister of the Interior: two years' hard labour; for shooting at the Foreign Minister: three years' hard labour; for shooting at the War Minister: four years' hard labour. *The Prime Minister must not be shot at at all.*'[12] The classic schizophrenic can't manage the abstractional levels at all; the really bright child loves the joke for its essential insanity.

All jokes contain this element of paradox. It is the silliness that is funny; but for many convergent people silliness isn't funny at all – on the contrary, it threatens a rigidly constructed world view, put together at a time (latency) when control of the environment is uppermost in the infantile mind. In the 1920s and 1930s many commentators pointed out the essential silliness of Nazism – the overblown rhetoric, the Ruritanian stage-sets and the recourse to the world's silliest composer, Wagner, himself a spectacular nut-case. They did not reckon on a convergent, masculine-dominated nation homing in on a pre-ordained, collective nemesis with terrifying purpose and accuracy, just like a particularly silly opera.

From all accounts, the Hitler household was not exactly a riot of humour. Hitler's father was 52 when young Adolf was born, having risen steadily through the Austrian Finance Office as a customs official. He was 'strict, precise, even pedantic' and insisted that people addressed him by his correct title.[13] Even his poor third wife (Adolf's mother), once his housekeeper, possibly his niece and twenty-three years his junior, referred to him as 'Uncle Alois'. He was, of course, a social climber, having reached the highest Civil Service rank open to someone of his education. Four of Adolf's siblings died in infancy, and the family moved four times before he was 6 years old, at which stage his father retired – 'suddenly he [Adolf] was continually running into the powerful figure of his father, who insisted on respect and discipline, and who translated his pride in his own achievement into inflexible demands for obedience.'

---

[12] Arthur Koestler, *The Act of Creation*, New York, Macmillan, 1964.
[13] Joachim C. Fest, *Hitler*, Harmondsworth, Penguin, 1977, p. 23.

The near-absence of national leaders with any sense of humour at all may be the most dangerous of all our problems. The party conventions in the USA have raised silliness to unprecedented levels, yet the leaders who emerge from them cannot afford to be funny. Indeed, to be in the running at all you must have put in years of dedicated seriousness, not to mention very serious quantities of cash. It is not that we need funny leaders, though it is an attractive idea, but rather that leaders without a feel for paradox are always dangerous because they are always at risk of accepting circumstances at face value.

It has been recognized for some time that we need planners and executives with 'systemic' minds – that is, minds capable of sensing the interconnectedness of things. There is no sense in a road-widening scheme if it solves one problem by transferring it elsewhere (like a projection of a family's collective neurosis into one anorexic) or, worse still, simply by increasing the number of vehicles on the roads. Professor Parkinson's famous law was systemic; need does not dictate expenditure.

Jokes are important for fun and because they stretch our minds, force us to juggle frames of reference so as to render ourselves the moving target in the imagined situation. Or, we could say, intelligence is the same thing as a grasp of paradox. The English are funny because, as Ralf Dahrendorf remarked, 'Britain is essentially at one with its history.'[14] It isn't that England is not afraid to grow old; she is simply used to it. The English do not spend a fortune in an effort to stay young, nor do they worry over much about preserving (on the couch) a healthy mind. They seem to know that life, apart from being deadly serious, is also a joke. To see the joke, you need to accept your own frailties for what they are and, ultimately, to see death as the companion of life, what gives it its meaning.

But this is a book about leadership, and leaders need energy. If you have seen it all before, as the British have, why bother with anything but jokes? How can we bring

[14] Ralf Dahrendorf, 'Not by Bread Alone', *Financial Times*, 30 December 1976.

forward people with the wit to see the paradox or the joke *and* the energy to pursue causes?

GRATITUDE AND MISCHIEF

Before we leave the family we must consider the odd relationship between 'aggression' and mischief. Psychologists and social workers are inclined to confuse the two, as a result of their difficulty in distinguishing the o–o and ⟨ modes of thought. Emphatically, not all mischief is aggressive. Aggression, as the ethologists remind us, is a fight/flight drive, useful when our survival is at stake. Some very disturbed people, whose survival, as they see it, is always at stake, are consistently aggressive. The aggression is then projected on to whatever person or object happens to be in the immediate purview.

Aggression or (as it is occasionally called) aggressiveness is sometimes useful at work – for example, in union negotiations, courts of law or salesmanship. Calling it aggressiveness implies that it can be turned on and off at will, like tap water. Selling is almost always aggressive, even during those phases when the salesman practises seduction. Even then, he has to know when to pounce and how to read the signals of weakening resolve. In fact, selling is a promiscuous activity because of the necessity to simulate depth and feeling in a series of brief o–o couplings. As systems theorists say, every victim requires a murderer.

If aggression is an adjunct of the o–o mentality, mischief is actually the opposite because it depends on the existence of the 'third corner'. When a child plays mischievously, he tests the nature and strength of the boundaries in an authority structure presumed to exist in the first place. He may simply be reassuring himself that the boundaries are still there. Paradoxically, once he can be sure he is bounded, he is free to be free again. If his parents don't notice, or don't bother, or simply indulge him, he will, quite naturally, carry the experiment to its next phase, until he elicits a satisfactory explosion.

Much the same thing happens when 'management' opts
for a quiet life by:

(1) giving way to wage demands, to ensure supply;
(2) failing to create ⌑ institutions for determining relative
     fairness in wages; and
(3) spending too long at lunch.

The silly manager is inclined to see all labour unrest in ○─○
conspiracy terms, as if the workers were a vast cheating
spouse. At about this point, the 'communists' begin to
seem credible as scapegoats. The truth is, although some of
the agitators are truly aggressive, the vast mass are simply
mischievous (and very likely bored) and are conducting an
absorbing experiment, carried over from childhood, on the
authority structure of the organization. When humourless
managers fail to see this, they inevitably make matters
worse, thus satisfying their internal ○─○ need for evidence of
conspiracy.

The very essence of mischief is the dependent acceptance
of authority, at least in provisional form. There is a world
of difference between the Anglo-Saxon conception of 'a bit
on the side' and the French *affaire*, a full-blown *institution*,
celebrated in verse and song. Sociology ought to provide us
with an answer to the question: why does so rigidly
authoritarian a culture as France institutionalize marital
infidelity, while a benign, though pagan, culture like
Britain treats it as a flaw or aberration? Of course, the same
issues touch on sex itself. The act of love can be combative
(○─○) or institutional, not just you and me but you, me and it
(⌑).

Once again, we must not argue for mischievous leaders
just because, at base, they accept authority. But we do need
people capable of sympathizing with the experimental curiosity of the lower ranks; who see it as not much more than
the testing of boundaries of younger siblings.[15] When such
people win through to high position, often by chance,
people instantly recognize their virtues and wonder why

[15] It is an important capability also among senior policemen – see Chapter 6.

there aren't more such people. As a matter of fact, there are.

John and Elizabeth Newson's studies of growing up show a remarkable split between the approach of some parents to others in their attitudes to infants.[16] Some view their own babies as 'artful' right from the moment of birth and treat them accordingly, picking them up less often, for example, because crying is seen as just another 'crafty' way in which the baby is trying to exert its power. Such parents generalize about all children, assuming, for example, they will be 'awful' in their teens – and so in due course, of course, it comes to pass. You *do*, after all, have to be crafty with such parents as these. Once that craftiness is learned, it is the begetter, naturally enough, of a deep and instinctive suspicion of, and in, the next generation, and so on.

Here, perhaps, are the roots of paranoia. If you are generalized half to death before you even declare your personality, and assumed to be plotting before you know what a plot is, then it is a perfectly rational thing to suspect parents and others of plotting against you. As you grow up, you naturally strive to control events by any means you can, but your trust in others has been shot to hell. If you can trust no one, then you can trust nothing, because all institutions, however innocent on the surface, must be seen as in the grip of those who cannot be trusted; the institution is thus denied its separate and neutral identity.

On the other hand, there is the parent who waits with curiosity for the infant to announce itself and allows a modicum of control to pass to the child – enough perhaps to counteract or mollify the inevitable terrors of its unfamiliar and confusing existence. The child may grow up crafty enough for a crafty world, but it will not project a meaningless suspicion on to others. More important, it has the chance to love itself and so, eventually, to love others fully and vulnerably.

Here is the link between craziness institutionalized by the family (see pp. 77–8) and the internalized 'bad object'

[16] J. Newson and E. Newson, *Four Years Old in an Urban Community*, Harmondsworth, Penguin, 1976.

or Original Sin school of human nature. There is a class link here too; the 'criminal classes' are drawn, on the whole, from the ranks of the 'artful' working-class babies. Horrifyingly, the same kind of projection crops up again in certain kinds of schools (see p. 94). If you are doomed to be presumed a criminal, it seems a pity to waste that state in unrecognized and unrewarded virtue. Likewise, if you are doomed to feel guilty, you might as well do something frightful.

In this context we must consider another phenomenon: gratitude. Gratitude is like a drug to some people. Unmindful of money, power, love, sex and the other temptresses, they will do almost anything to get you grateful. These are the people who will, if they can, manoeuvre you out of clear contractual relationships into interpersonal obligations. Their need to get you in their gift is a carry-over from a family life in which no one was particularly grateful for their existence. Children from very religious families, in which the Deity gets all the credit, frequently end up like this. But sheer parental indifference can achieve the same effect.

The importance of this, in later life, is that those afflicted invariably try to place organizational subordinates in a super-dependent interpersonal (hence o—o) relationship. For them, the ⟟ way of relating is anathema, precisely because it rules out personal gratitude; once you establish a formal regime which is fair to everybody, nobody has to feel personally grateful for anything. As the philosopher Lao Tze remarked, 'People say of great leaders – "We did it ourselves".' The wise leader is often unsung in his time, just as the teachers for whom one is grateful afterwards may seem a little forbidding close to hand.

THE WORLD OF OBJECTS

After the primal encounter with the breast in particular and the mother in general, children pass on to an appreciation of other sorts of objects. Here, the advantages of a middle-class upbringing may be nullified or even reversed. The middle-classes have a weakness for literacy, on the logical grounds that a superior facility with symbols represents the safest bridge to security in later life. There is nothing new in this. A few millennia ago, in Egypt, Duauf advised his son thus:

I have seen him that is beaten, him that is beaten; *thou* art to set thine heart on books. I have beheld him that is set free from forced labour: behold, nothing surpasseth books. Every artisan that wieldeth the chisel, he is wearier than him that delveth. . . . Let me tell thee, further, how it fareth with the fisherman. Is not his work upon the river, where it is mixed with crocodiles? Behold, there is no calling without a director, except that of the scribe, and he is the director.[17]

For the children of ambitious, upwardly mobile parents the universe of physical objects is dominated by the quest for the mastery of symbols. The new physical object in focus becomes a book, but it is essentially a means to other delights, not an end.

It is thus unlike a tree, a billy-cart, a speeding and dangerous car (or an abandoned one), a derelict building, a loony tramp, a vigorously 'courting' couple or any mechanical object purloined by unorthodox, street-wise means. At best, a parent with a craft and a communicable enthusiasm for it opens up a tactile and experiential world largely unknown to the bookworm. Even the child left to amuse itself in the street encounters a richness of experience, including boredom, unknown to children cosseted by safer and more rarefied stimulations.

Being good with your hands matters, as Lady Chatterley discovered. You need a certain love for physical objects to make them properly, even in big factories. In fact, a good manufacturing supervisor stands in relation to his employees much as the craftsman/father to his clumsy and curious child. It is a matter of communicable enthusiasm about the object and the process (☞) rather than the attempt to 'motivate' somebody directly. 'Motivation' is

[17] R. W. Revans, *Action Learning*, London, Blond & Briggs, 1980, p. 183–4.

interpersonal and always potentially manipulative or exploitative. The smart worker sees a dose of 'motivation' coming a mile off.

All of these themes – relations with a loved object, creativity, the Micawberish postponement of identity, the integrity of mess – are summed up in two stories from the childhood of the philosopher R. G. Collingwood.

my first lesson in what I now regard as my own subject, the history of thought, was the discovery, in a friend's house a few miles away, of a battered seventeenth-century book, wanting cover and title page, and full of strange doctrines about meteorology and geology and planetary motions. It must have been a compendium of Descartes' *Principia*, to judge by what I recall of its statements about vortices; I was about 9 when I found it, and already knew enough about the corresponding modern theories to appreciate the contrast which it offered. It let me into the secret which modern books had been keeping from me, that the natural sciences have a history of their own, and that the doctrines they teach on any given subject, at any given time, have been reached not by some discoverer penetrating to the truth after ages or error, but by the gradual modification of doctrines previously held; and will at some future date, unless thinking stops, be themselves no less modified. I will not say that all this became clear to me at that childish age; but at least I became aware from reading this old book that science is less like a hoard of truths, ascertained piecemeal, than an organism which in the course of its history undergoes more or less continuous alteration in every part.
During the same years I was constantly watching the work of my father and mother, and the other professional painters who frequented their house, and constantly trying to imitate them; so that I learned to think of a picture not as a finished product exposed for the admiration of virtuosi, but as the visible record, lying about the house, of an attempt to solve a definite problem in painting, so far as the attempt has gone. I learned what some critics and aestheticians never know to the end of their lives, that no 'work of art' is ever finished, so that in that sense of the phrase there is no such things as a 'work of art' at all. Work ceases upon the picture or manuscript, not because it is finished, but because sending-in day is at hand, or because the printer is

clamorous for copy, or because 'I am sick of working at this thing' or 'I can't see what more I can do to it.'[18]

On the 'third corner', the internally sensed something or other in the shadowy depths of 'out there', Collingwood is even more startling:

one day when I was 8 years old curiosity moved me to take down a little black book lettered on its spine 'Kant's Theory of Ethics'. It was Abbott's translation of the *Grundlegung zur Metaphysik der Sitten*; and as I began reading it, my small form wedged between the bookcase and the table, I was attacked by a strange succession of emotions. First came an intense excitement. I felt that things of the highest importance were being said about matters of the utmost urgency: things which at all costs I must understand. Then, with a wave of indignation, came the discovery that I could not understand them. Disgraceful to confess, here was a book whose words were English and whose sentences were grammatical, but whose meaning baffled me. Then, third and last, came the strangest emotion of all. I felt that the contents of this book, although I could not understand it, were somehow my business: a matter personal to myself, or rather to some future self of my own. It was not like the common boyish intention to 'be an engine-driver when I grow up', for there was no desire in it; I did not, in any natural sense of the word, 'want' to master the Kantian ethics when I should be old enough; but I felt as if a veil had been lifted and my destiny revealed.[19]

No doubt Collingwood was born 'bright' – so far as such things can be measured – but suppose we could replicate his extraordinary childhood circumstances in the case of just a few 'ordinary' children, might we not preserve their blessed ⌐ intellectual vulnerability to the point where it is too late for a school regime to destroy it? (Einstein remarked: 'It is nothing short of a miracle that modern methods of instruction have not yet entirely extinguished the holy spirit of curiosity!') As we pass on now to consider

[18] R. G. Collingwood, *An Autobiography*, Oxford, Oxford University Press, 1978, pp. 1–2.
[19] ibid., pp. 3–4.

the ⚬–⚬ and ⥁ dimensions in school, it is worth recalling that Collingwood was finally sent off to school, in an absent-minded sort of way, at the age of 13. By then he was safe.

4
School for Scoundrels

The institutional flavour of school may conflict with that of the family, though it is much more likely to fortify it. This chapter attempts to show how, in certain circumstances, the only creative (and institutionally minded) members of a school may be its subversives. The problem about school goes to its very heart : what's it for? If we don't really know, the school and its functionaries are without clear authority ([⊃). In that case the kids are subject to power (∘–∘). They will learn about that, even if they learn nothing else.

So far, I have argued that the ∘–∘ and [⊃ modes of thought are well set in the individual child by the time school comes along. Yet school is crucially important because of its power to contradict or to reinforce the prevailing pattern.

A child from a power-dominated home may be 'difficult' in school, but if the school has a stable, institutional feel, and if the first couple of teachers the child encounters have the containing capability that mother may have lacked, then the child's world view may be softened and his aggressions corralled into the form of mere mischief. Yet there is a high risk that such a child may pass on later to less beneficent schools or teachers. His disappointment then will be tinged with a sense of betrayal. The Lord gave, at long last, and the Lord then took away. At that point, anger may be so great that it cannot be contained and must be projected on to any satisfactory scapegoat, perhaps violently.

Then there is the child from a beneficent home who is pitched into a tough school with no sense of institution at all. This is a kind of schizoid nightmare – a Jekyll and Hyde existence within which the powerlessness of the beloved family is increasingly apparent. A generation ago the family as an institution was strong enough to preserve its special identity against competing interests. As Edward Shorter points out, the links between generations are much weaker now, and the couple at the centre (if it still is a couple) is an increasingly fragile sub-institution.[1]

But culture clash between home and school is the exception rather than the rule. Kids from tough homes usually go to tough schools, and kids from gentler backgrounds are likely to live near gentler schools or to have the kind of parents prepared to pay for a slower passage to adulthood. The middle-class household doesn't only delay gratification; the *quid pro quo* for the child is the delay of basic-assumption fight. It is as if the up-market parent says, 'You don't have to grow up yet, provided you so control your short-term desires that you learn to be a replica of me. If we do a deal on this now, many benefits will accrue to you later.' It is, on the whole, a fair offer, and the long-term benefits are indeed considerable. There are costs too, of course, because it is a narrowly convergent path to embark upon, and it turns many children into insufferable prigs.

The translation from dependence in the family to fight in the world outside is timed differentially by class. The whole point of the family is that as you do have to fight, among other things, in the real world, you need time to get ready to fight and to think about probable friends and enemies in the fray (see Figure 19).

(I assume here that going to work = *some* fight. But, arguably, the cosseted middle-class son who enters a 'management training scheme' in an organization whose chairman is a friend of his father, spends a deal longer in a dependent state.) Most university teachers never grow up in this sense, which accounts for their characteristic uselessness for most students (i.e. those not destined for university jobs).

Not all parents who elect to pay for education do so in

[1] Edward Shorter, *The Making of the Modern Family*, London, Fontana, 1977.

	dependent phase	encounter with basic-assumption fight
downmarket	family ──────────────→	school ──────→ work
upmarket	family → school → (university) ──→ work	

Figure 19

cynical pursuit of social preferment for their children. Some of them at least simply want their children to have a childhood. That is a humane and legitimate aim. Shorter makes it clear that the peer culture has largely taken over children from family culture in a way that could not have been foreseen immediately after the war. That, and materialism via the media, means that adulthood, of a kind, is encroaching further and further into innocence.

Let us pursue a likely biography – the child from a o–o family going to or ending up in a o–o school. What can we say about such schools?

(1)   They are big, confusing and frightening.
(2)   The teachers have a control model of the institutional process (o–o) and some are downright bullies.
(3)   Many teachers (like industrial first-line supervisors) are first-generation 'middle-class' and fundamentally scornful of their most obdurate pupils.
(4)   Staff frequently engage in a welter of complex (and trendy) curricular and 'pastoral' activities, at the expense of the school's central authority structure.[2]
(5)   There is massive negative peer pressure on the individual child who wants simply to work.
(6)   Parents are viewed by staff as at best irrelevant or at worst a nuisance.

What do children learn in such schools? Why, to survive in a naughty world. The school reinforces an image of a certain kind of family and gives it a gross institutional flavour. This, it says, is what the world is like, so you'll

[2] Elizabeth Richardson, *The Teacher, the School and the Task of Management*, London, Heinemann, 1973.

have to be quick or very, very clever. As children rarely feel clever in school (the cards aren't stacked that way), they conclude, most of them, that you've got to be quick. It is the survival or adversary ∘─∘ world view in the purest form.

At this stage the ∘─∘/⅀ dispositions become rather confused and confusing. One would expect the school 'counter-culture' (like any revolutionary cell) to be firmly ∘─∘ in character. What, after all, are difficult or delinquent children up to, other than simply 'rejecting authority'? But an examination of the evidence suggests that the leaders of such school counter-cultures (and it is leadership which concerns us) sometimes have a distinctly more ⅀ perspective than their teachers.

Paul Willis's book *Learning to Labour or How Working-Class Kids Get Working-Class Jobs*[3] provides us with a detailed and loving account of the 'lads', a cohesive group of a dozen uncontrollable youths in a British provincial boys' school. It should be borne in mind that while 'Hammerton Boys' is a tough, working-class school with substantial West Indian and Asian minorities, it has the reputation of being a 'good' school (see p. 104), which means that it maintains 'reasonable standards of behaviour and dress', enforced by a relatively interested and competent senior staff. It is certainly not a 'bad' school, in local parlance, and can fairly be compared with any inner-urban state school with a working-class intake in, for example, the USA or Australia. Indeed, there are echoes in Willis's work of William F. Whyte's *Street-Corner Society*.[4]

The most important point about the 'lads', notwithstanding their violence and unattractiveness otherwise, is their creative management of time and space within the school and their ultimate rationalization or justification of their attitude. Naturally, the 'lads' play truant for much of the time, having developed to a fine art the practice of checking in to register before 'wagging off'.

The 'lads' developed the ability of moving about the school at their own will to a remarkable degree. They construct virtually their own day from what is offered by the school. Truancy is

---

[3] London, Gower Press, 1980.
[4] Chicago, University of Chicago Press, 1955.

only one relatively unimportant and crude variant of this principle of self-direction, which ranges across vast chunks of the
syllabus and covers many diverse activities: being free out of
class, being in class and doing no work, being in the wrong class,
roaming the corridors looking for excitement, being asleep in
private. The core skill which articulates these possibilities is
being able to get out of any given class: the preservation of
personal mobility.[5]

The timetable-bound teacher, encountering one of the
'lads' on some unofficial and probably delinquent pursuit,
is met with one of a huge repertoire of vaguely convincing
explanations. The very complexity of the timetable, posited
on 'subjects', is an ally in this.

Willis :   But doesn't anybody worry about your not being in
            their class?
Fuzz :   I get a note off the cooks saying I'm helping them ——
John :   You just go up to him [a teacher] and say, 'Can I go
            and do a job?' He'll say, 'Certainly, by all means', 'cos
            they want to get rid of you like.
Fuzz :   Specially when I ask 'em.[6]

The originality and variety of explanations, subtly derived
from an appreciation of school culture and teacher psychology, serves only in the end to reinforce an understandable
teacher paranoia.

In the corridors, there is a foot-dragging walk, an over-friendly
hello, or sudden silence as the deputy passes. Derisive or insane
laughter erupts which might or might not be about someone who
has just passed. It is as demeaning to stop as to carry on. There is
a way of standing collectively down the sides of the corridor to
form an Indian gauntlet run – though this can never be proved:
'We're just waiting for Spansky, sir.' . . . In class . . . there is a
continuous scraping of chairs, a bad-tempered 'tut-tutting' at the
simplest request, and a continuous fidgeting about, which
explores every permutation of sitting or lying on a chair. During
private study, some openly show disdain by apparently trying to
go to sleep with their heads sideways down on the desk, some
have their backs to the desk gazing out of the window, or even

[5] Willis, *Learning to Labour*, p. 27.
[6] ibid., p. 28.

vacantly at the wall. There is an aimless air of insubordination ready with spurious justification and impossible to nail down. If someone is sitting on the radiator, it is because his trousers are wet from the rain, if someone is drifting across the classroom, he is going to get some paper for written work, or if someone is leaving class, he is going to empty the rubbish 'like he usually does'. Comics, newspapers and nudes under half-lifted desks melt into elusive textbooks. A continuous hum of talk flows around injunctions not to, like the inevitable tide over barely dried sand and everywhere there are rolled-back eyeballs and exaggerated mouthings of conspiratorial secrets.[7]

Teachers, in the end, are reduced to the 'class insult'. Outraged by the breakdown of the accepted educational order, their verbal attacks on offenders refer explicitly and belittlingly to class origins.

As the 'lads' saw it, after leaving school for good:

I thought that we were the artists of the school, because of the things we did, I thought definitely we had our own sort of art form, the things we used to get up to. And we were definitely the leaders of the school. . . . if we were all separated and placed among groups of the ear'oles [non-delinquent conformists] we could have been leaders in our own right. . . . Something should have been done with us, I mean there was so much talent there that it was all fuckin' wasted. I mean X, he was thick as pigshit really, but if someone had took him and tutored him . . . he'd got so much imagination.[8]

In fact, the 'lads' see the joke, or the paradox, in the very idea of school. Their appreciation of the institution comes from outside, so that, delinquent dunces as they are, they represent a higher-order 🏷 frame of reference. By contrast, most schoolteachers have never left school at all; the 'lads' never really entered it in the first place. Their reference was always the fight/flight outside world, alongside which school seems to be an irrelevance. It is quite different for the conformist pupils who really are inside the institution.

[7] ibid., p. 13.
[8] ibid., p. 195.

Willis says of these:

It is not so much that they support teachers, rather they support the *idea* of teachers. Having invested something of their own identities in the formal aims of education and supported the school institution – in a certain sense having forgone their own right to have a 'laff' – they demand that teachers should at least respect the same authority. There are none like the faithful for reminding the shepherd of his duty.[9]

We find, therefore, a bewildering array of perceptions of this world (see Figure 20). As depicted, this is too static, because perspectives shift over time according to circumstance. It is clear, for example, that while teachers harbour a three-part prestige model of school, their view of the 'lads' is distinctly adversarial (o–o):

teachers personalize, and base observations about kids – themselves lost in social and class processes – on what are taken to be concrete individual characteristics. Verbal comments start with 'I like' or 'I haven't much time for', and accounts are interrupted – in a way which is presented as illuminating – with '. . . a bloody good lad too' or '. . . a bad lot altogether – have you seen his Dad?'[10]

The lads have, after all, explicitly rejected the basis of the school's authority. Worse still, for teachers who, privately or part-consciously, have themselves begun to see schools as anti-educational child-minding institutes it is all doubly threatening; the lads, in their curious anti-heroic leadership role, have lodged in such teachers' consciences. The ⊱ teacher, like the conscientious bakery/brewery executive, asks, 'What's it really for?'

In Figure 20 it may seem odd to have established the 'lads' as the institution which regulates traffic between people at school; yet it is quite clear that they were well aware of their existence as an institution within the school, even though they would not have put it that way. There is even evidence of complicity with well loved mothers. On

[9] ibid., p. 13.
[10] ibid., p. 62.

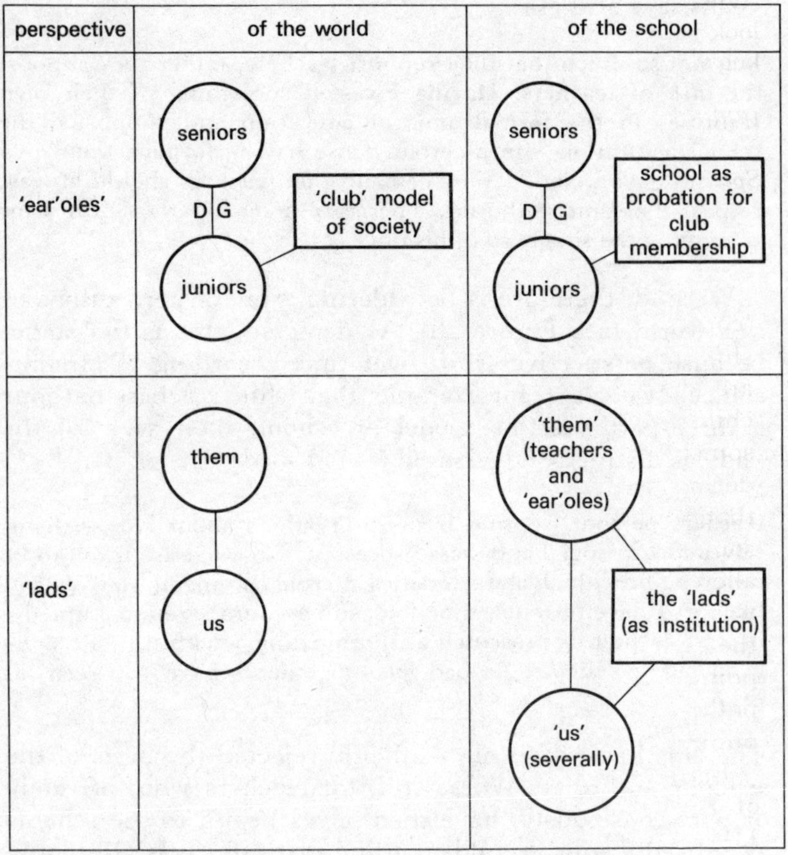

DG = delayed gratification

Figure 20

the last day of school the lads went on a spectacular lunch-time bender and reeled back to school very late, to be met, after a brief chase, by the police, who had been called in by the headmaster. Afterwards the head wrote to the parents of the 'lads' suggesting a meeting before 'any further action'. None of the parents bothered to turn up, and one 'lad' revealed later:

Our Mum's kept all the letters, you know, about like the letters Simmondsy's [the headmaster] sent [about the drinking]. I says,

'What you keeping them for?' She says, 'Well, it'll be nice to look back on to, won't it? You know, 'Show your kids like, you know, what a terror you was.' I'm keeping 'em, I am.

Willis :   Did your old man understand about having a drink
            for the last day of term?
Spansky :   Oh, ah . . . he laughed, he said, 'Fancy them sending
            a letter', you know. Joey's father came and had a little
            laugh about it, you know.[11]

When teachers, surprisingly often, confuse the terms 'corporal' and 'capital' punishment, it is clearly a Freudian slip. The teachers' views (see p. 96) of society and of school are similar. Indeed, like the world view of the first-born child (see Chapter 2), it is an inheritance model. But when somebody goes outside your frame of reference, thus rendering you powerless, it is, almost literally, maddening. At that point you may want to fight fire with fire – to seek out some ultimate sanction because people ought not to be allowed to 'get away with it'. The area bombing of Dresden was thus the caning of Germany; it wasn't a lot of fun for the civilian and refugee population, and there was no real point to it, but it did a power of good for certain senior politicians and air force officers, brought up in British public schools.

Early in 1982 a small primary school in the Toxteth area of Liverpool in England suddenly went crazy. Eight- to 11-year-olds broke windows, started fires, poured slops over teachers' cars and generally refused to take staff authority seriously. The teachers were reduced to tears and the head (for thirty years) to a rest-cure in the Lake District and early retirement. The spark which ignited the flame was the mass caning of seven children for some lesser misdemeanour (educationalists elsewhere in Europe are usually flabbergasted to discover that teachers in Britain are still empowered to beat 8-year-olds).

The post-mortem (especially that in the gutter press) was revealing: it was the work of 'left-wing pamphleteers', it was the knock-on effect of earlier youth riots in the same

[11] ibid., pp. 21–2.

city, it was the baleful effect of television, it was the influence of a small group of malevolent ringleaders and in particular of one girl (described, no doubt libellously, by one newspaper as 'big, black and nasty'). The post-mortem revealed, in fact, a crude and mindless attempt to cast the whole affair in paranoiac ∘–∘ fight/flight terms. It said, in effect, if only the head had caned the seven children a little *harder* (remember Vietnam?) the whole thing would never have happened. The *institutional* (⬭) story crept out, slowly, through the cracks. Staff turnover in the preceding year had been almost total, and one class had had more than four official class teachers in a year; at a time of gross cash shortages, the school had managed to *under*spend its allocation by a wide margin; the local authority educational official responsible for the school had been on paid suspension for a year and, above all, there was the caning – the threat of violence hanging over young children, some of them from homes and neighbourhoods where that threat was constantly present and for whom school might, just, have represented a haven of gentle dependence. At least the 'lads' made it to puberty before locking into anti-authoritarianism.

Willis describes exploits of the Hammertown 'lads' with such affectionate relish (or allows them to reveal all through their own pungent language) that we must assume he wasn't exactly an angel at school himself or, at the very least, wished afterwards he'd put up a better fight. Yet there is a poignant hopelessness about the 'lads'' small triumphs. The know they are destined for mundane factory jobs, if any job at all, and that they could so very easily have got themselves qualifications as a hedge in the outside world – something to depend on.

Willis makes it clear that their school experience is an almost conscious rehearsal for unskilled work in industry. There the main thing is to impose one's own meaning on the 'harsh conditions and external direction' of the factory floor. Brilliant as the lads are in the subversion of school routine, they subscribe to the profound anti-intellectual prejudice of their class. 'The rejection of school work by the "lads" and the omnipresent feeling that they know better is also paralleled by a massive feeling on the shop floor, and in the working class generally, that practice is more important than theory.' In Britain and Australia at least, that prejudice is shared by many members of junior management with working-class origins.

THE THREE-PART SCHOOL

Now we must consider the shift of middle-class children, many of them destined for leadership roles in society, into ⋎ꜱ schools. Here we must be careful in our use of the ⋎ꜱ symbol. The good ⋎ꜱ school is an *authority structure*. That is what distinguishes it from a school experienced as a *power system*, where survival is all. For the purposes of this distinction, all people have power, more or less of it, and absolute power does corrupt absolutely. In a coherent institution, people agree to limit their personal power in the interests of collaborating to effect institutional outputs. Thus power is a property of people and authority a property of institutions.

Elizabeth Bott has shown how class perception tends toward two-part power and three-part prestige models.[12] Solidly working-class people see the world as two-part, with themselves in the lower and disadvantaged position. Almost everybody else, and especially the upwardly mobile ambitious conformist, sees himself as located in the middle of a three-part prestige system. To say that a ⋎ꜱ school is a good thing because it provides children and staff with an institutional coherence, is too simple. We have to consider three possibilities.

The first is the ⟳ school – 'Hammertown Boys' will do as an example.

The second is the ⋎ꜱ school built on para-military assumptions, where the primary task is to be unlike the first type; this we may designate the 'club' model of schooling.

Clubs do not exist to achieve anything at all; they exist in

[12] Elizabeth Bott, 'The Concept of Class as a Reference Group', *Human Relations*, vol. 7, 1954.

order to exist. All you ask of the club of your choice is that it admits you in the first place and excludes those with whom you do not wish to associate. The club doesn't really have to do anything; it simply has to be there. We must designate it ⟨⟩ because members relate to one another, and to officials, within a clear institutional framework, for which there is general assent. There are also usually very clear rules for changing the constitution and very explicit membership rights in this respect.

If, as is likely, parents have to pay a great deal of money to gain school entrance for their children, so much the better. They may also feel better (see p. 23) buying an expensive shampoo. Reichenbacher, the father of American advertising ballyhoo (the man who persuaded *September Morn*, the famous prurient nude painting, into thousands of American interiors), once advertised two identical pairs of shoes in a shop window, one of them at half the price of the other. He even inserted a notice saying: 'The pairs of shoes are guaranteed to be identical; we just want to see which ones you choose.' Nearly everybody chose the expensive pair.

Lionel Tiger's studies of male bonding[13] suggest the powerful impact of single-sex high-status schools on subsequent political and commercial activity. The posh school creates a network of 'young males who are offspring of dominants and who expect dominance for themselves. Their strongly forged links with similar individuals co-operate to produce a cadre of distinctive, mutually-supporting persons, widely (and correctly) regarded as privileged.' Some such members of a high-status male bond group may later on find themselves in an institutional relationship to others – for example, as non-executive directors in relation to managing directors. When the managing director proves to be incompetent, it is not necessarily that the crony consciously protects his friend (thus screwing the corporation) but that he is without a higher-order conception of competence; he can't tell the difference between sub-standard performance and competence

[13] *Men in Groups*, London, Nelson, 1969.

because he is (still) within a survival (o–o) system, though in the driving seat within it.

This aspect of high-status schools is usually missed by the disputants on education policy. It isn't the *content* of education that matters but the *process* of coalition among powerful people, many of whom are bound, statistically, to be quite incompetent. They comprise systems which are much more than just the sum of their modest parts.

Properly speaking, the 'club' school should be represented as reflecting authority *and* power, but of different orders of abstraction (see Figure 21).

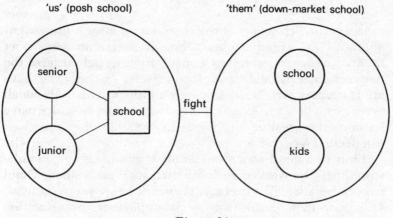

Figure 21

The third possibility is *good school*; that is, the school with those qualities that nobody can define but which everybody recognizes. Here the 'third corner' is a little more substantial than in a club. The educational output is the focus, seen as a transformation in the capability of children in line with their special abilities and the realistic demands of the world outside. Such a school, though conforming to the ⌾ pattern in its general coherence for pupils, is quite unlike a club. It can be compared more realistically with the relationship between an artist and his material (see Figure 22).

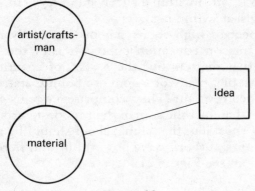

Figure 22

In art the behaviour of the materials is always unpredictable and the creative ideas, though rooted in some core
mental structure, develop constantly through interaction
between material and hand. Ironically, it was only the 'lads'
at 'Hammertown' who saw their nihilistic creativity as an
art form. To that extent – i.e. the extent to which they
harboured a creative idea about the school – they exercised
intellectual *leadership*.

Thus in a good school materials (from ideas to blocks of
wood) may be worked with for their intrinsic value and not
simply because, like literacy, they will help you to 'get on'.
It is not that 'getting on' is unimportant, but that life
denuded of all but 'getting on' is an emotional and intellectual desert. Good heads know this and sculpt good schools
accordingly. All this is made clear in an excellent report
from the Inspectorate of Schools in the UK, *Ten Good
Schools*.[14] The approach was refreshingly simple and
obvious.

Everybody knows a good school when he sees it, but no
one can define it. You can almost smell the calm and the air
of quiet purposefulness when you walk in the door. Her
Majesty's Inspectorate said, simply: let's make a list of fifty
schools known to be 'good', select ten for diversity and try

[14] Department of Education and Science, *Ten Good Schools : A Secondary School
Enquiry*, London, HMSO, 1977.

to figure out what they have in common. There are no prizes for the correct answers; it is much too easy. Good schools have good heads. In fact, a failing school can be 'turned round' in an astonishingly short time, probably because the parents' grapevine works even faster than the informal networks of customers, suppliers and others that surround a commercial organization in the process of transformation.

These, bear in mind, were not fee-paying schools. Included among them were schools facing very unpropitious circumstances as to size, location and history. In fact, the teachers' unions in Britain, distinctly ∞ bodies for the most part, have usually tried to suppress evidence that good schools can achieve miracles with unpromising intakes. Their preferred view is that teachers are powerless against the influence of brutish parents in particular and deprived communities in general. Yet even the 'lads' admitted their need for discipline:

[Referring to teachers in general] They're tryin' to pull themselves up. . . . all they'm tryin' to do is win us over. . . .

[Referring to one particularly approachable teacher] His whole manner, the way he carried himself . . . I think that closeness has to be tempered with a correct amount of discipline. . . . What we needed was someone like us who was just older, more responsibility.[15]

It may be worth quoting the final words of *Ten Good Schools* at length on the matter of the characteristics of those schools generally agreed to be 'good' ones:

The schools see themselves as places designed for learning; they take trouble to make their philosophies *explicit* for themselves and to *explain* them to parents and pupils; the foundation of their work and corporate life is an acceptance of shared values.

Emphasis is laid on *consultation*, team work and participation, but without exception the most important single factor in the success of these schools is the quality of *leadership* at the head.

[15] Willis, *Learning to Labour*, p. 197.

Without exception, the heads have qualities of *imagination* and *vision*, tempered by realism, which have enabled them to sum up not only their present situation but also attainable future goals. They appreciate the need for specific educational aims, both social and intellectual, and have the capacity to communicate these to staff, pupils and parents, to win their assent and to put their own *policies* into practice. Their sympathetic understanding of staff and pupils, their acceptability, good *humour* and sense of *proportion* and their *dedication to their task* have won them the respect of parents, teachers and taught. Conscious of the corruption of power, and though ready to take final responsibility, they have made power-sharing the keynote of their organization and administration. Such leadership is crucial for success and these schools are what their heads and staffs have made them. [My italics]

In talking about schools there is always the risk of making the teacher's task sound easier than it ever can be. None the less, we can be fairly sure there is an adequacy of such leaders within most school systems. Unfortunately, most of them are not occupying headships. Many of them have been too dedicated to the intrinsic ⋗ demands of education to pursue the ∘–∘ imperatives of 'getting ahead'. Once a ∘–∘ type reaches the top, the school is on the road to ruin. The head then projects the fight/flight survival model back on to his institution, and that creates the sub-institution represented by the 'lads'.

Such head teachers are often frightened to confront their own staff as to standards and thus are in flight from task. Sometimes they even live in fear of the teachers' unions. As in the universities, this pussy-footing approach is justified, or rationalized, in terms of 'academic freedom' or some such mantra. The children, often in the disturbing throes of a first, and confusing, encounter with a truly stupid adult (the class teacher), feel vaguely betrayed by authority, though few have the gumption to respond as the 'lads' do. Thus does the ∘–∘ school, mirroring the psychology of its head, teeter between fight and flight. The good head, of course, makes life intolerable for the irredeemably incapable teacher; he is 'cruel to be kind' or (see Chapter 1) 'tough but fair'.

But, at base, the point is that a 'good' school built on the notion of output and constitution (⊐) affords a proper role relationship to its teachers. Because such teachers can understand and influence their responsibilities and accountabilities in relation to institutional task, they are in a position to extend the same felicity to their pupils. When that happens, the kids actually assume authority in the role of pupil – and why not, since they are the principal con-sumers? In the 'club' model of private schooling (the image of a 'good school' in the eyes of the upwardly mobile) the pupil is not consumer but product – reassurance, in fact, that the parent has won his personal fight for advancement.

At 'Hammertown' all the 'lads' changed from Jekyll to Hyde at the end of the 'latency' period and at the onset of adolescence. Up till then most of them had been academi-cally successful and reasonably co-operative. They were, as well, strong enough and bright enough to have kept their options on personal identity open. In the space of about a year the *absence* of an intelligible and adaptable ⊐ frame-work and the incessant incursions of the mindless peer culture converted them to a crude mirror image of harsh authority, irrevocably damaged their career prospects and, ultimately, seeded a small cell of fiendishly inventive sub-versives into the industrial process.

The so-called 'crisis of leadership' is caused by too many people, particularly the young, realizing you don't have to obey inadequate authority figures. This is probably the most important lesson our young people learn nowadays, despite the efforts of our schools. Once it dawns on the young that you don't have to obey, that authority (or crude power masquerading as authority) has no effective sanc-tions, then the office holders are driven to repression, which leads to authority becoming a 'bad object', which discourages good people from seeking office and so on. Most British schools, for example, are of two kinds. With inspiring exceptions, both kinds produce ignorance, but of quite different kinds. Tough state schools tend to produce anti-authoriatarian anti-intellectuals. Cossetted private schools tend to produce conventional authoritarians with an exaggerated respect for book learning and a mindless deference towards figure-head leaders of dubious competence. It is hard to say which form of stupidity is the more pernicious. But then the authority of school itself is suborned if we are unclear what school is really for. The ex-pupils of these different kinds of schools often meet up again (in new roles) later on, usually with disastrous results. In bad schools you learn (without knowing it) to survive or to dominate. The good school constantly poses the question: 'What's it *for*?'

As a postscript, some years ago I conducted a study of a long (ten-week) middle-management course at a major British business school.[16] Even in those august halls a few 'lads' were in evidence – that is, a sub-group of middle-aged men, all from working-class origins, who had suffered a progressive 'de-skilling' as the course progressed. These were people whose quintessential skills were in *doing*, surrounded by clever *talk*. It was enough to make you sick; in fact, two were hospitalized with vague, but alarming, thoracic pains during the depressive 'dip' in the middle of the course. The remaining 'lads' even tried to introduce a striptease artiste into the school to liven up a 'gentleman's evening' arranged near the end of the course. However, the school's director, to the 'lads'' immense relief, put a stop to that.

I interviewed all the participants a few months after the programme; all but the two 'casualties' elected to come to my office in the Tavistock Institute in London, glad of the chance to get away from their own offices to talk of higher things. But these two insisted on my visiting them at their factories (both, predictably, were manufacturing managers). The transformation was startling; they seemed, for one thing, 6 inches taller and a whole lot healthier. Before being ushered into the great presence, and after a few minutes in the hands of subservient flunkeys, I sensed that I was observing a process of *re*-skilling. This, they were saying to me, is real life, and what's more, we know how to do it!

[16] Alistair Mant, *The Dynamics of Management Education*, London, Gower Press, 1981.

There is a poignant concurrence between the comments of these highly successful but socially risen middle-aged managers and those of the 'lads' at 'Hammertown Boys'. The very first business school alumnus I talked to was a graduate civil servant of impeccably middle-class origin – a classic 'ear'ole'. When I asked about social mingling during the course he said:

One aimed to cultivate those who were attractive people [lists six ex-private school pupils] – their personality made an impression!

Next, I spoke to a 'lad' – a sales manager from working-class stock and a party to the striptease fiasco:

I mixed with the men of the world – people who had suffered some of the bad things of life as well as the good, who savoured learning how to do things . . . who had learned to mix with all sorts of people.

Compare these with Joey, one of the 'Hammertown lads' from a big family known as a fighting family, son of a foundryman and acknowledged as a 'troublemaker' with 'something about him':

The ear'oles . . . they've got it all to come. I mean look at Tom Bradley. Have you ever noticed him? I've always looked at him and I've thought, well . . . we've been through all life's pleasures and all its fucking displeasures, we've been drinking, we've been fighting, we've known frustration, sex, fucking hatred, love and all this lark, yet he's known none of it. He's never been with a woman, he's never been in a pub. We don't know it, we assume it – I dare say he'd come and tell us if he had – but he's never been with a woman, he's never been drinking, I've never known him in a fight. He's not known so many of the emotions as we've had to experience, and he's got it all to come yet.[17]

There is a sad, envious, world-weariness about these words. Here is somebody who has grown up too quickly and knows it. Delayed gratification has its drawbacks, but

[17] Willis, *Learning to Labour*, pp. 15–16.

there is, at least, something to look forward to. It is a great irony that the 'ear'ole'/'lads' split should emerge not only in adulthood but also among managers in business schools.

Before we leave the subject of school, we should refer to one of the 'lads'' wistful imaginings of a useful teacher: 'What we needed was someone like us who was just older, more responsibility.' By this he meant someone as unlike the typical teacher (or, for that matter, 'careers master') as possible. In Chapter 5 there is a reference to the problem of preparing children for *un*employment in a world in which full employment (in the traditional sense) has probably vanished for ever. School ought to prepare children for adult life. Instead many leave school in a state of 'resourceless dependence' – able to fill an employment slot in another large and meaningless bureaucracy but quite unable to manage the potentially creative unemployed state. Work, after all, is not the same thing as employment.

A creative response to this problem is offered by a remarkable experiment in three British inner-urban areas. Funded by the Manpower Services Commission and carried out by the Grubb Institute of Behavioural Studies in London, this project has provided school-leavers and young unemployed people with the services of coaches on a once-a-week basis.[18] The coaches are not middle-class counsellors or 'experts' on job search, but ordinary (though experienced) shop-floor workers capable of representing, in a simple, uncluttered way, the adult world and its values in the local community. The coaches are simply released for one day a week by collaborating firms; some of them, unpredictably, turn out to have a positive genius for this unusual form of 'work' – that is, they succeed in conveying an adult perspective on work and employment and the relationship of both to life in a particular community.

The beauty of the scheme is that it fudges the boundary between school and adult life; it provides a space within which young people can try out versions of responsible adulthood. More to the point, the Grubb Institute argues,

[18] Grubb Institute of Behavioural Studies, *TWL Network in Practice 1978–81*, Report to MSC, London, 1981.

this is a natural process. This is what young people do with older, more experienced role models (and vice versa) in 'normal' circumstances in coherent communities. Only the distortions of our educational and employment bureaucracies, and the fragmentation of urban community life, have prevented it from happening. In a way, this experiment parallels the slow revolution in hospital obstetric wards; it is a matter not of imposing order and structure on chaos but of making space to allow something perfectly natural to occur. This important breakthrough in 'education', needless to say, did not emanate from schools.

5
Getting In

The routes to the top are many and various. This chapter touches on the relationship between situation and person which permits the ascent to power, beginning with Thatcher, Reagan and Fraser and passing on to other eminent politicians. In Chapter 6 we resume the pursuit of leadership and followership among more or less ordinary folk.

On 20 January 1981 Ronald Reagan assumed the Presidency of the USA with the support of less than one in four of the American electorate, the smallest proportion ever to vote in a Chief Executive. He achieved this through the apathy of non-voters and the unpopularity of Jimmy Carter who, only five years previously, had triumphed, as a virtual unknown, over other better-established political figures, because people saw in him a return to simple, old-fashioned virtues. Shortly after Reagan's inauguration he was shot by the son of a prestigious oil-company director because gunning down a cowboy President seemed to the lad the best possible way to demonstrate his passion for another film star. Later on, the boy's father opined that the event was unlikely to have financial consequences for his company as serious as the 1973 oil squeeze.

On 11 November 1975 Malcolm Fraser became caretaker Prime Minister of Australia in circumstances which still reverberate unpleasantly in constitutional circles. The Governor-General of the time (the Queen's representative), Sir John Kerr, was subsequently hounded from office by jeering protesters on account of his dubious part in the constitutional crisis. To many people, irrespective of their political persuasions, the event looked like a power play by Fraser, the Chief Justice, Sir Garfield Barwick, and the Governor-General against Gough Whitlam's democratically elected Government. To others in the legal profession it resembled nothing so much as an undignified brawl between three ageing and pugnacious lawyers with a few scores to settle.

In February 1974 Prime Minister Edward Heath, a grocer's son from Deal in Kent, unwisely accepted the advice of some of his aristocratic advisers to 'stand up' to the British coal miners on the matter of pay. There are institutions in Britain that it is safe to confront in this way, but the monarchy and the National Union of Miners are not among them. After Heath's election defeat, the Conservative Party fell into disarray around succession. A year later another relative unknown, Margaret Thatcher, entered the leadership lists and, via the vagaries of tactical voting in favour of other candidates with broader appeal, suddenly found herself Prime Minister.

In the space of two years, together with her guru, a plausible American economist, she succeeded in running down British industry and running up unemployment handouts to levels not seen since the Great Depression. In the end only a brawl with an Argentinian military dictator served to restore her flagging electoral popularity; the same brawl propped up *his* tottering regime.

I single out these three national leaders not because they are particularly unappetizing by modern international standards, but because their electors, and those who didn't vote at all, are so unexcited by them compared with some past leaders. Even their supporters might blench at the idea of the three countries being managed conjointly by a Thatcher/Reagan/Fraser troika. Together, they look a little terrifying, representing as they do a massive and simultaneous rightwards lurch in three of the major English-speaking countries. In early 1980 when I was planning a book on new attitudes to leadership, Thatcher and Fraser were already in situ. I confidently (so it seemed to my publisher) predicted a Reagan landslide because it seemed to me that the political pulse in the three countries usually pumps in concert.

For Truman you may safely say Curtin/Chifley and Attlee. There is something about wartime and reconstruction that calls forth the 'parties of conscience', although the Democrats' claim to the title is less clear or well established than that of the two 'Labour' parties in Britain and Australia. When the post-war booms came, Macmillan and Menzies raised *laissez-faire* complacency to an art form, with Churchill (briefly) and Eisenhower also supplying military nostalgia. Inevitably, a new generation of better-educated and (frankly) bored electors came along to install Kennedy, Wilson and Whitlam, though it took an unconscionable time to happen in Australia. There are a few other political figures in between, but there can be little doubt that the decisive rightward swing of the pendulum is with us now, at least among those who bother to vote.[1] It is arguable whether massive abstentions from the democratic process represent a leftwards or a rightwards shift of opinion. At a simple level, it looks leftish in the sense that it is the lower-income groups that tend not to vote. But, as history has shown, the decline of democracy usually leads towards the dictator. By subverting the process you may ensure, more or less consciously, the drift to authoritarianism.

The authoritarian personality usually exists on the paranoid/xenophobic right, especially among upwardly mobile, status-seeking immigrant groups and old-stock, declining middle classes. Richard Hofstader identified the German-Americans and Irish-Americans as traditional elements of the former group.[2] Both Britain and Australia now have substantial new immigrant sub-cultures, but the issue is never simple; the 'pseudo-Conservative' described by T. W. Adorno and others in the America of the 1950s was

---

[1] In the other English-speaking countries, at the time of writing, the amazingly bellicose and right-wing Muldoon remains in power in New Zealand, and Charles Haughey, once tried for IRA gun-running (and acquitted), teeters on the edge of power or lurks in the wings in the Republic of Ireland.

[2] Richard Hofstadter, *The Paranoid Style in American Politics*, London, Jonathan Cape, 1966.

conventional and submissive to authority at a conscious level but at the same time violent, anarchic and destructive at the sub-conscious.[3]

It looks rather as though very few people actually wanted Thatcher, Reagan or Fraser in particular as national leaders but that very many people couldn't think what else to do. They *did* know that they had run out of patience with Carter, Callaghan and Whitlam. As Godfrey Hodgson commented on the American electors' dilemma in 1968, 'It wasn't that the majority liked Nixon; its members just didn't feel that things were bad enough that you had to put up with McGovern.'[4] I have always argued that the real trouble with Nixon was not so much his wrong-doing as the public's rage with itself and its guilt about electing him after having viewed the 'Checkers' speech on TV. Anyone who watched that speech, way back in 1952, knew in his heart that you could not, indeed, 'buy a used car from this man'. Nixon's real sin was to expose the complicity. No doubt many people 'forgot' afterwards how they voted, just as after Kennedy's murder far more people believed they had voted for him than actually had.

It is also clear that it is dangerously misleading to interpret the election of national leaders in terms solely of personality or style. If most of us are hell-bent on the acquisition of wealth, the climbing of social ladders and the sublimation of our consciences, then the leaders we deserve will be those who promise to deliver all these things, but accompanied by high-sounding and reassuring platitudes.

What actually happened was that the electors in all three countries came to the view that 'things had gone far enough'. It was almost as if the 'liberal' leaders – Carter, Whitlam and Callaghan – were envisioned as children who had been allowed to become over-excited before bedtime. Enough, self-evidently, was enough. This is precisely the collective state of mind which obtains immediately before the advent of a dictator (who is seen as a firm, or even autocratic, father, stepping in to get things back to

[3] T. W. Adorno *et al.*, *The Authoritarian Personality*, New York, Norton, 1969.
[4] Geoffrey Hodgson, *In Our Time*, London, Macmillan, 1976.

'normal'). As a state of mind, it can be created and sustained artificially, as the Americans demonstrated in Chile, but it still requires a public conception of going 'too far' and therefore of the dividing line between normal and abnormal.

Our problem is that the world is now normally abnormal. Governments can no longer control events, if ever they could. Their incapacity to make things happen the way a stern father does is increasingly obvious now, thanks to modern communications media. Reagan, Thatcher and Fraser won't do any better because they can't really, but we still crave the 'firm hand' – some of us. As John Gall points out (see below), it takes about the length of a term of office to shift the populace back to square one, once we remember what a firm hand feels like.

Circumstances in the three countries are far from identical. For one thing, Britain is peculiarly inclined to masochism just now. It is no coincidence that the primary fetish of the British ruling class has usually been caning by disciplinarian ladies of the night. What Margaret Thatcher has said, with the greatest clarity, is, 'The more it hurts now, the nicer it will be in the end.' The problem is, of course, that, as with the caning fetish, you are corrupted in the process, whatever the outcome. The true equation is the cost of process versus benefits (assumed) of outcome. Why Britain should be bent on masochism now is hard to say; possibly it has to do with guilt about the easy money from oil revenues. Unlike the Australians and Americans, the British do not on the whole regard oil as a God-given national right, and the Australians and the Americans are not, on the whole, masochists.

In America too, the role of the 'right' is difficult for others to understand. Anywhere else big business is always the bastion of the 'right'. Only in America are multinational giants disapproved of for making money anywhere they can, if that anywhere should include the pinker countries. Patrick Buchanan, at one time President Nixon's speech writer, one criticized the 'obscene haste' with which big business acted to meet Soviet requests for the latest Western machinery or technology. Buchanan had been shocked by Alexander Solzhenitsyn's reference to what he called the 'alliance' between the communist leaders and the capitalists. Some have put American right-wing xenophobia down to the old American combination of fundamentalist Protestant churchmen and successive waves of non-Protestant and sometimes non-white immigration. At any rate, 'communism' has always been, and remains, the favourite American bogey; a rightward shift in America means, among other things, a resurgence of militarism, memories of Senator McCarthy and, most important of all, more money for industrialists.

There are similarities in the Australian social setting. The lurch to Fraser felt like a conflict across the generation gap, with the balance held by the new, ambitious, upwardly mobile immigrants. For many of them Australia is a place where you shouldn't need a conscience – a place to divest yourself of European memories and history if you possibly can. One respected commentator referred to the events of 11 November 1975 as marking

the signal of success for the politics of ruthlessness and opportunism. . . . both parties have suffered a further denial of quality recruits because the manner of the Whitlam Government dismissal has reaffirmed the anti-intellectualism, the crudity and bitterness of Australian parliamentary politics. The venom is still in the system.[5]

By 1982 that judgement on quality had been massively confirmed. One senior Australian politician even suggested the creation of a new Ministry of Scandals to take responsibility for the quite remarkable scale, consistency and range of ministerial corruption within the Fraser Government.

THE ORIGINS OF EMINENCE

Reagan, Thatcher and Fraser – an ageing screen cowboy with a terrible memory, propped up by an unlovely cabal of

[5] Maximilian Walsh, *Poor Little Rich Country*, Harmondsworth, Penguin, 1979, p. 100.

reactionary Californian millionaires (to quote one eminent American observer: 'Anyone who says we could have much worse presidents hasn't seen *Bedtime for Bonzo*') a socially risen lawyer/chemist with (by her account) an infallible memory and a wealthy, bullying agribusiness tycoon responsible for *fifteen* Cabinet resignations and sackings in the space of five years (and that before the 'Ministry of Scandals') – are not the first political leaders about whom people have felt somewhat lukewarm. We ought none the less to ask where they came from and how they rose through party ranks in order to be ready for the call. Are they really any worse than their predecessors, preserved in nostalgia? James Cameron, the distinguished British journalist, in a piece on nostalgia, asked:

Whatever happened to politicians? The old pros of yesteryear may not have been noticeably wiser or prettier than today, but at least they had recognizable and enduring personalities and characteristics. Compare a Churchill with a Thatcher, a de Gaulle with a Giscard, a Gandhi (M) with a Gandhi (F), a Roosevelt with a cowboy, a Stalin with a Kosygin, a Mao with a Hua, a Mussolini with whoever it happens to be this week. As well compare a Charlie Chaplin with a Woody Allen, a Hot Club de France with a pop group, a Segovia with a ukelele player. It is more than a difference in quality, it is a difference in kind.[6]

As is the case with many successful men (and especially American presidents – look at Lilian Carter and Rose Kennedy), the biggest parental influence on Ronald Reagan was his mother. The classic entrepreneurs tend to be sons of not very successful and somewhat distant immigrant fathers but with powerful mothers. To quote Reagan:

My father was likeable but not successful. He had various jobs; he worked some time in a shoe store but he didn't succeed at anything; he was good-natured, easy-going and he liked his drink, but my mother was a strong character and a very good Christian woman. . . . She was a great lady.[7]

This, as we shall see, is a persistent theme in the childhoods of political leaders: the distant and sometimes ideal-

---

[6] James Cameron, 'Nostalgia', *Guardian*, 31 December 1980.
[7] President Reagan interviewed by Kenneth Harris, *Observer*, 26 October 1980.

ized parent, plus careful nurturing from some other source – another parent perhaps or another person entirely. In the case of recent English political leaders that nurturing often came from an unrelated working-class nanny, into whose hands, (sometimes competent, sometimes grossly not so), children were placed completely. Jonathan Gathorne-Hardy even suggests[8] that the characteristic splitting of idealized women (distant mothers and frigid wives) from sexy women (working-class nannies and whores) can be attributed to this odd, and now largely discontinued, practice. Respectable ladies were distant and seen only in rigidly compartmentalized time slots; common ladies were associated with all intimate and pleasurable physical contact. That splitting is not the exclusive preserve of the English, though it is probably a little less striking in the USA and much less so in Australia.

Another persistent theme is the failed father. What the entrepreneur-to-be seeks is not really money, though that is the obvious goal, but control over a naughty world. If father can't hold the family boundary against adversity, the infant ingests a terror of encroaching uncertainty. When he grows up he is to be found, if successful, encased in a veritable cocoon of flunkeys, yes-men and bodyguards. Their function is to ensure that the great man is insulated from surprises – for ever. From now on, he is the one who administers the surprises to others.

Among leading artists a miserable childhood seems almost to be a help, particularly if characterized by brutality and solitude.[9] The list of such people is remarkable and includes Ruskin, Shaw, Turgenev (his mother appears to have achieved her orgasms by thrashing young Ivan, which didn't help matters), Delius, Kipling, Gorky and many others. Of course, in earlier times harsh treatment of children occurred matter of factly. It was the child with a certain genius who realized instinctively how extraordinary such treatment was – which must have signified an intuitive

[8] In his book *The Rise and Fall of the British Nanny*, London, Hodder & Stoughton, 1972.
[9] R. S. and C. M. Illingworth, *Lessons from Childhood : Some Aspects of the Early Life of Unusual Men and Women*, Edinburgh, Livingstone, 1966, p. 9.

grasp of some other 'normality'. The struggle towards that alternative vision of normality became the art. Most of these artists, of course, were thought to be dull at school; their minds were already elsewhere, further on. Gogol, a forerunner of Joseph Heller's character Yossarian in *Catch-22*[10], feigned madness in order to escape the harsh punishments of his school. Once in the sanitorium, he resumed a kind of contented normality, until the doctors came to look at him again.

The drive to succeed frequently comes primarily from the attempt to please the distant parent. Where the drive is not ameliorated by some nurturing force, it becomes a stern and persecutory tyrant. Hitler was of this type; so too was Mussolini:

I require to *be* somebody, do you understand me? I want to be not only the man I am. I want to rise to the *top*. In my youth I wanted to be a great musician or a great writer but I understood that I should have remained mediocre. The environment in which I was born enslaved me. I shall never be content. I tell you, I must *rise*, I must make a bound forwards, to the top.[11]

Mussolini's father was more devoted to his socialism than to young Benito, who was expelled, or nearly, from both of his first schools, both times for stabbing another boy. Even then the old Italian spirit of the vendetta could be determined in him. His school report said:

His character is passionate and unruly. He places himself in opposition to every rule and discipline of the school. One personal motive guides him, and this is the principal streak in his character; he wishes to requite every injury inflicted by an older schoolmate. He cannot support an injury; he wants revenge.[12]

Pugnacious the Reagans, Thatchers and Frasers may be, but they are not quite of this ilk. We must look to Colonel Gadafi, Generals Amin and Pinochet and the Ayatolla

[10] Joseph Heller, *Catch-22*, London, Corgi, 1972.
[11] Graham Tayar (ed.), *Personality and Power: Studies in Political Achievement*, London, BBC, 1971, p. 47.
[12] ibid., p. 45.

Khomeini for the modern equivalents of the 1930 dictators. We are happy enough, however, to accept their money in exchange for armaments. It is a bit like giving children dynamite to play with, and we ought not to complain when, as with General Galtieri, our own missiles are turned on us. It is, in fact, the triumphant vindication of Milo Minder-binder's[13] vision of free-market capitalism: it's OK to bomb your own base, *provided everybody has a share.*

The Australian press barons Rupert Murdoch and Kerry Packer, like young Mussolini, also followed in their fathers' footsteps but more so. In these cases the fathers were successful and tough but just respectable enough for knighthood. Sir Frank Packer used to force his sons into boxing gloves and clout them around a home-made ring. It toughened them up, no doubt, but there must have been other side-effects too. The Packer and Murdoch sons, born wealthy enough, have aimed on the whole for money rather than respectability. What they seem to like most of all is *winning* (see p. 47 and Sammy Glick).

TAKING UP POSITION

There is an extensive literature on the origins of national leaders. The purpose of this book is not to cover all that territory, nor to confine attention to political or national leaders. Some of the most interesting and relevant 'leaders' are those who, in small ways, provide models of power and authority in more homely settings – in families, gangs, schools, work places and so on. We ought, however, to pay some attention to another crucial period in the lives of most prominent people – that time in early to middle adulthood when they begin to take up positions in their chosen field. (Levinson's work on this matter is referred to in Chapter 1.)

At this stage there seems to be a necessity for most people to subjugate, to a limited extent, whatever independent instincts they may have developed in earlier life. They

---

[13] The eponymous capitalist/hero of Joseph Heller's *Catch-22.*

have not lost their distrust of authority, but they are able to take some kind of institutional role on trust, as it were, in order to get in. This really is where luck plays a part; the system may be overcrowded, and overcrowded with talent. Indeed, an entire generational cohort may be overcrowded as a result of an enthusiastic birth rate years before.[14]

The late 1930s were excellent years in which to be born and the 1950s absolutely terrible. No doubt the 1950s babies are now more competitive than their elders and very much more influenced by survival instincts – and why not? There is so much more competition for far fewer prizes.

The luck lies in being born at a nice, uncrowded time and, in the case of national leaders, in being at about the right age at points of important political discontinuity. It is also, of course, a matter of luck to have parents like Orson Welles's, who succeed in convincing the child that everything he does is touched by genius. The 'getting in' phase does demand a sympathetic patron for the late twenties and early thirties, and that may be a matter of luck too, though those who ensure high visibility for themselves very much increase their chances of attracting a suitable patron. One of C. P. Snow's characters advised: 'Never be too proud to be *there*!' If those crucial years are missed, the recovery of a successful career requires enormous energy, or luck, or both.

Khrushchev, for example, caught the eye of Lazar Kaganovich, the notorious head of the Ukrainian Communist Party, when he was just 33. When Kaganovich was transferred to Moscow he took his protégé with him. Later Khrushchev served as Stalin's faithful hatchet man, just as Stalin himself had grafted away in the wings awaiting his chance. Even later Khrushchev was to charm Western observers with his forthright humour. But in those early days 'it was not sufficient to be energetic, hard-working and loyal – one had to take on any assignment, however grisly, and carry it out with the utmost enthusiasm.'[15] The

[14] Richard A. Easterlin, *Birth and Fortune : The Impact of Numbers on Personal Welfare*, London, Grant McIntyre, 1980.
[15] Tayar, *Personality and Power*, p. 34.

late President Brezhnev, likewise, was Khrushchev's protégé in the Ukraine.

The spectacular rise and fall of General Alexander Haig (whose illustrious forbear, that *other* General Haig, is inspected in Chapter 6) is a good example of the courtier's route to the top.

The Pentagon's army of the 1950s and 1960s was designed to facilitate the promotion only of the ticket-punchers; of those officers who plotted their careers from West Point teaching post to staff college course, from being an aide to the kind of bureaucratic general who had the muscle to assign his own aides to ever more powerful postings, to marrying their daughters. It helped if, somewhere along the career trail, there was a combat command. Such men were more courtiers than professional soldiers. Al Haig spent his career as an intriguer and flatterer at the courts of General MacArthur in Japan and Korea, at the court of Cyrus Vance . . . , of Kissinger, of Nixon, and finally of Reagan.[16]

The striking thing is that the man whose troops 'trod the edge of atrocity' in Vietnam, who helped to protect the CIA from exposure of its illegal operations and who was involved, to some extent, in the Watergate-era wire tappings, ended up as the nearest thing to a 'liberal' in the Reagan cabinet.

Baldwin, a rather unlikely British Prime Minister, was, in a quite different and entirely British way, a courtier. He was nearly 50 when his father's old friendship with Prime Minister Bonar Law catapulted him into the corridors of power. As Law's Parliamentary Private Secretary (PPS) 'Baldwin's qualification for position as PPS was that he could (as the only son of a wealthy Worcestershire ironfounder) give his full time to the job, and above all, *keep his mouth shut.*'[17] Later on his only real competitor for leadership of the Conservative Party was Lord Curzon, an intellectually arrogant peer emotionally crippled in infancy by the sadistic ministrations of a mad nanny.[18]

---

[16] Roger Morris, *The General's Progress*, London, Ronson Books, 1982.
[17] Tayar, *Personality and Power*, p. 11.
[18] Gathorne-Hardy, *The Rise and Fall of the British Nanny.*

Baldwin, according to Sir Oswald Mosley (himself a leader of the best eccentric British type), was 'the yawn personified. He was a man who represented above all England asleep.'[19] Of course, he rose to power at a time when most of England *wanted* to sleep, to deny the grim realities of unemployment, housing decay and social injustice at home, as well as the horrors of Continental Fascism (see pp. 12–14 on basic-assumption flight). Baldwin was *exactly* what Britain deserved. He also exhibited another tendency of the obsessionally energetic but intellectually indolent leader: when the thinking got complex or abstracted, he would 'go out of gear'. Lord Swinton once told the tale of a long and important conversation between Baldwin and Neville Chamberlain about the 1926 Trades Dispute Bill. Baldwin forgot about it completely. Lord Swinton quotes Chamberlain:

Well, I simply cannot make head or tail of this. I started on him when I got there before dinner and argued it with him and put it very strongly to him and then we went at it again after dinner, and went on pressing it, and his reactions seemed favourable, until then I saw he'd gone out of gear. He started sucking blotting paper.[20]

Chapter 3 has touched on the question of intelligence in leaders and, in particular, the *mode* of intelligence. People with a reputation for incisiveness (those, for example, whose diaries are always overcrowded or who require completed 'staff work' on a single piece of paper) are sometimes incapable of concentrating on a complex issue for longer than half an hour (at which point, a kind of glazed portcullis descends over previously alert eyes or, more likely, the diary comes to the rescue). Most of us have met senior people who go 'out of gear' on occasion. It is not at all uncommon.

Like Baldwin, F. D. Roosevelt was well connected and even married his own cousin, a niece of President Theodore Roosevelt. He always wanted and intended to be

19 Tayar, *Personality and Power*, p. 15.
20 ibid., pp. 15–16.

President and didn't mind who knew it. (There is an engaging story about Margaret Thatcher, née Roberts, at Oxford. When a friend suggested she join the Univerisity Labour Club where, at that time, all the best and brightest young things congregated, she replied, 'You're just playing at politics. . . . I want to be Prime Minister some day – there's no competition down at the Tories!' And so it proved. When it came to the crunch thirty years later, Margaret Thatcher went through the male/Tory competition like an axe through butter.)

It helps to be single-minded in your ambitions, but the cost is usually single-mindedness – an incapacity to deal in a creative way with complexity and, perhaps worse still, an incapacity to see the joke. Roosevelt at least kept his charm. Sir George Catlin said of him that he possessed the magnetism and vitality of him who seems 'entirely present'. Catlin recollected that Lord Louis Mountbatten had the quality too, so did Pope Pius XII. Perhaps that is why Roosevelt is remembered as a great leader. He had sufficient wit (though not a lot to spare) to pursue important issues; he had the charm, plus the usual 'duplicitous' political skills. Catlin said:

The story is told by a certain person, let's call him Smith, who went in and talked to the President and put forward proposals and the President said, 'Well now, it's most interesting, Mr Smith, and I heartily agree with what you have to say; I'm deeply concerned with this – thank you so much.' And then Jones came in, put forward almost exactly the opposite and again he got the same reply from the President: 'I'm delighted to hear what you have to say, it's most interesting.' Eleanor Roosevelt then said, 'Franklin, you really do shock me. Here are these two men with quite opposite proposals and you told them that you agreed with both of them. I do think it's shocking.' And the President paused for a while and he said, 'Well, my dear, I entirely agree with you.'[21]

Churchill had the single-mindedness; it was really just a matter of historical events catching up with it. He came to

[21] ibid., pp. 28–9.

supreme political power even later than Baldwin – at 65. His childhood had obvious parallels with that of Lord Curzon except that, by chance, Churchill's nanny was as kind and nurturing as Curzon's was brutal and loony. Neglected by parents whom he none the less idolized, Churchill lent on Nanny Everest, who gave him 'total love and undiluted attention' for the first five years of his life. His nickname for her, with Freudian prescience, was 'Woomany'.

Later, when his aristocratic relatives summarily dismissed the poor woman, Churchill did his best to look after her financial needs. He was even at her death-bed;

Death came very easily to her. She had lived such an innocent and loving life of service to others, and held such a simple faith, that she had no fears at all, and did not seem to mind very much. She had been my dearest and most intimate friend during the whole of the twenty years I had lived.[22]

Nanny Everest gave Churchill something. What exactly it was we will examine below. He had one experience of British flagellatory lunacy, at an appalling prep school, whose headmaster was quite as mad and sadistic as Lord Curzon's nanny. Young Winston's Nanny Everest got him out of that, but not before he had been beaten mercilessly a few times. By the time he got to Harrow, he was ready for Hitler. Sir Harry Verney writes:

He was a little senior to me, and when I got to Harrow, I found there was a well known tradition of a very stupid little boy who would not learn Latin – nothing would induce him to. And of course we had to start by declining *mensa*, and when we had *mensa* ('a table') and then vocative *O mensa* ('Oh , table'), Winston went off the deep end. 'I'm not going to learn rubbish like this.' He would not learn any more. I don't think he ever learned the accusative, *mensam*. Never got as far as that. And he wouldn't learn and he didn't learn. He was immensely stupid, and known as the most stupid little boy but one in the whole of Harrow. The other, stupidest boy of all was the brother, Jack.[23]

[22] Winston Churchill, *My Early Life*, London, Thornton Butterworth, 1930, p. 86.
[23] Tayar, *Personality and Power*, p. 77.

Churchill knew better:

My teachers saw me as at once backward and precocious, reading books beyond my years and yet at the bottom of the form. They were offended.[24]

Chapter 3 deals with different meanings of the concept 'bright' or intelligent. The same goes for 'stupid'; we must remember that Einstein was hopeless at school too – which tells us something about Einstein and a whole lot about schools. In fact, the list of eminent scientists who were flops at school is remarkable – Newton, Watt ('dull and inept'), Darwin (the family produced five generations of Fellows of the Royal Society, all without much academic distinction until the post-graduate stage), Edison, Marconi, Pasteur and many others.

But Churchill always maintained the classic British anti-intellectualism, except when it came to writing and painting. Here, as with his brick-laying, there was a physical output. His observation that unemployment had no more to do with the Gold Standard than the Gulf Stream might have been modelled on his father's famous query (as Chancellor of the Exchequer, on a first encounter with the decimal system): 'What are those damned dots?' Admittedly, Churchill was ambitious. As Mrs C. F. G. Masterman remarked, 'I think he was terribly afraid of failing. He'd seen his father go down.'[25] Yet he had the kind of intelligence to seize on, and stay with, an issue – something which transcended political ambition. That is why bricks and (in Chapter 3) object relations are important to our analysis of leadership. Once the object occupies centre stage, leadership is no longer merely transactional; it assumes a 'transformational' character. It was said of Charles Gray, for example, that 'he had foreseen at 30 the necessity for a measure [the Reform Acts] which he carried at 70. . . . he seemed to be raised up to carry reform.'[26] (As a child, Gray had been taken, as a treat, to Tyburn to

[24] Churchill, *My Early Life*, p. 56.
[25] Tayar, *Personality and Power*, p. 77.
[26] James McGregor Burns, *Leadership*, New York, Harper & Row, 1978.

witness the public hanging of a group of Jews found guilty of fraud. He was a sensitive child, and the experience seems to have reinforced his innate loathing of injustice and naked power.)

Eminent people do seem to have much in common – perseverance, intelligence, self-conviction, verbal fluency, energy and the capacity to cope with stress. Many seem to have had at least one distant and perhaps unsuccessful parent, and almost all seem to require patronage at the point of consolidation in the chosen field. A period in the political wilderness is a common theme too. One expert divides successful politicians into obsessionals (Baldwin, for example), controlled hypermanics (like Khrushchev, Churchill, Roosevelt and Mussolini) and, finally, controlled sociopathics (Hitler and Stalin). You do, in other words, require enormous energy to sustain high position, though the sources of energy may differ from person to person.

Displaced people tend to be energetic, sometimes pathologically so. Their marginality, which is moral as well as broadly cultural, allows them to cut across the existing order. It is exciting to see what you can do/get away with. It was Henry Kissinger who once said, 'Power is the ultimate aphrodisiac!' But he started life as Heinz Kissinger, a very orthodox Jew in a very unfortunate place, the town of Feurth in Nazi Bavaria. He was born, in fact, quite close in time and space to the Beer Hall Putsch. When the time came to escape from Germany, one of those who didn't get away recalled later: 'In 1937 I tried to go to America. I got an immigrant number that said I would have to wait seven or eight years – it was all sold out. Henry was smart and he could see (at the age of 15) what was going on. He was thinking alien.'[27] Later, in America and at the height of his power, Kissinger actually cultivated that heavy German accent.

Many presently successful people were made by the dislocations of the Second World War, just as a striking number of the Asian businessmen expelled from Uganda

---

[27] R. Blumenfeld *et al.*, *Henry Kissinger: The Private and Public Story*, New York, Signet, 1974, p. 33.

by General Amin quickly recouped a fortune, from scratch, in Britain. The Hungarians, as I have noted elsewhere,[28] more or less run the Australian economy, while the original (but not Aboriginal) Australians laze about enjoying the benefits. There is an apocryphal tale about the sale of Mr Robert Maxwell's Pergamon Press publishing house to the American entrepreneur Saul (Leasco) Steinberg. Steinberg, so the tale goes, thought that Maxwell was probably the offspring of another Robert Maxwell, perhaps also an MP. His suspicions about Pergamon (quite well founded as things turned out) surfaced only when he learned that the vendor was none other than Ludwig Koch, a refugee from the nether parts of Czechoslavakia and known affectionately to the satirical magazine *Private Eye* as the 'Bouncing Czech'.

Once you achieve the first step to high visibility, the system works for you. The media require names the way supermarket shelves require stock. There is only so much space next to the check-out at eye level; the trick is to be there. In career systems, once you begin to be promoted on the basis of reputation rather than output, you will be difficult to stop. Even attempting to stop you will be newsworthy. You have become part of an informal coalition of visible persons, part of an Establishment. All you then require is a modicum of talent (sufficient to avoid very embarrassing blunders) and immense sustaining energy. A lot of talent (see Rab Butler, pp. 132–3 below) may be a positive hindrance.

MARGARET, RONALD AND MALCOLM

Before we pass on to less eminent leaders, it is instructive to consider the professional callings of the three national leaders with whom we began. Though rather different people, Thatcher, Reagan and Fraser appeal, in their different ways, to a similar yearning in the populace – a yearning for firm and simple government and for the projection

---

[28] See Alistair Mant, *The Rise and Fall of the British Manager*, London, Pan, 1979.

of bad feelings on to others, foreigners, minorities or whoever. After Carter the USA wished to fantasize. President Carter, as I have pointed out, emphasized the Chief Executive aspect of the President's role. The dominant and quite conscious image then was of a shirt-sleeved President slaving all night over the cables.

It was all too much like real life, and especially so when the US cavalry failed to save the Iranian hostages' day. Then the dinner suits returned to the White House lawns and, according to the Press Corps, the new President slept through most of the executive activity. The President as Chief Executive was dead (or sleeping); long live the Head of State. If you had deliberately set about wreaking this change from ignominious reality back to romantic fantasy, where would you have gone? To Hollywood, of course, for a cowboy from Central Casting.

In Australia Prime Minister Fraser, probably the most intelligent of these three national leaders, used to present himself as a simple farming man (the periodic cropping of Cabinet Ministers supported this image). In truth, Fraser, like President Carter, is an agribusiness tycoon. His ascendancy represented a return to agrarian 'normality' after the effete, intellectual Whitlam years. What Australia does is sell the land – the crops that grow on it, the meat that fattens and the wool that thickens on it, and the minerals that constitute it. When the prestigious Jackson Committee called for a 'general debate' on participation in the management process in Australian industry, the appeal might have been shouted from the top of Ayer's Rock on a wet Thursday. The whole idea was complicated, unfamiliar, a bit pink and, above all, abnormal. The constitutional problems remain and eat away at the effectiveness of the vital (and grossly over-protected) Australian industrial sector.

In this respect, Margaret Thatcher is perhaps most interesting of all. Her social and professional make-up is as follows.

(1)   Like Reagan (but unlike Fraser), she has risen from modest lower-middle-class origins (by repute, her

father was a notably tough employer of the Grantham
ladies who worked in the family grocery business).

(2) She trained, in the first instance, as a chemist – a field
in which you set up experiments in the laboratory
and, if you get it right, they work. It is a go/no-go
world of perfection or complete failure. The trick is to
get the experimental design right. ICI, Britain's top
chemical company, turned her down for a job, possibly for want of the flexibility you need to work with
messy industrial reality.

(3) She trained, latterly, as a tax lawyer. As Chapter 6
reminds us, barristers in particular have to convince
themselves absolutely of the rightness of their case (no
matter how villainous the client may be) and the
absolute inadmissibility of all contrary argument. The
barrister is the Fuller Brush salesman of the professions; for a fee, he will sell *anything*.'

All this can add up to a lethal combination in a national
leader. The socially uprisen often harbour a distaste, even
contempt, for those they have left behind in the lower
orders. In truth, the Thatcher Government is a government of and for the ambitious, rising, managerial elite. It is
also a government of experiment, treating complex society
as if it were a machine which, after a period of down time,
can be got to work again. Also, unlike the old blue-blood
Tories, able to accept left-wing politicians at face value
(Butler, for example, regarded Aneurin Bevan as a political
giant), the new breed tends to experience all shades of grey
as bright pink.

But society is not a machine. You need a special kind of
intellect to grasp that the system upon which you experiment is affected, in the meantime, by the process of experimentation. Human beings, unlike machines, don't spend
periods in down time; they simply lament the passing of
time and the missing of opportunities. The older and wiser
they are, the better they recognize the irrecoverability of
time. In truth, the lawyer/chemist employs a simple space
metaphor for the world, where all the elements are fixed
and none more so than the lawyer/chemist himself. In a

world of fixed elements (like a properly conducted chemical experiment), the notion of 'reality' makes sense. In the real world of political events, where everything moves constantly, including one's own vantage point, reality is a matter of opinion.

There is a revealing account of Margaret Thatcher's visit to Peking in 1976. In a Sunday briefing with three of the favoured journalists covering the tour, she was asked by one of them if her daughter Carol was to meet Chairman Hua's daughter or (also in Peking at the time) Chip Carter, the American President's son, a recent law graduate like Carol herself. Later, in her meeting with Chairman Hua, Mrs Thatcher got her facts muddled and said, 'I understand you have a daughter who is a lawyer?' Chairman Hua responded, inscrutably, 'I have no *son* who is a lawyer!' At which obscure joke all the Chinese present grinned broadly.

Afterwards, on the train to Shanghai, the 'offending' journalist (OJ) was carpeted by a furious Margaret Thatcher.

MT :   You told me that Chairman Hua had a son who was a lawyer!
OJ :   No I didn't – I said President *Carter*'s son is a lawyer.
MT :   (*Tapping forehead*) Mr —, I have a filing system here. I always remember these things correctly!

At this stage the two other journalists chipped in and corroborated the version of their hapless colleage. Still the Thatcherian 'filing-system' resisted any contrary version of reality. Finally, all three journalists, by now quite angry, wrote down what had happened, signed the document (even the local Foreign Office man, also present at the original incident, signed at some risk to his career prospects) and sent it down the train. Mrs Thatcher never spoke to the poor OJ again, nor for a long time to the other two journalists. They were scribblers of such eminence that she had little choice there, but the 'filing system', no doubt, remained unruffled, impeccably consistent (from within).

This really is the point about the simple binary mind and

the secret of its attractiveness to voters. It reflects a kind of reassuring, consistent *certainty*, immensely appealing after too much wallowing in the mire of reality. Mrs Thatcher, for example, is much given to extolling the virtues of Housewifely Thrift in the nation's affairs (notwithstanding Britain's massive international debt). Jean Hayward, a Grantham contemporary of the young Margaret Roberts, put it succinctly in a letter to the *Guardian*:

Having shared the PM's Grantham upbringing, I think I can shed light on her housekeeping policies.

She was raised Chapel, and Alderman Roberts would never have owed a ha'penny to anybody. His shop served a neighbourhood of neat houses, tenanted by lower-middle and upper-working classes who would face hunger rather than the shame of tick.

There was, however, nearby New Street, a condemned slum where dwelt a mucky lot whose reliance on the dole, the never-never and boozing on the slate was a horrid example to us all. Some of their children were fed in a soup kitchen, paid for by honest citizens who stood on their own two feet and owned bikes. These kids could be pitied, but not played with, by the clean ones.

Margaret left them behind by passing a scholarship to the Girls' High, which was a bit posh. The girls were divided into scholarship-passers and paying pupils, most of whom had come up from the kindergarten or the Misses Bailey's Private School. Paying parents bought uniforms on credit accounts from the approved drapers. Scholarship parents paid cash, but tended to buy cheap – not Jaeger – knickers. Their girls were thus clearly at a disadvantage, however clean and clever.

Superiority could be attempted by winning all the prizes, taking elocution lessons, and becoming head girl. The ploy did not impress those who were born with the right accent and knew they were top anyway.

Some of us have outgrown this childhood view of the socioeconomic system; others manifestly have not.[29]

It is a rare leader indeed who can inspire while facing boldly towards the essential messiness, unpredictability and frustration of the real world – what *can't* and *won't* happen

[29] *Guardian*, 26 November 1982.

rather than what is *supposed* to happen. Still, such people
exist. We have to know how to recognize them and provide
a bit of elbow room for their progression to high rank. We
cannot allow them simply to opt out, out of sheer boredom
with the competing simpletons.

THE EXPOSED JUGULAR

Who are the political leaders with a more subtle turn of
mind, and what happens to their careers? At this point
most people seem to refer back to Adlai Stevenson in the
USA and in Britain, to Hugh Gaitskell and Iain Macleod
(both of whom died prematurely). All these were liked and
trusted but perceived to lack 'killer instinct'; they were nice
guys. (A scrutiny of the Australian political scene has not
yielded any nice guys at all, but perhaps they exist.) Possibly, Stevenson's great 'failing' was his incapacity to relate
everything that happened in the Third World to the cold
war and therefore to the inevitability of military solutions.
Twenty years later, post-Vietnam, that looks like a healthy
'failing'; at the time Stevenson just seemed like a 'soft-line'
man in the era of 'hard-nosed' lawyers, bankers and
systems analysts clustered around Macnamara, Rusk and
others. We may have entered a similar era in American
politics now.

In Britain nobody quite understood why R. A. (Rab)
Butler never became leader of the Conservative Party and
therefore (in the 1950s) Prime Minister. He was so obviously streets ahead of his Conservative contemporaries in
intellect and lucidity and could, had he been better
organized and more resolute, have succeeded Churchill.
Churchill himself feared at the last that Eden might not be
up to the job, and Butler had been the principal architect of
the Conservatives' narrow election victory in 1951 and also
a highly successful Chancellor of the Exchequer for four
years. Butler, of course, knew from the start that the Suez
war was a lunatic act (about as pointless as Vietnam, and as
misconceived) but made the mistake of *saying* so. Macmillan, who got the job, was more cunning about expressing
his misgivings.

In 1956, Eden had invaded at Suez and then retired ill, leaving
Butler for three weeks in control. Butler withdrew the troops and
restored the pound. He was then taken by surprise by Eden's
resignation, but Macmillan was not. Butler, as he puts it, was
plugging away at his job [my italics] trying to save what he could
out of Suez, while Conservative backbenchers by subtle propa-
ganda were told that the withdrawal had been his fault, and
Macmillan, '*a most able politician*' [Butler's italics] courted the
younger members of the Cabinet. Butler writes: 'I suffered very
much at this time. . . . I do not think there have been many
occasions where the blame was more wrongfully attached.'[30]

Many people take the view that Butler's downfall was really
his incapacity to tolerate humbug and stupidity. In this he
resembles a more recent Conservative Cabinet casualty,
Norman St John-Stevas. Butler was not only contemptuous
of the pompous fools around him; he was, much worse
still, very funny about them. The capacity to see the joke,
as I have argued above, is not only important in leaders; it
is a *sign* of intelligence, at least, the kind of intelligence
which grasps complex systems. St John-Stevas is reputed
to have coined two of the more popular epithets for Mrs
Thatcher, 'the Leaderene' and 'the Blessed Margaret' – so
much for St John-Stevas.

In hindsight, it seems likely that if Stevenson and Butler
had come to power, then neither Vietnam nor Suez would
have happened. Why not? Because both men were bright
and level-headed enough to see the folly beforehand, and
neither could believe in President Nasser or the 'communist threat' as the anti-Christ. They fell short of power
because they both lacked 'killer instinct' and, perhaps more
important, were seen to lack it. The wonder of it is that
Stevenson ever got the Democratic nomination in the first
place. The people sensed they were unsatisfactory glad-
iators, yet many of them knew they were wise men. In the
end the people got the leaders they deserved.

Now, there is a curious phenomenon, observable in the
competitive rituals of large organizations, to do with the

---

[30] Terry Coleman on R. A. Butler's *The Art of Memory* (London, Hodder &
Stoughton, 1982), *Guardian*, 22 April 1982.

killer instinct and its corollary, the submission impulse. What is more, the phenomenon is clearly the counterpart of aggressive display and response in the wild. The animals, by and large, manage to establish pecking-orders without undue loss of life. When, somehow, dominance is established between combatants, the subordinate beast bares his neck in an attitude of submission – the equivalent of 'OK, OK, you win', or 'Pax!', or throwing in the towel. At this signal the dominant beast stalks off, honour satisfied. Humans, as Lorenz suggested, are rather more inclined to press on to the kill. (It helps, of course, to be distanced from victims by technology and a few thousand feet.)

People who are gunning for the top almost invariably signal the fact to others. The implicit signal is: 'I am ambitious. Watch out for me because I will do whatever is necessary to secure my career interests, whether it contributes to organizational aims or not. I have no shame.' The Butlers of this world, to quote Woodrow Wyatt, writing in the *Sunday Times* in 1982, are too proud, or too decent, to scrabble in the dust for the highest prize. They stand back, baring the neck as it were, and leave the field to the aggressors, sometimes with amused contempt, more often in bewilderment. Almost invariably, hidden in the retreat are strong, sensible people whose leadership capacities are destined to outgrow and outlast the aggressors. These people are passed over.

Butler's reluctance to 'scrabble in the dust' is paralleled by that of Paul Hasluck in Australia. When Prime Minister Holt (as accident-prone, in his way, as Anthony Eden) contrived, at the second attempt, to drown himself in 1967, many took the view that Hasluck, then Minister for Foreign Affairs and later Governor-General, was a logical successor. But he confined his leadership campaign to one dignified letter to each party member. The extravert John Gorton got the job after what has been described as a 'presidential campaign on television'.[31] He lasted just two years, until his own inglorious and lubriciously scandalous departure, largely engineered by (surprise, surprise)

[31] Maximilian Walsh, *Poor Little Rich Country*, Harmondsworth, Penguin, 1979.

Malcolm Fraser, then his Minister for Defence. What Hasluck thought of it all is not clear but can be imagined.

Most ambitious people proceed by attaching themselves to patrons just a few years further along the same path. Such patrons may be on the point of running out of steam intellectually and morally, in which case the protégé is a source of succour and a reassurance that ambition is a worthy god. Most interestingly, those whose job it is to advise on promotion and succession, usually quite *nice* people, frequently collude with all this on the mistaken assumption that the 'killer instinct' is more important than wit. By 'wit' I mean brains *plus* common sense. There is an important distinction to be made between what psychologists call 'operating intelligence' and the kind of frigid intelligence that comes from cramming data and impressing dim-witted university professors but is of no earthly use.

However, there are organizations, notably the British Civil Service, that go out of their way to prefer gentle, amateurish souls who wouldn't hurt a fly. In Civil Service Selection Boards some of these souls get through to become straightforward incompetents, but the vast majority of successful aspirants, perceiving the rules of the game, simply succeed in concealing their brutish ambitions with greater skill than their adversaries. Thus the extraordinary blend of amateurishness and crude ambition that distinguishes some parts of the British Civil Service is sustained.

6
Getting On

*We garner the fruits of our formative institutions (the family
and school) in the world of work (or, more correctly nowadays, of employment and unemployment). In fact, the connection between getting a job (survival – ∘–∘) and what wants
doing (real work with real, valued outputs – ⊐) is tenuous at
best. Here we examine the work of a variety of institutions –
politics, law, the military, the police, diplomacy, sport, the
Church, the arts – and the problems of bearing authority
within them. The chapter concludes with an account of a
remarkable historical figure who relinquished employment and
risked survival in order to do* what wanted doing.

WARRIORS AFTER THE FRAY

The reader may wonder why I have devoted quite so much
time to the primal origins of behaviour, attitude and
pattern of thought. There are several reasons for doing so:

Leaders are exposed. Whatever their own hang-ups
about dependence, and they may well be considerable, the
dependent projections of everybody else rest upon the
leader. Most people feel personally involved with their
leaders, even though, at a rational level, their relationship is
purely institutional. The leader speaks for the follower, and
when he is perceived to fail the failure is felt, like as not, as
a personal betrayal. When followers turn nasty on charismatic leaders (witness Mussolini's mutilated corpse, strung
up by the toes for public vilification) they turn very nasty
indeed.

Without adequate education in these matters, people are
inclined to seek out the kind of leaders who have always
had difficulty with dependent relationships – people, for
example, who could not tolerate their fathers and who
cannot now tolerate the giving up of dependence to
anybody. Such people usually need, however, to be depended upon, as others need drugs. Once installed in power,
they rule by division. The very interpersonal association
with leadership that the followers crave is the means by
which they are kept separate from one another and without
institutional coherence. As I believe Speer commented
about Hitler, 'He had always carried out the old principle,
divide and rule. There were political groups who were
always ready to do away with others. A few critical words
from Hitler, and all Bormann's enemies would have
jumped at his throat.'[1]

Relationships characterized by super-dependence are
regressive; that is to say, they re-enact earlier childhood
experience. Under extreme pressure, and without adequate
institutional buffers, leaders are inclined to regress. James
McGregor Burns recounts the poignant tale of a dinner at
the White House in the winter of 1968.[2] Present with
Burns were the President, Lyndon Baines Johnson, a
White House staff member, an ex-Governor of Texas, plus
all the wives. After a long stiff pre-dinner period in which
all scrupulously avoided the subject of Vietnam, LBJ began
to reminisce about his boyhood years in Texas.

He talked until dinner — about his parents, his mother's expectations of him, his father's discipline, his brothers and sisters. He
talked during dinner, hardly bothering to eat, about his life and
troubles growing up. He talked on and on after dinner, while his
wife and friends listened with apparent interest to stories they
must have heard many times.[3]

---

[1] The quotation is broadly accurate; I regret that its source eludes me. To
pursue, see Albert Speer, *Inside the Third Reich*, London, Sphere, 1981, p. 138.
[2] James McGregor Burns, *Leadership*, New York, Harper & Row, 1978.
[3] ibid., pp. 422–3.

Finally, exhausted by the flow of words, Burns excused himself. The President accompanied him to the elevator and then

announced and conducted a tour of the family living quarters, including a look at the presidential bedside piled with memoranda and reports.[4]

On the following day, they talked again. Burns gained the impression that the President was, 'seeking a final victory before the bar of history' and that, though he himself was but a humble academic, 'every juror would count.' Later, Johnson recounted a recurring dream of impotence. He apparently dreamed he was lying in bed in the Red Room of the White House, paralysed from the neck down, listening to his aides in the next room, quarrelling over the division of power. In the dream he could hear but not speak. Waking, he would make his way through the empty corridors of the White House to Woodrow Wilson's portrait.

It soothed him to touch Wilson's portrait, for Wilson had been paralysed and now was dead but Johnson was still alive and active. In the morning the fears would return – of paralysis of the body, paralysis of his presidency. And soon he would quit.[5]

Johnson was perhaps the archetype of what McGregor Burns calls 'transactional' leadership – that is, leadership built upon a huge network of ○–○ interpersonal transactions. People who looked to be of use were given the 'Johnson treatment', 'the powerful application of varying concoctions of supplication, accusation, cajolery, exuberance, scorn, tears, complaint, the hint of threat'.[6] Godfrey Hodgson described the phenomenon thus:

a legislator whose vote was needed would find himself literally surrounded by a one-man army of Lyndon Johnson. His birthday would be remembered, his vanity flattered, his shoulder

[4] ibid., p. 423.
[5] ibid.
[6] ibid., p. 345.

squeezed. He would be reminded, subtly or brutally according to the estimate made of his temperament, of his political problems at home or of his hopes of advancement on Capital Hill. Every scrap of information would be retrieved, every tactic used, until the wretched man did what was wanted of him; then he would be overwhelmed by signs of the majority leader's gratitude and admiration.[7]

The tragedy of Lyndon Johnson was not that he was without vision, but that the survival aspects of his character triumphed in the end. Hodgson puts it succinctly.

He was proud, domineering, insecure, persuasive, egotistical, subtle, coarse, sentimental, vindictive, intelligent (though not at all intellectual), insistent upon loyalty (yet capable of the most brutal ingratitude to those who had been loyal to him), needing love (yet not always able to repress upwelling bitterness and anger). Of the three very able and complex men who occupied the White House during (the post war period), he was perhaps the ablest, and surely the most complex. Yet the origins of his tragedy can be traced to two simple characteristics: he was passionately ambitious to be remembered as a great President. And big and leathery as he looked, he was as sensitive to what others thought about him as a man with no skin.[8]

The transactional or ○—○ leader tends to end up a bit like LBJ, not really understanding the past and desperate for justification, as Burns puts it, before the 'bar of history'. Sir Garfield Barwick, acknowledged as one of the finest advocates of the Australian bar and one-time Attorney-General, Foreign Minister and Chief Justice, provides a curiously similar example of the adversarial personality after the action is over. As Chief Justice, Barwick was a principal actor in the unseating (described above) of Prime Minister Whitlam. His advice to the Governor-General (another ex-member of the Sydney Bar) was that he could, and by implication ought to, withdraw the commission of the democratically elected Prime Minister if it seemed likely that the Senate (the Australian Upper House) would

[7] Godfrey Hodgson, *In Our Time*, London, Macmillan, 1976, p. 170.
[8] ibid., pp. 167–8.

refuse money supply to the Government. Barwick went
further and advised that the Governor-General's duty
would then be to invite the Leader of the Opposition to
form a caretaker Government. (It could be predicted that
the sitting Prime Minister, as o—o a character as Barwick
himself, might decline to be so unseated if allowed to
remain in office.) This is, in fact, what happened.

Australian constitutional law was vague enough to permit
all this ambiguity. In truth, the Leader of the Opposition,
Malcolm Fraser, had already observed some time before:

> If we do make up our minds at some stage that the Government
> is so reprehensible that an Opposition must use whatever power
> is available to it, then I'd want to find a situation in which we
> make that decision and Mr Whitlam woke up one morning
> finding that decision had been made and finding that he had been
> caught with his pants well and truly down.[9]

(Much Australian political debate is conducted at this sort
of level.) After this sort of remark, the great suspicion
among Australians was that there might have been some
collusion between Barwick and Fraser beforehand. Barwick
had become increasingly reactionary in his opinions in
recent years and increasingly disturbed by the line taken by
Prime Minister Whitlam. Barwick was also, of course, an
ex-Government Minister of Fraser's Liberal (i.e.
Conservative) Party. In the event, the sitting Labour Government was not permitted to exhaust all the available
options to obtain supply before the money actually ran out.

Afterwards an ex-Attorney-General and High Court colleague of Barwick's dissociated himself from the Chief
Justice's advice to the Governor-General as follows:

> In my view, a Chief Justice, or any other Justice of this Court,
> should not act as a constitutional advisor to the Governor-
> General on a subject such as this which would always be
> intensely controversial and involve the whole country in an
> extreme degree of political partisanship. I am not discussing the

[9] David Marr, *Barwick*, London, Allen & Unwin, 1980, p. 251.

question of a Chief Justice giving advice to a Governor-General
in any circumstances, only on extremely political events, and
particularly where he knows that the advice he is giving to the
Governor-General is in direct opposition to that being given to
the Governor-General by the Prime Minister. The advice was, in
my opinion, wrong, and by its disregard of the options open to
the Governor-General, seriously prejudicial to one side in the
political confederacy. I dissociate myself completely from your
action in advising the Governor-General and from the advice you
gave.[10]

Barwick's reply was typically curt:

You have entirely misconceived my purpose in informing the
members of the Court of my actions. . . . I did so merely out of
courtesy and not in any sense to seek support or acquiescence. I
need neither. . . . I note your remarks. I fundamentally disagree
with them, both as to any legal opinion they involve, and as to
any matter of the propriety of my conduct. I see no need to
discuss with you either question.[11]

As Barwick remarked later, one of the advantages of being
Chief Justice was that he was 'not accountable to anyone'.
    The echo of LBJ resonated a few months later at a
National Press Club lunch in Canberra. Barwick, the guest
speaker, led with his chin in a battle with the assembled
press corps. As he slugged it out with his questioners, the
grounds of his constitutional decision became less and less
secure. Yet Barwick could not leave off. 'It seemed,
observed [one of the journalists present]: "as if he wanted
to spill his guts. He seemed upset by the hostility and skill
of the questions and he felt himself under attack. He was
anxious to talk. It was like a confessional." ' After the lunch
Barwick stood on the footpath outside the Club speaking
with journalists for three-quarters of an hour. The engine
of his car was running, and the president of the Club inter-
vened a number of times to allow the Chief Justice to get
away but he brushed the interruptions aside and went on
talking: about the old days with Lang and about Whitlam's

[10] ibid., p. 282.
[11] ibid.

duty to resign the moment supply was deferred. He accused Whitlam of 'threatening' Kerr and remarked, 'If I were Kerr, I would have sacked Whitlam on the first day.'[12]

Barwick's biographer, David Marr, describes the Chief Justice's closing professional years in terms strangely reminiscent of James McGregor Burns's White House encounter with the failing President Johnson.

In his social round, Barwick found himself an object of curiosity. His talk was anecdotal, breaking off occasionally to remark out of the blue what the Queen Mother had said to him the year before. He spoke of the law as if he stood at its font. He talked of sailing as if he once sailed before the mast and circumnavigated the globe. His flow of stories rarely faltered. It was as if he feared silence, as if he feared that responding to his listeners might reveal something of himself that he wished to keep back. He did not discuss ideas. Here was an old man who appeared to enjoy few of the satisfactions of age: he was not reflective, did not read, and the past had little interest for him beyond anecdote. His tales were principally about his victories; while listening to him, it seemed that being able to beat anyone, whether on the floor of the House, in a yacht, or in court, was his idea of what life was all about.[13]

It is as poignant a description as one could ask for of the adversarial mind, a mind professionally canalized to inflate one view and to discredit absolutely the opposing view. It is always a decisive mind, but no less prone to error than any other.

As an advocate [o—o] he had very great skill at solving his clients' problems, at getting them out of a fix, but as a Judge [⊃—⊃] he faced a different task; to set out the true position of all the parties, to identify and expound the truth. Few judicial ideas and principles emerged from the mass of his judgments. It was always easier to guess Barwick's response to a case than to predict what principles he would use to decide it.[14]

---

[12] ibid., pp. 287–8.
[13] ibid., pp. 283–4.
[14] ibid., p. 291.

Barwick, a survivor to the last, came through the constitutional crisis in better shape than his fellow lawyer, Kerr.
The Governor-General was hounded from office within
two years, a victim of jeering crowds wherever he went.
Paint was thrown over his car, and mounted police had to
escort him even to cocktail parties.

Barwick had been careful to leave Kerr and Fraser in the
limelight, yet no one doubted he was the strong, decisive
figure in the eye of the storm: 'It was a matter for *him*
[Kerr] to be satisfied that there was no chance of getting
supply. The rest was for him – not me.'[15] Fraser, however,
did become Prime Minister and at least as ∘—∘ a Prime Minister as Whitlam had been. (It is probably more than coincidence that they are both physical giants.)

Perhaps on 11 November 1975 Prime Minister Whitlam
ought to have invoked the ⊱ model and simply telephoned
the Queen. But by then his eyes were glinting with battle,
and anyway his quasi-Republican sentiments were a matter
of public record. It would have been galling, when salva-
tion might have been a phone call away, to invoke a tiny
woman on the other side of the world. At that moment
Whitlam (and all Australia by extension) was in the
awkward predicament of the teenager who has rejected parental authority yet still needs something to be 'out there'
when the chips are down. The Queen is a sensible woman,
and soundly advised, but very difficult indeed to envision
as a protagonist at the OK Corral.

THE MILITARY-INDUSTRIAL IDIOT

Most of the examples in the first part of this book are
drawn from the worlds of family, school and industrial
work. These are the experiences most of us share. But the
∘—∘ and ⊱ dimensions are present in all walks of life – in the
professions, in sport, in the military, the police, the
Church and so on. We have dwelt on early infancy, and in
particular on the theory of 'good' and 'bad' objects, because

[15] ibid., p. 285.

so many eminent figures rise to eminence as a result of infantile conditioning and then, under stress, replay those experiences repeatedly, purposelessly and, sometimes, destructively.

I have spent many years tinkering with the workings of organizations large and small in the hope of making things happen *despite* the people ensconced in the power networks. Age, weariness and constant frustration have led me to conclude that it is always more efficient to go for the people – that is, to remove those who will never have the wit or strength of character to shoulder the leader's burden, and to replace them with better men and women. What then divides sheep from goats is easier to sense than to describe, which means, probably, that it derives from the primal core of personality.

Perhaps the obvious place to pursue a discussion of the ∘–∘/꠸ꠦ polarity, and especially the former, is in the military. We all move, quite naturally, from one pole to the other according to circumstance and usually on fairly short cycles. The problem for military forces is that the cycles are usually longer and quite unpredictable. Behaviour and leadership style appropriate to peacetime tend to fail in war and vice versa. Of course, it matters which war: wars of aggression and conquest are essentially ∘–∘ in character. The best that can be dredged up as a 'third corner' tends to be rather woolly and unconvincing – *Lebensraum*, or the 'communist threat', or whatever. The defence of the homeland is another matter again. Then the basis of authority is a shared experience of threat to a valued 'third corner' or 'good' object. Once that institutional condition is satisfied, armies are freed to fight as fiercely as may be in the ∘–∘ survival mode. (Wilfred Bion went so far as to argue that even in peacetime the armed forces act as a subconscious container for our aggressions, just as the police act as containers for our delinquent urges.)[16]

[16] W. R. Bion, *Experiences in Groups*, London, Tavistock, 1961, p. 157.

The problem with armies, navies and so on is put neatly by Norman F. Dixon:

Those very characteristics which are demanded by war – the ability to tolerate uncertainty, spontaneity of thought and action, having a mind open to the receipt of novel, and perhaps threatening, information — are the antitheses of those possessed by those *attracted* to the controls, and orderliness, of militarism. Here is the germ of a terrible paradox. Those very people who, because they have adopted attack rather than submission or flight as their preferred psychological defence against threat, are in theory the best suited to warring behaviour, may be the very ones *least* well equipped for other components of successful fighting.[17]

This is Dixon's polite way of stating that a remarkable number of generals, admirals and so on, past and present, have been very thick indeed. It is in the nature of peacetime to attract to the military those authoritarian personalities most defended against ambiguity and complexity and most needing a container for aggressive instincts. Because such people think in a ∘–∘ way, and because they need war to give coherence to their tunnel-like perspective on the world, it is easy for them to believe in the absolute Satanic evil of the adversary, whoever it happens to be. Because such people are very energetic, they usually succeed collectively in shifting the national consciousness towards the likelihood, the inevitability and, finally, the desirability of war. The war, when it comes, releases their own internal tensions and, ironically, reveals their absolute incompetence. After a while, perhaps a few years, the awfulness and pointlessness of war act as antibodies and the countervailing anti-war forces emerge. By this time, inevitably, a new and more competent breed of military leaders has emerged, most of them destined to get out of the peacetime military as soon as they possibly can. Thus peacetime tends to tug us into war, and war, after a while, pulls us back to peace again, like the ebb and flow of the tides.

[17] Norman F. Dixon, *On the Psychology of Military Incompetence*, London, Futura, 1979, p. 194.

Dixon argues that many military leaders (for example, those of the First World War) display behaviour symptomatic of weak ego function. In this light:

their behaviour typifies the neurotic paradox in which the individual's need to be loved breeds, on the one hand, an insatiable desire for admiration with avoidance of criticism and, on the other, an equally devouring urge for power and positions of dominance. The paradox is that these needs inevitably result in behaviour so unrealistic as to earn for the victim the very criticism which he has been striving so hard to avoid.[18]

Anyone puzzled by Richard Nixon's compulsion to commit his undoing to magnetic tape should be no more surprised than the policeman who understands the urge of the criminal to return to the scene of the crime. It isn't that he wants to be caught so much that he cannot tolerate the uncertainty of not knowing when a nemesis, in which he believes absolutely, will catch up with him.

On the theme of nemesis, I worked once with a senior manager in the computer industry, renowned for his aggression and energy. He was very successful, very unpopular and very ○—○. One night he broke down and confessed to me some of his background. His father, it seems, used to beat him fairly regularly and more or less illogically. When he went to school – a very tough one, naturally – he began to be beaten up there too, more or less for sport. After a time his world view came to focus not on *whether* he would be beaten up but *when*. Accordingly, the only way to reduce the intolerable anxiety about that was to hit first. He did, and it worked. He had done the same thing ever afterwards, metaphorically speaking, in all his relationships. It had brought him considerable success, so it was scarcely easy for him to fault it as a world view.

Dixon takes the view that there are two principal classes of military incompetence. The first class includes Generals Elphinstone (first Afghan war), Raglan (Crimea), Buller (Boer War) and Percival (Singapore), who appear to have been careless, to say the least, with the fighting forces entrusted

18 ibid., p. 115.

to their command. These were all 'mild, courteous and peaceful men' paralysed by the burden of decision-making under fire. The other class is characterized by 'overweening ambition coupled with a terrifying insensitivity to the suffering of others'. This group includes Haig (alarmingly, a close relative of General Alexander Haig), Joffre and a number of the other First World War generals. These, far from becoming paralysed by decisions, were actively 'vain, devious, scheming and dishonest'. Cecil Woodham-Smith's marvellous *The Reason Why* describes the catastrophic results when an incompetent of type 1 (Raglan) has authority over type 2 (the Earl of Cardigan – reputed by one contemporary to possess the 'brains of a horse').[19]

In fact, anyone struck by the predominantly military rhetoric of big business (and the experience of very senior executives) cannot fail to be impressed by the elements of military incompetence listed by Dixon:[20]

(1)   a serious wastage of human resources (look at most factories);

(2)   a fundamental conservatism and clinging to outworn tradition (or, as Peter Drucker would argue,[21] to past successes);

(3)   a tendency to reject or ignore information which is unpalatable or which conflicts with preconceptions (e.g. company yes men);

(4)   a tendency to underestimate the enemy;

(5)   indecisiveness and a tendency to abdicate from the role of decision-maker;

(6)   an obstinate persistence in a given task despite strong contrary evidence (reference Concorde);

(7)   failure to exploit a situation gained and a tendency to 'pull punches';

(8)   failure to make adequate reconnaissance;

(9)   a predilection for frontal assaults, often against the enemy's strongest point (reference the gross over-crowding of once profitable markets);

---

[19] Cecil Woodham-Smith, *The Reason Why*, Harmondsworth, Penguin, 1968.

[20] Dixon, *On the Psychology of Military Incompetence*, pp. 152–3.

[21] Peter Drucker, *Managing in Turbulent Times*, London, Heinemann, 1980.

(10)   a belief in brute force rather than the clever ruse;
(11)   failure to make use of surprise or deception;
(12)   an undue readiness to find scapegoats;
(13)   a suppression or distortion of news from the Front, usually deemed necessary for morale or security (see Frank Snepp on the Vietnam débâcle, below);
(14)   a belief in mystical forces – fate, bad luck, etc.

THE TROLLOPE PLOY AND THE ART OF REFRAMING

If we place these tendencies in a politico-military context, there are disturbing parallels in the conduct of the Falklands war. There was a point, just before the sinking of the Argentine battle cruiser *General Belgrano*, when it seemed that the Argentine President, General Galtieri, had finally seen the light, had realized that the invasion had been misconceived in the first place, largely due to the Junta's failings with respect to points, 3, 4, 6, 8, 10 above. But by that time his navy colleagues were reluctant to budge. A certain amount of subtle diplomacy over the next few days probably would have got the Argentines back to the UN resolution. This was the moment for the 'Trollope Ploy' (see below).

Instead Margaret Thatcher's natural predilection for items 1, 2, 3, 4, 6, 8, 9, 10, 13 and 14 led to the sinking of the *Belgrano*, with the loss of several hundred lives (blamed incidentally on the fleeing Argentine escort vessels – see item 12) and to the inevitable escalation of the war. Embarrassingly, the warship was well outside the exclusion zone and known to be steaming home (the Americans had cracked the Argentine's codes).

The Cuban missile crisis was a very similar stand-off. The difference was the presence of Robert Kennedy and the application of the 'Trollope Ploy'. On Friday, 26 October 1962, at the height of the crisis, a senior member of the Soviet Embassy in Washington had semi-officially sounded out the Americans on a formula for resolving the conflict. This involved the supervised withdrawal of the Russian missiles in exchange for a US promise not to invade Cuba. But by Saturday the heavies in Moscow had linked the deal with the dismantling of US rockets in Turkey. At this point, recounts Robert Hilsman:

It was Robert Kennedy who conceived a brilliant diplomatic manoeuvre – later dubbed the 'Trollope Ploy', after the recurrent scene in Anthony Trollope's novels in which the girl interprets a squeeze of her hand as a proposal of marriage. His suggestion was to deal only with Friday's package of signals – Khrushchev's cable and the approach through Scali – as if the conflicting message on Saturday, linking the missiles in Cuba with those in Turkey, simply did not exist. That message, in fact, had already been rejected in a public announcement. The thing to do now was to answer the Friday package of approaches and make the answer public – which would add a certain political pressure as well as increase the speed.[22]

As the world knows, it worked, thanks to Kennedy's and Khrushchev's preference for the subtle ruse over brute force (see item 10); Krushchev needed a way out by then, too, just like Galtieri.

The point is, if you are confronted by a Galtieri (an obvious case of Dixon's 'overweeningly ambitious' type) the one thing you must *not* do is to allow yourself to be drawn into his web of adversarial illogic, his 'ballpark'. At all costs you must 'reframe' the situation, which means, of course, retreating or ascending to at least one higher order of abstraction. By then, unfortunately, Margaret Thatcher, buoyed up by her military yes men, had the glint of battle in her eyes. The same thing seems to have happened to Gough Whitlam (see p. 143) the day he forgot to telephone the Queen – the adversary was at the door and the blood was up. Of course, if the real primary task was re-election, Margaret Thatcher's instincts were perhaps rather clever. In 1982 the British people were glad of a foreign bogey and happy to fly now and pay later or, more correctly, to *punish* now and pay later.

Watzlawick and his colleagues recount a number of delightful examples of 'reframing' in their book *Change*.

---

[22] Robert Hilsman, *To Move a Nation*, New York, Doubleday, 1967, quoted in Paul Watzlawick, John H. Weakland and Richard Risch, *Change : Principles of Problem Formulation and Problem Resolution*, New York, Norton, 1974, p. 108.

There is, for example, the tale of the commander of an army detachment in Paris during one of the many nineteenth-century riots. He received orders to clear the city square by firing at the *canaille* (rabble). He commanded his soldiers to take up firing positions, their rifles levelled at the crowd, and as a ghastly silence descended he drew his sword and shouted at the top of his lungs: 'Mesdames, M'sieurs, I have orders to fire at the *canaille*. As I see a great number of honest, respectable citizens before me, I request that they leave, so that I can safely shoot the *canaille*.' The square was empty in a few minutes.

This is an excellent example of 'reframing' and you have to be clever (i.e. operating from the 'third-corner' vantage point) in order to achieve it, as in the case of the American police officer surrounded by an ugly and hostile crowd while issuing a ticket for a minor traffic violation. As the mood turned uglier, the sergeant began to doubt whether he could make it safely back to the security of his patrol car. But this cop had had some experience of 'talking down' potential suicides. In a flash of genius he announced in a loud voice: 'You have just witnessed the issuance of a traffic ticket by a member of your Oakland Police Department!' While the bystanders reeled back, fathoming the deeper meaning of this, the patrolman made it back to his car and drove off. It is a good example of what Stephen Potter calls the 'boldly meaningless' in the description of wine: 'Too many tramlines' was his favourite, guaranteed to stop most wine buffs in their tracks. The policeman was both in the situation and fearful for his survival but at the same time able to see it as from a great height *as a situation*. That latter vantage point is the 'third corner'; occupying it is a little like an 'out-of-the-body' experience.

The problem, or paradox, is that the very skill employed in cranking a fixed situation, like the Front Line in the First World War, to a higher-order solution is the same skill that reveals the *activity* of war to be absurd in the first place. Clearly, the arms race is absurd.

Our political and military leaders have been virtually unanimous in public assertions that we must go ahead and stay ahead in the armament race; they have been equally unanimous in saying nothing about what happens then. Suppose we achieve the state of ideal mutual deterrence . . . what then? Surely no sane man can envisage our planet spinning on into eternity, divided into two armed camps poised to destroy each other, and call it peace and security! *The point is that the policy of mutual deterrence includes no provisions for its own resolution.*[23]

It is like a game with no end, and no possibility of end. Like all games, it requires resolution by changing the rules, and that can be done only by a higher-order authority and from an oblique (external) perspective. E. P. Thompson, the historian, is attempting just this in leading the European nuclear disarmament movement. Europe, he points out, has been chosen as the venue for a violent ∘–∘ game between two forces locked in endless conflict.[24] It is as if two rival street gangs had chosen an elderly couple's sitting-room, replete with mementos and valuables, for a final, definitive rumble. Or, to shift the metaphor to an American setting, whatever happened to the protagonists, the OK Corral no doubt ended up in an awful mess. The folklore of the West never tells us who tidied up afterwards.

We could select any of Dixon's fourteen fatal flaws to indicate that they all spring from the ∘–∘ mind and to illustrate the effects of it in positions of great power. Perhaps the fall of Singapore provides us with the best example of the curious problem that the ∘–∘ mind faces over the matter of vulnerability (see p. 76) and defence. Singapore fell, with hardly a struggle, because the British military simply failed to defend it. Nearly 140,000 British, Indian and Australian soldiers (including young James Clavell – see p. 31) died or went into totally unnecessary captivity. The speed and ease of the capitulation staggered, even nonplussed, the Japanese, many of whom had *cycled* all the way down the

[23] Charles E. Osgood, 'Reciprocal Initiative', in *The Liberal Papers* ed. James Roosevelt, Chicago, Quadrangle Books, 1962. Reprinted in Watzlawick *et al.*, *Change*, p. 15.

[24] E. P. Thompson (ed.), *Protest and Survive*, Harmondsworth, Penguin, 1980.

Johore Peninsula. The economic loss ran into hundreds of millions of pounds: elaborate and expensive dock install-ations were forfeited; stores, fuel and, into the bargain, a couple of new battleships were lost (although the last was the result of the Navy's committing blunders 8, 9 and 10 above rather than the Army's committing 2 to 6 inclusive and 13).

In fact, the weakness of the Singapore defences had become apparent long before the Japanese attack. But not even the pleas of the Prime Minister could shift General Percival's obdurate refusal to defend the island adequately. At the eleventh hour the chief engineer, Brigadier Simson (with the engineer's characteristic grasp of reality), tried one last-ditch attempt to persuade Percival that defences could and ought to be erected. As usual, Percival refused his pleas.

It seems that Simson was past taking no for an answer, for he said to the General: 'Sir – I must emphasize the urgency of doing everything to help our troops. They're often only partially trained, they're tired and dispirited. They've been retreating for hundreds of miles. And please remember, sir, the Japanese are better trained, better equipped, and they're inspired by an unbroken run of victories. . . . And it has to be done now, sir. . . . Once the area comes under fire, civilian labour will vanish.' The plea was forceful, respectful and logical, but amaz-ingly, the General remained unmoved. Simson, his anger rising, said: 'Look here, General – I've raised this question time after time. You've always refused. What's more, you've always refused to give me any *reasons*. At least tell me one thing – why on earth *are* you taking this stand?' At long last the General Officer Com-manding Malaya gave his answer. 'I believe that defences of the sort you want to throw up are bad for the *morale* of troops and civilians.'[25]
Simson was 'frankly horrified'. He stood there in silence.

suddenly feeling quite cold, and realizing that, except for a miracle, Singapore was as good as lost. As he put on his Sam Browne, Simson could not forbear to make one last remark –

[25] Dixon, *On the Psychology of Military Incompetence*, p. 139.

'Sir, it's going to be much worse for morale if the Japanese start running all over the island.'[26]

There is, it seems, an analogy between the defended fortress and a certain kind of military mind. Indeed, Hudson (see p. 74) uses precisely this analogy to describe the way in which identity is shaped in those who become their mature selves in the latency period – that is, between the ages approximately of 6 and 13.[27] Percival may well have held at bay anxiety about his own morale by displacing it on to the civilians in Singapore. In his fantasy Singapore was as 'impregnable' as his own mind was to disagreeable news. Simson, by contrast, had a realistic 'third corner'/object – the island itself and all who dwelt on her, real people about to disappear into real, and horribly cruel, captivity. On Singapore Dixon ought to have the last word.

Defensive, as opposed to offensive, responses rank low in military esteem. Defensive activity is protective, womanly, one might almost say maternal. In sex, to use a particularly trite but apposite metaphor, it is the male who penetrates the fortress of the female; he is the attacker, she the defender. For the male to carry out elaborate preparations for his own safety is to some extent effeminate, an admission of weakness. For the male who has doubts about his own virility, whose life and choice of career are governed by unconscious doubts about his own masculinity and sexual adequacy, such effeminate activities may be anathema. By the same token it is possible that there is an affinity between the behaviour of the generals in Singapore and the refusal on the part of male industrial workers to wear protective clothing, ear-plugs and the like.[28]

Hitler, we should remember, never allowed for greatcoats in Russia because he couldn't bear to think about the possibility that the campaign might stretch on into the winter. Erich von Manstein pointed to Hitler's absolute lack of understanding of defensive warfare. J. P. Stern concluded[29] that Hitler, all along, 'knew the truth about

[26] ibid., pp. 139–40.
[27] Liam Hudson, *Human Beings*, St Albans, Paladin, 1978.
[28] Dixon, *On the Psychology of Military Incompetence*, p. 141.
[29] J. P. Stern, *Hitler : The Führer and the People*, London, Fontana, 1975, p. 224.

himself' – the truth that not conquest but indiscriminate
annihilation was his aim'. In the deepest recesses of the ⚬⚬
mind there is no safe haven from the struggle – simply the
certainty of triumph or, more certain still, disaster.

We must be careful however not to typecast people, even
generals, as irrevocably either ⚬⚬ or ⟨symbol⟩. Bernard Montgomery, unarguably a great general, demonstrated the wonderful human capacity for adaptation. From the start he
was a candidate for the military – dominated by his mother,
from whom he inherited a passion for order and discipline,
yet denied the reciprocal love he craved. His father was a
bishop, much older than his mother and, as with the fathers
of so many eminent sons, a distant figure. As Montgomery
himself recorded, his early life was a series of 'fierce
battles' from which his mother invariably emerged the
victor.

At the age of 37 he was still preaching that the Army,
like the Church, demanded celibacy if the profession was to
be taken seriously: 'You can't make a good soldier and a
good husband.' Yet he suddenly fell head over heels in love
with a girl less than half his age. When she, very sensibly,
rejected him, he rebounded into the arms of a highly intelligent and artistic widow his own age with children of 13
and 11. He was lucky; Generals Auchinleck and Gort had
both married girls half their age and both of those marriages ended disastrously. Montgomery married at 40 and,
until his wife's tragic death ten years later, enjoyed a bliss-
fully happy and transforming life with the only person in
the world who could pull his leg. When his beloved Betty
died the light of his life had gone out. He withdrew completely for a few days and then, as suddenly, he emerged in
his new role as Commander of the Ninth Infantry Brigade
at Portsmouth. It was the end of 1937 and he had some
urgent work to do.

John Carver, Monty's adopted son, reflected that marriage to his mother might well have saved Montgomery not
only from a stiff asceticism but also from an incipient tendency towards the milder forms of madness. But, ten years'
exposure to artists, mess and Bohemian tomfoolery taught
Montgomery a subtlety vouchsafed very few military

leaders. Above all, he had developed an eye for character and a feel for the uses of diversity and irreverence.

Returning for a moment to Dixon's comments on deception in the interests of 'morale' (blunder 13 above), there is a strange parallel in the last days of the American presence in Vietnam, except that CIA disinformation served the purpose not only of preserving civilian morale but also of persuading Congress to carry on funding the war effort long after it had become clear that this would be to throw good money after bad. As Frank Snepp wrote of the CIA Chief of Station in Saigon: 'Trained in counter-espionage, he viewed 'political action', the manipulation of both information and individuals, as part of the natural order of business. But like so many other professionals in his trade, he seemed to have learned his skills almost too well'. A few months before Saigon's collapse some of the junior CIA staff started to complain about 'the increasingly polemic tone of CIA reporting to Washington and our willingness to supply [Ambassador] Martin with whatever propagandistic data he needed to influence Congressional votes'.[30]

In the end the disinformed Vietnamese friends of the USA were left, in the same way as the locals in Singapore, to the tender mercies of the advancing North Vietnamese. As to Ambassador Martin himself, the principal architect of the disinformation, here is Snepp's assemblage of comments from within the CIA station:

He's a born conspirator – he habitually schemes, has a conspiratorial and clandestine mentality and immediately tries to put you under his control. He's always searching for weakness, like a shark going for blood.

If [General] Curtis Le May had invented an ambassador, he would have invented Martin. You know: 'Bomb them back to the Stone Age.' [Martin was notoriously insensitive to the wastage of civilian life.]

In a sense Martin was a perfect extension of the Nixon White House. He had an almost instinctive appreciation of power and

---

[30] Frank Snepp, *Decent Interval*, Harmondsworth, Penguin, 1980, p. 83.

how to parley it into certain objectives, and like the President himself, he was a dedicated anti-communist, almost religious in his fervour. 'To him', said a friend, 'there was nothing so loathsome as being a communist. His attitudes were formed at a time when communism was the nemesis of all that was good, and Vietnam was a psychological battleground for him.'[31]

For the student of these matters, Martin appears to fulfil the requirements for incompetence type 2 (see p. 146) and Percival for type 1. Either way, the innocent bystander tends to get it in the neck.

PLAYING BALL (DISPLACED WAR)

Let us pass on now from war to sport, a fundamentally similar activity, provided you are able to take the Geneva Convention seriously. Nowadays, unless the Russians and Americans finally decide to slug it out, war is largely a matter of guerrilla insurgency and indiscriminate but scientific torture by repressive regimes. The days when warfare approximated to the ▷ model are long past. Perhaps the last vestige was demonstrated by the reluctance, even refusal, of British military leaders to follow through the prosecution of Nazi officers guilty of war crimes. Once again, a Prime Minister's demands were virtually ignored by the military. Even the old soldier Churchill wrote to Prime Minister Attlee to suggest that the execution of mass murderers had exhausted any usefulness it may formerly have had.[32]

In truth, many of the criminals themselves were amazed to get away with it all. Some of the British military took the view that they had simply obeyed orders and that had the war been lost, the whole exercise would have amounted to a sporting contest in which the only casualty was a poor decision.[33] The American Army was rather less forgiving and rather more inclined to prosecute, whether or not the victims of genocide had been British or American.

[31] ibid., pp. 70–1.
[32] Tom Bower, *Blind Eye to Murder*, London, André Deutsch, 1981.
[33] ibid.

The crime, of course, was against humanity. That ⋺ fact hung like a pall over the international old-boy network of military commanders totting up the scores in their latest fixture. At this stage the ○–○ mentality emerged in a particularly grisly fashion, obscuring the major crime. First, the lawyers moved in. Now, it is a well established principle of advocacy that you must defend your client as ably as you can, whatever sort of villain he may happen to be. The law – that is, the 'third (institution) corner' – exists to free the advocates for their ritualized cock fight. Without the institution, there really might be 'blood on the ceiling'.

The problem for the British military officers defending the war criminals (or it ought to have been a problem) was that defence meant calling the holocaust survivors liars. One of the advocates defended a particularly unsavoury mass murderer on the grounds that he had to deal with the 'dregs of the ghettos of Eastern Europe', as if this constituted an especially disagreeable form of deprivation. In fact, the Belsen staff were accused not of murder at all but of failing to provide for the inmates' 'well-being' and of 'ill-treating' them. Advocates are salesmen and, like salesmen, are tainted, in the end, by their wares.

A year or so after the war another ○–○ consideration loomed in centre stage. The cold war was beginning to freeze up. Increasingly, the war crimes trials were being seen as counter-productive in winning German support against the communists. Somewhere between the amoral eloquence of the military advocates and the Russian threat the residue of the *big* crime filtered slowly back into the soil, like a slow degrading poison.

Sport is perhaps the best context in which to examine the release of ○–○ emotion in a safe ⋺ setting. Even boxing, the most survival-oriented and gladiatorial of sports, is ringed around with rules and conventions, most of them established by the same kind of aristocratic Englishmen who used to make up the rules of the world game. We all need to discharge or act out our dominance/submission fantasies, especially those of us who do not live in Argentina, Uganda, Poland, etc., etc.

Wrestling, the one activity in which it really is possible

for one man to kill another extremely quickly, has been surrounded, in the absence of the 12-ounce glove, by the most marvellous ritualized razzmatazz. It has assumed a position somewhere between the Elizabethan theatre in the round and modern ballet. The point is that a convention of the most bizarre and improbable kind has emerged to render the ∞ contest tolerable.

Team games are the most relevant for the practice of leadership in business and politics. The choice of leader lies, fundamentally, between the ∞ and ☌ poles. The ∞ leader has little detachment from the game. He *is* the team and, more significantly, he is an extension of the massed supporters in the bleachers. The destabilized personality of the charismatic sportsman (for example, the footballer) is some evidence of the massive psychological projections of the supporters. At such times the footballer is little more than a puppet on the end of a thousand invisible strings dancing to the ∞ tune. The other kind of leader remembers, most of the time, that it's 'only a game'. The true philosopher-leader knows that life too, given the inevitability of death, is a game, of sorts.

There is an ancient rivalry between the Australians and the English in the game of cricket. Cricket satisfies most of the conditions of a good game – it is fundamentally absurd, extremely complicated and very old. Having exported it to the Colonies, the English feel about Australian cricketers the same way a father does about his teenage son driving away in the borrowed family car. The Australians, I am afraid, do not have the good grace to let the old man win occasionally – at any rate, not deliberately.

Accordingly, there is a problem about leadership. The English, just like the Australians, want desperately to win. Unlike the Australians, they don't care to admit it – after all, it's only a game. This is, as Stephen Potter pointed out long ago, an attempt to 'win the losing', to make the victor feel that, in some higher-order and more stately game, he has actually lost. Of course, if you begin with this jugular-baring attitude, you are more likely to lose. The English response has been to oscillate between the attitude of gentleman captains with a good intellectual appreciation of the game and its history and a capacity for making urbane speeches and, on the other hand, provincial or colonial roughnecks with a more pugnacious and unsentimental approach to just winning.

In cricket, the game being what it is, I favour the former approach. In fact, one of the more successful English captains of recent times is a philosopher, though not particularly good at cricket. Then again, very few generals excel in hand-to-hand combat. Even in boxing the occasional Tunney emerges to out-think a Dempsey. Look at Muhammad Ali – an extraordinarily gifted athlete, and actually bigger than most of his opponents, but with hardly any killer instinct at all, nor an explosive knock-out punch. He did know, however, how to convert or reframe a ∞ contest into an *institution*, how to crank it up a point or two in the abstraction scale, like the Oakland City cop referred to above. Even Ali's little poems were a stroke of genius against opponents notorious for superstition. Fighting a man is one thing, but fighting a living legend, and according to some mysterious higher-order script, is quite another.

Cricket and the 'Merchant Marine' leadership model

Mike Brearley, the ⌐ philosopher-captain of cricket, stands in stark contrast to two of the less successful captains of recent times — a pugnacious 6′7″ South African and an equally pugnacious bruiser from Somerset with a little brush with an irritating fan in a pub, and subsequently with the British constabulary, behind him. The most extraordinary English victory over the Australians (not excluding the bodyline tour) took place with the Somerset bruiser (a failure as captain) in the role of subordinate hatchetman to the philosopher. The boss carried the dependence, and the underling (recently demoted from the captaincy) carried the fight. It was a lethal combination. Worse still, Brearley is training as a psychoanalyst. Cricket being the game it is, this will render him, in due course, in the role of captain. Fortunately for the Australians and others, the England selectors take the view that cricketing ability is a pre-eminent quality in a captain.

The combination of ⊳ leader and ∘–∘ 2i/c is known as the Merchant Marine model of leadership. There was a time, in the Australian coastal trade, when a disproportionate number of the ship's masters had Wurlitzers installed in their cabins. Most of them simply stayed there at the keyboard all day. A student of individual/abnormal psychology might argue that they were just loopy, probably as a direct result of too many years in the first mate's job (the bastard you love to hate). The student of systems psychology (most seamen fall into this category; after all, their systems are inescapable and the system boundary against the elements – half an inch of steel – all too permeable) sees that the arrangement works rather well. The first mate runs the ship and thus carries the fight, and the Master is there to go down with the ship, if need be, warbling 'Nearer My God to Thee' on the vibrato keys as the water gurgles up the pipes.

The present English ambivalence about the cricket captains harks back to the infamous days of 1932–3 when a variation of the 'Merchant Marine' model almost succeeded in reframing a series of cricket matches into an international incident. What happened is easily explained. The Australians, irritatingly and typically, had succeeded in breeding a batsman of freakish ability. Don Bradman possessed a speed of reflex which allowed him to play the game on a different plane from that of any of his contemporaries. He also loved to spend all day making runs; in fact, he gave the impression that only a well aimed hand-grenade stood a chance of removing him.

From this point on the imagery of cricket and war do indeed become entangled. (I must declare an interest here: it was, I believe, my own father, covering the tour as a journalist, who coined the immortal phrase: 'This isn't cricket; it's war!') The important thing to understand in what followed is the irreversible logic of unconscious processes of decision-taking. If Bradman played on a different plane, then a different plane of response was called for. The essential combination was (of course) a ∘–∘ English captain, a weak and ineffectual team manager (following the Merchant Marine model) and, down among the grimy 'professionals', a working-class bowler fast enough to kill a man.

The tour manager was Sir 'Plum' Warner, who later wrote of Douglas Jardine, the captain: 'He is a queer fellow. When he sees a cricket ground with an Australian on it, he goes mad. He rose to his present position on my shoulders and of his attitude to me I do not care to speak.' Jardine, a wealthy Scots/English solicitor brought up in India, was, apart from his ability at cricket and other sports, a very good shot. In fact, he spent his honeymoon in Africa slaughtering big game and always stalked a wounded animal himself on the principle 'Fear and be slain'. Educated at Winchester and Oxford, he was, to put it simply (and outwith the laws of libel), typical of his class. He was basically nice, but he said of the Australians: 'The only way you are going to beat these people is by hating them.'

One of the tour's fast bowlers was 'Gubby' Allen. His verdict on Jardine was similar to Warner's: 'A Jekyll and Hyde character. He had a very charming side. But when the test matches were on he was insane, utterly determined to win at any cost.'[34] Allen however was an amateur, which meant that he did not have to do as he was told by his captain – namely, aim *at* the batman's head so he would, in defending himself against injury, give a catch to a group of close-in fielders. Harold Larwood, the working-class professional from Nottinghamshire with the perfect fast bowler's physique (broad shoulders and arms almost trailing the ground), had no such scruple; in fact the idea of decapitating the odd Australian batsman quite appealed.

After the first few serious injuries, the Australians complained that it wasn't really cricket, which was a bit like telling your parents they are behaving childishly. England won the series, the most bitter in the long history of the contests between the two countries, and the game (☞) barely recovered. As the Australian captain said to Warner (who had dropped round to commiserate over his Larwood-induced injuries), 'The game is too good to be

---

[34] This quotation and other details have been culled from Peter Deeley's article, 'Was that Cricket?', which appeared in the *Observer Colour Supplement*, 7 November 1982.

spoilt. It is time some people got out of the game. Good afternoon!' A line almost worthy of Jardine's look-alike, Basil Rathbone.

The ∞ objective (winning) was achieved, but the cost was considerable. The cricket Establishment dropped Jardine as soon as it decently could; he had served its unconscious purpose. (The year after the tour it quietly changed the fast-bowling rules too, to save lives, though it never accepted responsibility for what it had permitted to happen.) Left with the obloquy, Jardine died, embittered, in a Swiss sanitarium in 1958. Larwood, ironically, emigrated to Australia, where, after all, his class sympathies ought to have lain. (People forget that Australia's depression years were in many ways harsher than Britain's.)

The structure of these events ought to engage our attention in the light of contemporaneous events in Nazi Germany. (The year 1932–3 was, remember, the period of Hitler's legal triumph, abetted by an Establishment that wanted its dirty work done for it and that planned to ditch him once he had seen off the communists.) A leadership opportunity for the ∞ mentality sometimes arises when there is something shameful to be done (for which an Establishment is unprepared to assume responsibility) and there exists a ready supply of ambitious underlings anxious to promote their careers and needing to project their frustrations on to some external bogey. (This same structural theme is discussed, in the context of business and commerce, on p. 26.) Once Bradman appeared on the scene, the plot unerringly took on an almost Wagnerian impetus. Warner, Jardine and Larwood were simply typecast for their roles.

From the start some insightful souls saw what was afoot. When in April 1931 the news that Jardine had been appointed England captain reached Winchester College, his old cricket coach remarked that Jardine would make a good skipper 'but he might lose us a dominion'.

Other leading sports

The 'Merchant Marine' model makes sense only in team

games, and it is in these games that the obvious parallels may be drawn with leadership. Indeed, many Europeans get their main ideas about leadership (in any setting) from football. It isn't an entirely helpful model for government, and the football manager's job is about as secure as any junta in a banana dictatorship. It is a binary conflict model, fuelled by 'charisma' and absurdly dependent on luck.

When we consider the ⊶ and ⏛ dimensions, sports such as golf, sailing, skiing, mountaineering, surfing, hang-gliding, marathon running and so on are quite special. Here the unpredictable elements occupy the 'third corner'. Most involve some human co-operation, though an occasional Reinhold Messner (the man who climbed Everest alone without oxygen bottles) appears from nowhere to attack a mountain in hand-to-hand interpersonal combat. Even the single-handed yachtsman communicates with his craft in the context of ocean and weather. People drawn seriously to these sports relish the unpredictability and the beauty of them. Such people are of a special, and romantic, psychological type.

The remarkable resurgence of coarse marathon running requires some psychological/sociological explanation. It is an extraordinary social phenomenon. The mass marathons are about not the 'winners' but the mass in the middle of the bell-shaped statistical curve and, further, the masses who watch and experience it all vicariously. Like wars, almost everybody in the locality knows someone in the fray, and most are not very different from you and me. It may well be a popular reaction against the synthetic spectator sports in which the overpaid brats have taken over.

Tennis is perhaps the best example, where the court and the rules provide the context for an otherwise gladiatorial contest. Very ⊶ characters like John McEnroe and Ilie Nastase constantly convert that gentlemanly ⏛-ness into spiteful conflict with a detestable parental authority. When such people take on the game and all who sail in her, the opponent becomes almost an irrelevance. It seems that McEnroe and Nastase can't actually play well until they are locked into a grossly unfair and slightly paranoiac struggle with fate. Once plugged into that, like eccentric machines plugged into an electric circuit, the juice begins to flow (and heaven help the opponent – if not actually beaten, he may be *bored* half to death). Of course, at this level huge sums of money are involved. The real game is displaced to the Swiss bank. The Swiss bank and the mass marathon are thus connected by the notion 'sport', but it is a mercifully tenuous connection.

General Haig is a tennis fanatic; ex-President Carter likes to run and ex-Prime Minister Wilson to paddle in the sea; Ike and Willie Whitelaw (the one-time British Home Secretary) have had their golf; and, of course, Lord Home of the Hirsel, the British Prime Minister after Macmillan, has blasted thousands upon thousands of innocent game birds from the sky. However, most politicians, despite their energy levels, are overweight and unsporting. Their health record is remarkable when this is considered. Most of their energy, sometimes manic, is channelled into o–o conflict in one form or another; the fickle elements do not appeal to them.

If I were pressed for a good national leader's game, I would plump for golf, which really does test character. But it would have to be Scots links golf, preferably in winter and certainly without those little electric cars that allow you to do the strategic work (like an armchair general) without any of the slog (like a foot soldier). Perhaps the greatest virtue of the game, apart from its sublime pointlessness, is the virtual irrelevance of the referee. The referee, if anyone, is Sir Isaac Newton; gravity dictates whether the ball drops into the hole or not, and there is no point in arguing. But golf will do nothing for the morally infirm in mid-life; we must find the people who are suited to the game in the first place and accelerate their advancement in politics. It could hardly be a worse method than leaving it to 'chance' so that the o–o raiders nearly always prevail.

Above all, sport is a way to fantasize efficiently. Within the convention of the game (the 'third corner'), you can act out anything you like, including fierce aggression, without actually killing your opponent(s). That works as long as you play; for the spectator the experience is less helpful – less cathartic. When rival spectators start to kill each other after the game, we know that vicarious sporting involvement has failed to help them to manage or contain their fantasy lives. They have poured fantasy into their players, and the players, inevitably sometimes, have failed them. At that point the convention cannot hold them; once they are stripped of the 'third corner', naked survival behaviour emerges uncontrolled. It is bad for the players too. Pumped full of mass expectation, their own meagre reserves of personality are sometimes swamped. They become, like petty demagogues, creatures of the mob. Still, what do we expect if our schools eschew fantasy and also fail to institute sensible conventions?

A further note on the 'Merchant Marine' leadership model

In a limited liability company the model is usually played out between chairman and chief executive; sometimes the game is played the other way round, with the chairman as bastard and the chief executive as the dependable figure. Either way, it helps to project fight and dependence on to different people. Only an unusual person can switch from one to the other in an unconfusing and supportive way, as the new army of one-parent families is discovering. Sometimes organizations lurch painfully from dependent chief executive to fight chief executive and back again in a five- or six-year cycle:

Alternating positive and negative feedback produces a special form of stability represented by endless oscillation between polar states or conditions. In human systems the phenomenon is best exemplified by certain committees whose recommendations slowly oscillate between two polar alternatives, usually over a period of some years. The period of the cycle has been found, on close examination, to be just longer than the time required for the advocates of programme 'A' to graduate, retire, or otherwise leave the scene of action, being replaced by a new generation whose tendency is (having been exposed to the effects of programme 'A') to demand programme 'B'. After some months or years of programme 'B' a new generation of postulants is ripe to begin agitation to restore programme 'A'.[35]

[35] John Gall, *Systemantics*, London, Fontana, 1979, p. 29.

Oscillation between dependent and fight/flight leadership isn't quite the same as that between ⟀ and o–o modes. Often it is a shift between two forms of *interpersonal* relationship, one combative and the other persuasive, cloying and super-dependent. The true ⟀ organization affords an *institutional* relationship; the people are grateful for the system and take the functionaries for granted.

Jimmy Carter's costliest tactical mistake was to stress the chief executive aspect of the presidency at the expense of the head of state role. Reagan reversed this, reintroducing the pomp and, according to the press corps, sleeping through most of the executive activity. This, after all, is no less relevant for a symbolic role than playing the mighty Wurlitzer, especially for a nation deprived of its monarchy. One misconceived Carter TV commercial depicted a single light burning in a White House window; the camera zoomed to the Oval Office and the solitary shirt-sleeved President. To camera he intoned: 'You're asleep now but I'm still here reading the cables; everything will be OK in the morning!' It was supposed to make people feel safe in the dependable hands of a conscientious chief executive officer. Most Americans took the view he ought to get more sleep. In due course, in oscillation, they got the somambulist Reagan.

SUPER-EGOS

Licking sin No. 1 : the Church

In our naughty materialist world, spiritual leadership is a vexed subject. What is religion for and what therefore ought its ministers to be up to? In superstitious cultures such as Iran we see a resurgence of zealot leaders like the Ayatollah Khomeini. Even in the sceptical West while church attendances dwindle, folk leaders arise, from the egregiously loony Jim Jones to the serenely venal Bhagwan.

At the crudest level religion helps with superstitions and fears. Conversion experiences peak in adolescence, when sex scares us, and in late life, when death looms.

Khomeini, leading a crudely male-dominated society, represents a doctrinal defence against the first of these. So too does the Pope's birth-control encyclical. But sex doesn't scare the new cults; they embrace it, so to speak. Instead, they seek the Answer to Everything – the answer which will settle the worrisome question of mortality. Jim Jones took the matter to its logical conclusion, pursuing a thought process similar to that of the sales manager referred to on page 146. If it is uncertainty about the *timing* of death that bugs you, that can be managed quite simply.

In practice, religion is a pure expression of the ⋊ mode, with God at the apex (see Figure 23), unless it is used just as a survival device against the world's naughtiness. Then it fails the believer and excludes non-believers as surely as a 16-stone bouncer at the door. Expressed in this way, God is seen, in a sense, as outside, independent of the people concerned, just like a formal constitution. The complication is that most faiths, and the Christian faith in particular, stress the incorporation of the 'good object' within the person. It is both outside and inside. You can, of course, say the same thing about constitutions; the Weimar Constitution was a sound enough *document*, but the *spirit* of the thing was not incorporated in a sufficient number of Germans, especially in the upper echelons of society. Constitutions, like lawns, need 600 years or so of fertilization

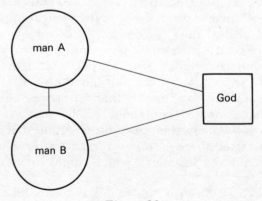

Figure 23

and tender loving care in order to enter fully into the
national psyche.

In theology the notion of the Trinity symbolizes the need
for ternary images in general when it comes to make sense
of subtle abstractions. Because religion draws us into the
vale of the imponderable, it is difficult to know whether
Father, Son or Holy Ghost ought to occupy the 'third
corner' as far as man is concerned. The point is that a
three-cornered structure appears to be necessary to contain
the central mystery.

The Bishop of Winchester, John V. Taylor has said:

The Holy Spirit is active in precisely those experiences that are
very common, of recognition, of seeing things in a new way, the
penny dropping. Not necessarily in a religious way at all. He is a
kind of current of communication between me and something
outside or beyond me; and every time a human being says, 'Oh, I
see it now!', I would claim that is what I mean by the Holy
Spirit. The man who says it is all part of *him*, going on in his own
brain, is just as likely to be wrong as I am when I say: 'No, I
think it is something independent of you.'[36]

When Bishop Taylor talks of 'the penny dropping' he
makes a whole series of links between religious belief, creativity (of the 'lateral thinking' variety) in the arts and the
largely atheistic world of psychoanalytic theory. (Freud, of
course, needed a ternary and vaguely theological model to
express the relationships between id, ego and super-ego.)

Chapter 2 makes clear, I hope, the central importance of
the 'good object' (and, of course, the 'bad object') in the
work of Freud, Melanie Klein and others. Where the
analysts and the clerics tend to part company is on the
matter of the location of the *real* 'good object'. They agree
on incorporation – on the fact that the sense of goodness or
badness is somehow contained *in* the person – but the
world of psychology then goes on to argue that that (after
the breast) is all there is to it – apart from Jung's notion of
the 'collective unconscious', which might be seen as a cul-

[36] Quoted in Gerald Priestland, 'The Ghost that Came to Dinner', *Listener*, 5
November 1981.

turally determined 'god'. God, we must remember, is thought of in our culture as a *man*, and that, as comparative religion teaches us, is a cultural quirk.

The most successful book I know among those which attempt to link the insights of psychology with religion is *The Dynamics of Religion* by Bruce Reed.[37] This is a fascinating essay into the process of religion with many implications for psychological well-being in general. Reed proposes an oscillation theory of movement between the ⚬⚬ and ⊳⚬ modes. In order to be creative and useful human beings, he argues, we need regular periods of regression to a state he refers to as 'extra-dependence' (a phrase chosen to suggest dependence upon something or someone outside oneself, perhaps unknowable, rather than 'dependence' which in common parlance implies some kind of weakness). It is a grown-up and symbolic version of the childhood experiences described by John Holt:

Not long ago I saw this scene in the Public Garden in Boston. The mothers were chatting on a bench while the children roamed around. For a while they would explore boldly and freely, ignoring their mothers. Then, after a while, they would use up their store of courage and confidence, and run back to their mothers' sides and cling there for a while, as if to recharge their batteries. After a moment or two of this, they were ready for more exploring, and so they went out, then came back, and then ventured out again.

In just the same way, this baby in the pool had his times of exploration, and his times of retreat and retrenchment. At times he let me tow him around freely, kicking his feet and paddling his hands. At other times, he gripped my arms fiercely, pulled himself towards me, and by his gestures and expressions showed me that he wanted to be held in the same tight and enveloping grip with which we had begun. Or he might even ask to go back to the steps, or to be lifted out of the pool altogether. Then, a few minutes later, he would be back in the water and ready for more adventures.

At one time or another, I have watched a number of parents trying to teach their very young children to swim. On the whole,

---

[37] Bruce Reed, *The Dynamics of Religion*, London, Darton, Longman, Todd, 1978.

they don't get very far, because they are so insensitive to this rise and fall of courage in the child. Is it because they don't notice? Or because they don't care? Perhaps they feel that the child's feelings are unimportant, to be easily overridden by exhortation and encouragement, or even anger and threats.[38]

Well, most of us have known parents and teachers and (especially) bosses who resort to exhortation and threat and who obviously don't notice the effect they are having on others. Employees of such bosses tend to experience their working lives in survival terms and to retreat each evening to the blessed humanity of the pub – a serious rival (as I suggested on p. 24) to the church for the containment of regression in communities.

The point about the oscillation, as Reed suggests, is not, during the working week, to move about in a godly cocoon (or an ungodly one, for that matter) but to be freed by worship to enter fully and energetically into the workaday world. When religious practice works, there is a mediation between man 'in his solitariness crying out for the meaning of existence' and man 'struggling to exist as one among many'. The implication of these ideas is that members of Churches ought to concentrate on worshipping God in churches, so that *outside* they can become absorbed in an efficient way with the affairs of humanity.

When the Church itself becomes absorbed in a proliferation of groups and clubs and so on, then the manifest purpose is to edify and maintain its members. The latent and unconscious purpose may be to preserve the Church against assaults from the environment and to erect barriers against other members of the community. The *useful* function of religion Reed defines thus: 'a social institution which provides a setting in ritual for the regulation of oscillation processes in a social grouping'.[39] Alternatively, he uses the notion of synchronization of oscillation, so that religion can be seen as a social process rather than an exclusively individual one.

---

[38] John Holt, *How Children Learn*, Harmondsworth, Penguin, 1970, pp. 110–11.
[39] Reed, *The Dynamics of Religion*, p. 52.

The synchronizing role extends way beyond the faithful, especially in coherent communities:

An elderly lady in the congregation said how surprised she had been when a neighbour had told her she was sorry she had been ill. She had not been ill, and discovered in the ensuing conversation that her neighbour had jumped to this conclusion because she had not seen her going to church the previous Sunday. Later in the week, several others had asked her whether anything had happened to her. She was amazed that people who did not go to church themselves should bother to notice whether she went or not.

As she reflected further, she realized that she often used to see people standing in their windows on Sunday, watching her walking down the road. There were others she used to meet because they were in their gardens as she walked by. By going to church regularly, it appears that she had become a *dependable* element in the worlds of her neighbours. When she failed to appear, they had to supply reasons.[40]

The old lady, in a sense was going to church *on behalf of* the unfaithful, though not consciously.

If we accept this view of the religious process, then the link with analytical psychology is obvious. Winnicott, the great psychotherapist, remarked:

People who are ill (and we are all ill to some extent) have a drive to cure themselves. Nothing is more important than to do that. This means they experience a great need to feel real, and they only come to feel real by doing something like regression to childhood dependence, to something which can *hold* them. This may be localized, for example, in the Church or in music.[41]

In other words, a sense of unreality is distressingly normal and so too is the necessity to regress. It is only in the case of some severe trauma that the individual has recourse to the therapist's consulting-room.

This is, in a way, the equivalent of saying, in the world of manufacturing, look after the product and all those

[40] ibid., p. 55.
[41] ibid., p. 21.

desirable outcomes like 'communications', 'motivation', 'industrial relations', profit and happiness will accrue in due course. But it doesn't work in industry if the product happens to be ill-designed, shoddily made or not particularly valuable in its end use. Likewise in religion God at the centre has to be 'good enough', in the eyes of the ministry, to render the doctrine, ritual and social activity surrounding the process less important – 'good enough' for their purposes or, in the case of the King James Authorized Version, superb. Of course, you have to work at your god continuously, just as every manufacturer has to work at his product.

The idea of regression crops up again and again in the arts and the sciences. Darwin dragged himself, over twenty years of obsessive resistance, to *The Origin of Species*. Alfred Russell Wallace performed the same task under the delirious influence of three nights of malaria. Likewise the French mathematician Poincaré described how he discovered a new class of mathematical functions:

For fifteen days I strove to prove that there could not be any functions like those I have since called Fuchsian functions. I was then very ignorant; every day I seated myself at my work-table, stayed an hour or two, tried a great number of combinations and reached no results. One evening, contrary to my custom, I drank black coffee and could not sleep. Ideas rose in crowds; I felt them collide until pairs interlocked, so to speak, making a stable combination. By the next morning, I had established the existence of a class of Fuchsian functions, those which come from the hyper-geometric series; I had only to write out the results, which took but a few hours.[42]

Ernest Newman described how Wagner arrived at the opening passage of the Ring cycle after years of worrying away at the problem:

His difficulty was to begin – to find the tiny point of matter which, introduced into the inchoate fluid of his thinking, would effect in a flash the needed crystallization. And that tiny point of

[42] H. Poincaré, 'Science et Méthode' (1908), in P. E. Vernon, *Creativity*, Penguin, 1970, quoted in Reed, *The Dynamics of Religion*, p. 17.

consolidating matter came to him, unbidden, unanticipated, during his disturbed half-sleep on that hard couch in the hotel in Spezia. Falling into the cataleptic state that is the prime condition of all artistic creation of the highest kind, he suddenly felt, he says, as though he were sinking in a mighty flood of water: 'The rush and roar soon took musical shape within my brain as the chord of E flat major, surging incessantly in broken chords; these declared themselves as melodic figurations of increasing motion, yet the pure triad of E flat major never changed, but seemed by its steady persistence to impart infinite significance to the element in which I was sinking. I awoke from my half-sleep in terror, feeling as though the waves were now rushing high above my head. I at once recognized the orchestral prelude to the Rheingold, which for a long time *I must have carried about with me*, yet had never been able to fix definitely, had at last come to being within me!*[43]*

Now, eccentric geniuses may seem far removed from the leadership capacities of humble clerics and department heads in manufacturing but the link between them is their conviction about the existence, if shadowy, of the 'third corner' – their belief, deep down, that there is something out there (and sometimes in the guts) that confers meaning on the workaday world. At that level there is no important difference between the department head identified with his output and the craftsman/artist utterly absorbed or lost in the object he is creating (or recreating, if you believe in Melanie Klein and the incorporated 'good' breast).

Looked at this way, it is not simply that the ⌇⌐ mind is capable of creative regression but that creativity and ⌇⌐-ness are the same thing. The regression is *to* the 'third corner'. It is downright dangerous to regress at all from the ∘–∘ position; if you regress, you may never again return to the haven of adult control. The ∘–∘ mind is wonderful at control (which is why so many bosses are thus) but absolutely hopeless at childlike vulnerability, where true creativity and true calm lie.

Mode of creativity is important too because it determines history. Bateson argues that it mattered, and matters still,

43 E. Newman, *The Life of Richard Wagner 1848–1869*, New York, Knopf, 1937, quoted in Reed, *The Dynamics of Religion*, p. 18.

that Darwin wrote the timely book on evolution, even though it was Wallace's psychedelic inspiration, and his helpful letter to Darwin about it, that got Darwin going.[44] The way Wallace put it was:

> The action of this principle is exactly like that of the centrifugal governor of the steam engine, which checks and corrects any irregularities almost before they become evident; and in like manner no unbalanced deficiency in the animal kingdom can ever reach any conspicuous magnitude because it would make itself felt at the very first step, by rendering existence difficult and extinction almost sure to follow.[45]

Bateson argued that, had Wallace's essentially cybernetic explanation gained favour, not only would we have a different view of evolution today, but the whole cybernetic movement might have occurred a hundred years earlier. Had that happened, the effects would have spread far beyond the evolutionary argument; somebody might, for example, have been able to view Europe as a system in 1914.

Licking sin No. 2 : A policeman's lot

Creativity is not confined to the arts and sciences, however. Consider the creative possibilities in the work of the police. It is no accident that the current debate about policing centres on two opposed views of society and hence of the role of the police within it.

One view says that society is divided, in a binary way, into decent people and 'villains'. (The truly subtle cop distinguishes, quite rightly, between villains and 'real villains'.) According to this view, 'Decent' people don't have to take account of their own villainous bits, and policemen don't have to worry about the bits of themselves in the villains. The logical role for the policeman is to prowl about in cars, armed to the teeth, looking for villainous types. Villainous types always have longer hair than policemen and frequently different-coloured skin too. Such

[44] Gregory Bateson, *Mind and Nature : A Necessary Unity*, London, Fontana, 1979.
[45] ibid., p. 192.

people invariably run away when you chase them. QED. A senior British policeman even pointed out recently that if people stay off the streets, they run absolutely no risk of being beaten to death by a policeman. This assertion is true but in some ways rather unhelpful.

The alternative view, and one that is being defended with some courage by other senior policemen, is that the local cop (if he has that ⟡ capacity) is a kind of container for delinquent urges. By simply *being there*, preferably on foot and unarmed, he symbolizes authority – the holding back of primitive forces. I had the opportunity to check this interesting thesis recently at the senior staff college of the British police force. Seated before me were some of the cleverest and most senior cops from all round the world. I asked if they, when young, used to feel that frisson of irrational guilt whenever they saw a policeman in the street. 'We still do!' they roared back, with one voice.

The point is that the local cop/bobby is both a recognizable person of the society and a symbol of authority. He has to be able to take in some of those feelings about authority, modify them and feed them back in a tolerable form. In that he performs almost the same function as the mother containing her infant's nameless dread. Accordingly, if you promote � policemen (and in the nature of it, many of those drawn to police work are concerned primarily with control – of others consciously and of themselves unconsciously), then they will simply build up the police armoury for the battle with the forces of villainy. It means more technology, more computer records and ultimately, of course, more villany. (The connection with the military mind, as Norman F. Dixon reminds us, is close).

All this is perfectly obvious. But is it obvious to those charged with appointing and selecting our senior policemen? Where, after all, did the selectors come from? The principle is clear to E. P. Thompson and his supporters in the European nuclear disarmament movement. All you have to do it to translate the rabid anti-communism of the US military industrial complex to a squad car and imagine the villains as Russians. It isn't what they have done that matters but what you can tell they are about to do.

It was Sir David McNee, the ex-Metropolitan Commissioner of Police in London, who pointed out that staying at home protects you from the violence of policemen. He never corrected the impression created by that rather unfortunate statement. On the whole, the 'free-born' Englishman does not take kindly to anybody (even the Police Commissioner) delimiting his access to the Queen's highway. But then, the Queen, who has to grasp the ⌐ model as she sits at its apex, probably does not take kindly to Mrs Thatcher talking of 'her' troops on the Falklands: the troops are Her Majesty's armed forces, and political leaders ought not to forget it.

Some senior policemen even argue that the police at work necessarily reflect the society from which they derive and, on this logic, condone a certain amount of racism in the ranks. They do not, however, take the argument to its logical conclusion and suggest that the police ought therefore to embrace a small number of axe-murderers, spies, child-molesters, drug addicts, madmen and so on. They confuse, in other words, the personal attributes (o–o) of human beings with authority in a formal role (⌐). A policeman may be a racist in his heart but he should never act that way on duty. It is a crucially important principle for the police to grasp.

By contrast, the Archbishop of Canterbury, the Very Reverend Robert Runcie, got into the most awful trouble for understanding perfectly certain principles with which some of those in authority apparently have so much difficulty. The Falklands Memorial Service was supposed to be a kind of triumphal assertion that God must have been on our side because we *won*. Runcie, a brave man on the battlefield in his time and a brave man still, remembered in his sermon the sacred principle illustrated by Figure 24.

Thus he reframed the orgy of o–o celebration as a higher-order act of mourning. That, after all, is his job. The Prime Minister was reported as 'spitting blood' with anger; the war, after all, was her *personal* triumph. The Archbishop took it all quite calmly, recalling perhaps Jesus's last few words on the cross. He too knew that the main problem wasn't the turpitude but the stupidity.

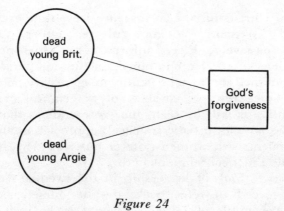

Figure 24

THE QUIET WARRIOR

This chapter, reviewing as it does the ∘–∘ and ⟆ dimensions in a variety of callings, began with an appreciation of two eminent and fundamentally similar men: Lyndon Baines Johnson, the former President of the USA, and Sir Garfield Barwick, the former Chief Justice of Australia. Their similarity lay in their ∘–∘ propensities, in the one case 'transactional' and in the other adversarial, though both occupied jobs which demanded ⟆ detachment. Thus their professional careers both ended under a few clouds, and both were found a little like beached whales when there was nobody left to seduce or to fight. The point, for them, had gone.

We shall end, by contrast, with an entirely ⟆ character of no eminence at all, whose life culminated in a violent political act. Georg Elser, of whom hardly anybody has heard, is one of the twentieth century's moral giants, a true leader of conviction. He rebutted, in a single extraordinary act, Jung's strange view of the German as one who cannot be held responsible for what he does; 'perhaps it would be more correct to regard him at least as one who *passively endures.*'[46] Jung was Swiss and much impressed by the

---

[46] Stern, *Hitler : The Führer and the People*, p. 109.

notion of Christianity as an insecure Levantine graft on to
the old Germanic/Wotanic culture. Other Germans
endured passively; Elser, informed by some persistent
inner voice, acted. He combined, in the one personage, a
number of nice contrasts: a gentle, unaggressive personality
with a fierce resolve; mastery of a technical craft (not
irrelevantly, as will be seen, the same craft as that of the
young Jesus) with artistic (musical) appreciation and skill;
a huge talent with women (lots of mistresses) with a profound and practical religious faith.

When we think of leadership in the twentieth century,
we are forced to refer back, despite ourselves, to the
awesome example of Hitler. It ought to be easy to lead
people in the direction of their best instincts; it must take a
prodigious act of leadership to lead millions, even passive
millions, away from them. Yet this is what Hitler achieved,
and we ignore his achievement at our peril. Adolf Hitler
and Georg Elser shared but one of the qualities listed above
– a fierce resolve – but for Elser the resolve was a matter of
selfless duty ($\female$), whereas for the Führer it was a matter of
life and death ($\circ\!\!-\!\!\circ$). They died, as it happens, within a
month of each other.

Who was Georg Elser? He was the man who some time
in 1938, at the age of 35, decided, à propos not much, to
kill Hitler. He was a good, apolitical German, very successful in his craft (as the artist *manqué* Hitler was not),
comfortably off, a part-time musician, attractive and
unconnected with any subversive political activity. He
simply saw, after Munich, not only that Hitler 'would make
further demands on other countries and incorporate
them'[47] but also that it mattered, that it would lead on and
on to unimaginable evil. Elser had, as some people do, a
feel for evil.

Quietly, and quite alone, he set about his plan, armed
with precisely the skills he needed – turning and cabinet-
making – and with an experience in clock-making and
explosives. He had never made a bomb before, but *this*
bomb, constructed entirely from drawings and without

[47] ibid., p. 142.

experimentation, worked beautifully. He had to give up his job completely in order to do it and spent many months on preparation. The fitting of the device to a concrete pillar in the Munich Bürger Bràu Keller took him about thirty-five nights of painstaking, secretive work. After the first few nights his knees went septic from the constant kneeling. This was in 1939, five years and millions of lives before the Prussian generals' botched attempt of 1944. In the event, he missed by thirteen minutes because Hitler left the hall earlier than scheduled. Fate, Elser decided, had not meant Hitler to die. After all, he had prayed to God throughout the period of preparation that what he was attempting was right and that he would have strength for it. He said afterwards:

I have never prayed to God in a personal way, that is, freely from the heart and in my own words. And I have never made my action – I mean the wish that it should succeed – the object of my prayer. When I was a child my parents took me occasionally with them to church, later I went alone a few times, but less and less often as the years went by. Only in the course of this year [1939] I went again more often, in fact perhaps thirty times since the beginning of the year. More recently I went even on weekdays, maybe into a Catholic church if there wasn't a Protestant one close-by to say the Lord's Prayer there. To my mind it doesn't matter whether one does this in a Protestant or a Catholic church. I admit that these frequent church visits and prayers were connected with my deed, which preoccupied me inwardly, for I am sure I would not have prayed so much if I had not prepared and planned that deed. It's a fact that after praying I always felt a bit more composed. If I am asked whether I regard the deed I committed as sinful within the meaning of the Prot-estant teaching, I wish to say, 'In a deeper sense, no!'[48]

Elser was caught at the Swiss border (the knees gave him away), but only because his perfectionism took him back to the Bürger Bräu, the day before Hitler's speech, just to check everything was working. He was tortured, of course, and finally murdered in Dachau on 9 April 1945 – the same day, oddly enough, as that on which Admiral Canaris and

48 ibid., pp. 146–7.

some of the other aristocratic bomb plotters were extermi-
nated. His captors never understood him, believing to the
last that he must have been implicated in subversive politics or in the pay of Germany's enemies. The truth was, as
J. P. Stern points out, he was 'Hitler's true antagonist – his
moral anti-self'. The true antagonist was

not to be found among the military leaders or the landed aristocracy with their illustrious names, all of whom shared with him
[Hitler] some political aim or patriotic fear; nor yet among the
clergy of the established Churches, whose martyrs chose self-
sacrifice rather than resistance; nor among the Jews, most of
whom were his helpless victims, forsaken by God and all men.
To find his true antagonist we must look for a Nobody like
himself, one who, sharing his social experience, yet lived and
died on the other side of the moral fence. . . .[49]

Georg Elser simply knew, just as Hitler did, what he had
to do. Yet Elser, the political assassin, we regard in hindsight as rational and Hitler, and all the numerical majority,
as collectively mad. If we look on madness as deviance,
then this poses us a philosophical, psychological and statistical problem: what if everybody is mad save one?
Elser's interrogators sensed that he was not mad and never
found a link with organized subversion. He was an incomprehensible phenomenon to them – it was as if he bore on
his slim shoulders the conscience, and the capacity to act,
of a whole nation. What is more, he accepted his fate – even
embraced it at the last – as the will of God. Odd that in a
Christian society obsessed by Nazism we should have for-
gotten him so completely.

[49] ibid., p. 138.

7
Culture and Industrial Institutions

This chapter explores the ○─○ and ⊃ dimensions in a variety of industrial cultures, including Japan, Germany, Sweden and the USA. It offers also a full account of the Great Teutonic Irony, or how the Germans got from us the idea for that most ⊃ of institutions, 'industrial democracy' – not (as the myth supposes) in 1947 but in 1848!

If it true that the ○─○ and ⊃ modes of thought have their sources in primal experience (mothering and so on), then, it might be argued, they are culture-free. Yet even mothering is culture-bound: witness the whole generation of Western mothers who accepted, against their instincts, the injunctions of silly and mostly male child-rearing 'experts' to ration and regulate time at the breast and to leave infants to cry their hearts out in the interests of 'learning' to shut up. It is, after all, only in the last few generations that we as a species have grasped the notion of childhood as a specific state at all. The otherwise kindly Victorian proprietors who sent 3-year-olds to spend more than half the day huddled in filthy pitch-dark mines simply lacked the *conception* that such conditions were, in one special respect, worse for children than for adults.

Recent history indicates that the ○─○ and ⊃ notions, ever present on our thinking, are disposed in quite different ways by culture. Elizabeth Bott[1] has shown how different classes think about class, the working classes viewing the

---

[1] Elizabeth Bott, 'The Concept of Class as a Reference Group', *Human Relations*, vol. 7, 1954.

world in terms of a two-part *power* model and the middle classes seeing themselves as inhabiting the middle of a three-part *prestige* system. In Chapter 3 I suggested that the firm is viewed in quite different ways by the English and the Germans, the English locating ○—○ fight within the firm and the Germans projecting it, quite sensibly, on to trade rivals. On the other hand, the English, as inhabitants of a dependency culture, have been relatively neighbourly since the nineteenth century, refraining on the whole from dropping bombs on other nations except under extreme provocation. The exceptions (Suez, the Boer War, the Crimea) tend to prove the rule by their extreme and perhaps partly conscious incompetence. It is as if, disliking the whole bombing business, the English have set out to 'win the losing' (see p. 158), thus ensuring the loss.

A colleague of mine, Dr Gert Hofstede, has made fascinating use of the collected opinion surveys of the IBM Corporation around the world.[2] He had the wit to see that this standard instrument, administered over many years in forty countries, represented a research goldmine. No one is suggesting that the typical IBM employee is typical of the population of any country. None the less, the evidence shows that the opinions of employees in Japan differ markedly from those of their colleagues in, for example, Sweden. In fact, the Japanese and the Swedish employees usually manage to cluster at opposite ends of any polarity you care to construct, and this cannot be without relevance for the wider populations of both nations.

Hofstede simply put together all the responses, asked the computer to cluster them and then labelled the four principal clusters that emerged. These were:

(1) *Power distance (PD) : large versus small* This reflects the rigidity or otherwise of hierarchical relationships. Hofstede defines it as 'the difference between (1) the extent to which the boss determines the behaviour of the subordinate and (2) the extent to which the sub-

---

[2] Geert Hofstede, *Culture's Consequences – International Differences in Work-Related Values,* London, Sage, 1980.

ordinate can determine the behaviour of the boss. The bigger the difference, the bigger the PD.' Some 58 per cent of the variance in PD in Hofstede's data can be predicted from geographical latitude, population size and GNP. More crudely, banana republics (and dictatorships) tend to have high PD. (The USSR, an exception, no doubt, to the latitude rule, is not an IBM stronghold.) As to latitude, the Belgians and French are the northerly exceptions, but their boss-iness can be put down to the inheritance of the Roman Empire; they tend, in fact, to resemble the other Latin countries in Europe and South America. The point about PD is the whole society's acceptance or rejection of the inequality of power distribution.

(2) *Uncertainty avoidance (UA)* This is a measure of activity designed to control the future or at any rate to create a reassuring fantasy of control. It is associated thus with Adorno's 'authoritarian personality' (see p. 112). High UA is linked with rigidity and dogmatism, intolerance of ambiguity and different opinion, tradi-tionalism, superstition and racism. Fromm described fascism and Nazism as the 'escape *from* freedom' – that is, the reaction of ○-○ people against the intolera-ble ambiguities of a *self*-regulating, democratic ⊳ system. Hofstede found that the 'young' democracies, those that developed their present form of government after the First World War or later (Austria, Finland, France, Germany, Ireland, Israel, Italy, Japan and Turkey) tend to show higher UA scores than the 'old' democracies (Australia, Belgium, Canada, Denmark, Great Britain, the Netherlands, New Zealand, Norway, Sweden, Switzerland and the USA). Most of the latter group may be said to have relinquished aggressive foreign policy long ago and to have got the hang of ⊳ government.

(3) *Individualism* This variable correlates quite closely with PD (above). That is, the most 'individualistic' countries – the USA, Australia and the UK (with individualism values of 91, 90 and 89 on the Hofstede data) – tend also to score lowest on PD, as might be

expected. Conversely, the most 'collectivist' cultures (on individualism – Venezuela 12, Columbia 13, Pakistan 14) have high PD. But measures of individualism and of PD are not the same thing. Some countries (France and Belgium again) combine individualism with large PD; others (e.g. Austria and Israel) combine small PD with only moderate individualism. Individualism here relates to emotional dependence on powerful groups or organizations, whereas PD refers to dependence in relation to powerful *people*. Where individualism is low, people expect in-groups (relatives, clans, organizations) to look after them in exchange for absolute loyalty; where individualism is high, you are supposed to look after yourself and your immediate family.

(4)   *Masculinity* Finally, Hofstede distinguishes the assertive versus nurturative elements in the questionnaire responses, labelling 'masculine' the ∘–∘ ambition to get ahead and to earn and own more and 'feminine' the ⌐ concern with interpersonal relations, with service and with the physical environment. The masculinity index is, significantly, negatively correlated with the percentage of women in professional and technical jobs (at least in wealthier countries) and positively with the segregation of the sexes in higher education. It is positively correlated with permitted traffic speeds and with traffic mortality. In Christian countries masculinity is associated with Catholicism rather than with Protestantism but negatively correlated with the percentage of GNP spent on government aid to the Third World. The masculinity index essentially counterposes quantity of things to quality of life. Whole societies differ in relation to it, but the men almost invariably incline to the quantity pole.

Undoubtedly, Hofstede is on to something, if only a way of treating the writings of management experts (all of whom come from somewhere or other) with due scepticism. His complaint is that most management theory is American; my observation is that most American experts have names like Drucker, Herzberg, Vroom, Maslow, etc, etc. I have suggested that we must distinguish between two kinds of 'third corner' when we consider the ⌐ mode of thinking (cf. Figure 5, p. 35):

(1)   the object, product or output, which gives meaning to human relations;
(2)   the constitutional form by which relations are regulated.

In the fully developed Germanic/Scandinavian form of industrial democracy both aspects are catered for:

(1)   the culture reinforces the technical specialisms, so that (for example) engineering is a respectable trade, not to be regarded as inferior to the 'arts' or to 'science'.
(2)   the factory is fully constitutionalized and the arrangements have the force of law.

This means that:

(1)   the products are well designed and carefully made;
(2)   the rules about employment are quite clear.

In Anglo-Saxon culture, we are prone to sloppiness on both counts.

In Japan, the product is cosseted with the same obsessive care as an essay in traditional calligraphy, but the human relations system remains a claustrophobic mixture of feudalism and family life (writ large). The new Japanese generations are unlikely to tolerate this rigidly hierarchical and paternal system for long. No doubt, in due course, the Japanese will buy a Scandinavian company constitution, dismantle it clause by clause to see how it works, then painstakingly replicate it. Irritatingly, it will probably work. But perhaps not: when Rolls Royce bought in the GM Hydramatic transmission system, they machined the surfaces too perfectly for it to function.

Figure 25 shows the irrelevance for us of Japanese culture in relation to the sort of human relations variables studied by Hofstede (himself a Dutchman and therefore, on the research evidence, close to the Scandinavian pattern). For the illustration, I have lumped together the UK, USA and Australia, as well as Denmark, Norway and Sweden, as they almost invariably cluster together on all four dimensions. The English-speaking nations appear therefore to be similar to the Scandinavians as to risk-taking; similar to the Germans as to masculine dominance and power distance; and unique as to individualism. The Japanese, spiritually as well as geographically, are a world apart. The Venezuelans, by contrast, are even more so on individualism and power distance, though close to the German pattern for uncertainty avoidance and masculinity. Hofstede will not thank me for labelling his dimensions in the following way by attaching heavily laden values to his admirably scientific nomenclature:

left-hand side		right-hand side
free-thinking	(individualism)	brain-washed
democratic	(power distance)	authoritarian
courageous	(uncertainty avoidance)	cautious
compassionate	(masculinity)	acquisitive

Once we do so, however, we can see both the attractiveness of the left-hand side for our cultural *ideals* and the explanation for the civilized standards of the Scandinavian countries. In the Anglo-Saxon world we diverge from them in individualism (which accounts for the sole British complaint about the Swedes – their unfunniness) and in masculinity because we split the aggressive/acquisitive industrial subculture from society as a whole. (Only in Stockholm, to quote an actual experience, will you find opera stars as ordinary guests at a party given by a safety match company.)

On the right-hand side lie the characteristics of the authoritarian personality – conformism, fascism and greed. The evidence, if Japan is a guide, is that this unlovely ∞ social order, allied with a true love for the production of objects, leads on to great collective wealth. (A Japanese

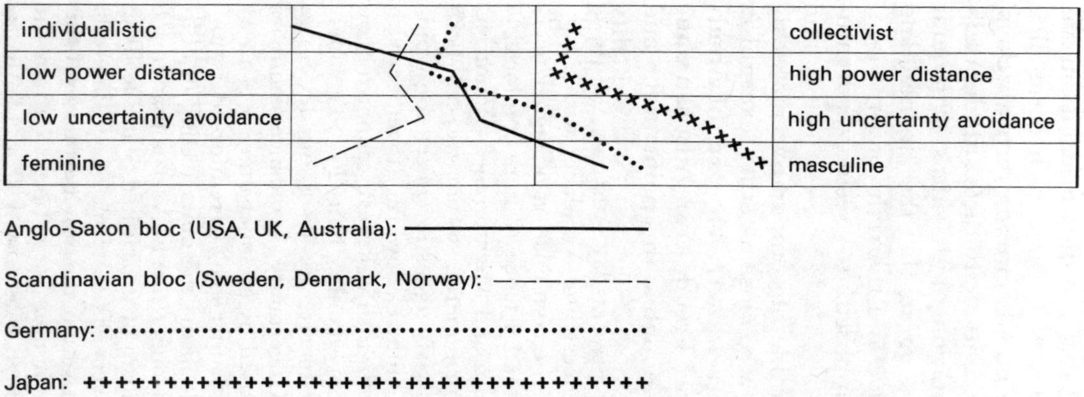

individualistic	collectivist
low power distance	high power distance
low uncertainty avoidance	high uncertainty avoidance
feminine	masculine

Anglo-Saxon bloc (USA, UK, Australia): ————

Scandinavian bloc (Sweden, Denmark, Norway): — — —

Germany: ···········

Japan: +++++++++++

Figure 25

The results for the USA, UK and Australia are so nearly identical as to justify the appellation 'bloc'. For the Scandinavians slightly more violence has been done to the countries' separate results: the Danes are slightly lower on power distance and the Norwegians noticeably higher on risk avoidance. On this scale, the polar *opposite* of the Anglo-Sacon pattern is the Yugoslavian, which raises a few questions for the many from that country to have settled in Australia since the Second World War.

The Anglo-Saxons are much more individualistic than anybody else in the sample, much less autocratic than the Japanese (though more so than the Scandinavians), quite inclined to risk-taking (more than the Germans and the Japanese, but less than the Scandinavians) and somewhat dominated (in the case of employees of big firms anyway) by 'masculine' values.

colleague of mine, in order to display his Europeanism, remarked that he had instituted a policy to dine with his wife twice per month. I was impressed, in a way.) Of course, with a conformist and risk-avoiding orientation, the Japanese ought not to be innovative – and so it turns out. Japanese business leaders are now beginning to research in earnest the topic of why the economic miracle still depends on the super-efficient exploitation of the ideas of others. (One Japanese scientist even suggests that the Japanese left brain is electrically hyperactive and the right brain, where creativity and fun are supposed to reside, virtually dormant.)

Hofstede's book is a rich mine of comparative material. Why do Austria and Israel hew so close together, except for masculinity (Austria high, Israel low)? Why are they both lowest of all in power distance? Freud, as an Austrian phenomenon, emerges naturally enough at this point:

The most striking thing about present-day Austrian culture is that it combines a fairly high Uncertainty Avoidance with a very low Power Distance. Somehow the combination of high Uncertainty Avoidance with *high* Power Distance is more comfortable (for us). (We find this in all Latin and Mediterranean countries, plus Japan.) Having a powerful superior whom we can both praise and blame is one way of satisfying a strong need for avoiding uncertainty. The Austrian culture, however (together with the German, Swiss, Israeli and Finnish cultures), cannot rely on an external boss to absorb its uncertainty. Thus Freud's super-ego comes naturally as an inner uncertainty-absorbing device, an interiorized boss. For strong Uncertainty Avoidance countries like Austria, working hard is caused by an inner urge; it is a way of stress release. The Austrian 'super-ego' is reinforced by the country's relatively low Individualism: the inner feeling of obligation to society plays a much stronger role in Austria than in the USA. The ultra-high Individualism of the United States leads to the need of an explanation of every act in terms of self-interest: and expectancy theories of motivation do provide this explanation: we always do something *because* we expect to attain the satisfaction of some need. The high Masculinity score of Austria may be one reason why Freud paid such a considerable amount of attention to sex as a motivator.[3]

[3] ibid., p. 375.

Why, in the same vein, is the Republic of Ireland (one important source, along with Germany, of American culture) so *exactly* the same as the Scandinavian group, *except* for its high masculinity index? Can it be simply, as Hofstede suggests, the persistence of Catholicism? Of course, the whole island is locked in o—o conflict between Protestant and Catholic values, the conflict displaced into the North. Both sides would argue it is not a simple o—o conflict but authorized from on high. If God *is* watching, Figure 26 must represent the view, and despairing He must

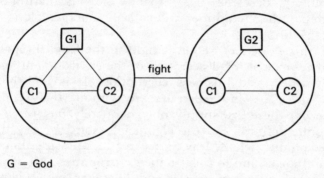

G = God

C = Combatant

Figure 26

feel about so much nonsense perpetrated in His name. My particular interest in Ireland stems from Egan's and Barron's study of leading Irish innovators and entrepreneurs a few years ago.[4] The interesting thing there was the positive correlation between religious fundamentalism and business creativity. It was as though, if you can leave the Creation to God, then you may be freed for vigorous and creative activity in the business mêlée. (This was the opposite of the o—o American pattern, in which innovativeness, aggression and philosophical turmoil tended to go together. Then again, many of the great American entrepreneurs have been refugees from elsewhere.) ·

---

[4] D. Egan and F. Barron, 'Leaders and Innovators in Irish Industry', *Journal of Management Studies*, 1968.

Primarily, Hofstede is useful because of the observed correlation between democratic forms and the ⌘ aspects of culture. Where the leaders think in a ⌘ way, there will be proper constitutional forms which, far from tying people up in red tape, will provide sufficient security for them to be individualistic, to be themselves and to take risks. Where the power is institutionalized, there is little need for the exercise of interpersonal power and the emergence of high power distance. Finally, where there is a concern for the physical environment ('nature', as the British revealingly describe it – that which is natural, not synthetic) the 'feminine' values will emerge, along with women's lib.

On this evidence, we get it right in the English-speaking countries except for desecration of the environment and for fairly widespread business corruption. It is not that the UK, the USA and Australia are without the 'feminine' concerns; these are simply not adequately *integrated* with economic activity. Self-proclaimed 'bastards' carry the ∘–∘ values on our behalf, leaving us free to fantasize about our cultural ideals and to misuse the ⌘ structures. All of which returns us to Reagan, Fraser and Thatcher, which is where we came in.

THE GREAT TEUTONIC IRONY

While there is meaning in the kind of data Hofstede provides us with, we run the risk of pushing national stereotypes further than the data will support. The statement 'Of course, your typical German . . . [fill the space with your fancy]' may contain truth but explains or predicts very little. Because of the two world wars, the mutual stereotypes of English and Germans have tended to take over. For the Germans the English symbolize smug laziness; in English eyes the Germans stand for humourless and heartless efficiency.

What is often left out of the equation is the institutions and their impact on stereotypical behaviour. Which came first – the institution or the behaviour? Do we get the institutions we deserve, or is it that everything we do, or choose not to do, is governed, without our knowing it, by the institutional setting that reared us? The 'cycle of deprivation' is well understood in the institution of the family; beaten children grow up to be child-beaters, as night follows day. The First World War, and the punishment it exacted, begat the Second World War once the grafted-on Weimar Constitution crumbled. Some historians even argue that the Thirty Years' War, which institutionalized the amoral mercenary soldier, was the true begetter of Hitler.

The truth is that the Nazi momentum had very nearly petered out immediately before Hitler's final accession to power. Yet the historical determinist is entitled to argue that the cycle of events was irresistible – that

the rapid, unopposed extinction of all political forces from left to right remains the most striking feature of the Nazi take-over. If anything could have demonstrated the sapped vitality of the Weimar Republic, it was the ease with which the institutions that had sustained it let themselves be overwhelmed. Even Hitler was astonished. . . . All these inglorious downfalls meant that the nation was inwardly bidding goodbye to the Weimar Republic.[5]

Here the contrast with Britain could hardly be greater. It is not so much a matter of formal institutions, though these are important, as the collective grasp of their spirit. The Germans, as to politics, lacked several hundred years of gut feel for anti-authoritarianism. England had been a discrete political entity for almost a millenium, and the English had begun to practise on the likes of Hitler in 1215. The important institutional difference is perhaps that in Britain Parliaments preceded the Civil Service. In Germany civil services of considerable sophistication and probity (and with a mercantile/militaristic bent) preceded the first vestiges of parliamentary democracy. The last British monarch to appoint his own Ministers was George III; the last German monarch to do so was Wilhelm II, just before Weimar.

[5] Joachim C. Fest, *Hitler*, Harmondsworth, Penguin, 1977, pp. 617–18.

Yet if we consider the situation in the industrial sub-culture, the positions are reversed. The Germans appear to have got the hang of industrial institutions in the middle of the nineteenth century while the British haven't caught on *yet*. What is the basis for this claim? The minority proposals to the Revolutionary Parliament in Frankfurt in 1848–9 ('Das professoren Parliament'), included one proposal for the 'proper ordering of industry'. This proposal set out the basis for the establishment of elected works councils and of a district and regional organization to link them. It was to be the basis for all subsequent German arrangements in this field, including the post-war structures supposedly installed by the victorious Allies in the late 1940s. In fact, the Americans *stopped* the Germans from reverting to the very enlightened Weimar arrangements for industrial democracy for fear that the communists might too easily infiltrate the new democratic structure. Even in 1891 a law was passed which, among other things, made it obligatory for each enterprise to establish a formal book of rules as a counterpart to the state constitution. The workers had the right to be heard on its contents. Carl Legien, the president of the united Social Democratic union movement, thought that the 'constitutional factory' was what obtained in Britain.[6] The truth was nearer to a crude ∘–∘ power struggle and hardly constitutionalized (⧄) at all.

Of course, industrial democracy always had a rough ride in Germany, first under Bismarck and later, rougher still, under Hitler. Yet the idea had been grasped that once your industrial institutions begin to be as big as towns, then it makes perfect sense to create institutions to perform those functions for which there is little call in a rural village. Why the Germans grasped this essential point is difficult to determine. It may well be linked with another odd juxtaposition: in Germany the educational revolution preceded the Industrial Revolution; in Britain the opposite was the case. To this day the British working class preserves a special form of insightful street-wise ignorance (see Chapter 4 on

[6] Alistair Mant, Lord Wilfred Brown, and Professor W. Hirsch-Weber, *Bismarck to Bullock: Conversations about Political and Industrial Contrasts in Britain and Germany*, London, Anglo-German Foundation, 1983.

schools). By the mid-nineteenth century most ordinary German children (or, more correctly most children of the German constituent states and kingdoms) were receiving compulsory state education in a broad range of useful subjects.

In Britain, if you got an education at all, it might be at the hands of a pupil-teacher in a class of several hundred. The English, as apart from the Scots, have never had a particularly good feel for educational institutions once you got beyond the privileged few. Today the British teacher is the only teacher in Europe legally entitled to assault children physically. What's worse, many are sufficiently ignorant of the implications of this to persist in supporting corporal punishment without evident embarrassment. Thus does the o—o mentality persist among the innocent, and thus is the notional coherence of the school institution subverted.

British industrialists continued to conduct huge enterprises on the basis of charismatic persuasion spiced with confrontation, as if the whole were indeed a tiny village nestling in some fold in the gentle Cotswold Hills. They prefer, on the whole, to do without red tape, as if any institutional arrangement must stand like an impregnable barrier between the leader and the followers. Yet the same individuals know exactly what to do when someone tries to site a motorway too near the bottoms of their own gardens. They will employ, with consummate and inborn skill, the pressure group, the petition, the deluge of letters to MPs and other tools of political influence. It all adds up to a massive blind spot — but precisely the blind spot you would expect within a split-off industrial subculture charged with carrying all competitiveness and aggression on behalf of society.

What, then, is the Teutonic irony? It is simply that when the Germans learned how to 'order' industry, they learned it from the British — not, obviously, from a study of British industry (Engels and Marx took a different line) but from observation of the political arena. They saw, some of them, that the transformation of the British populace via the successive Reform Acts represented a discovery about *human nature.* As Trevelyan remarked, in 1800 Britain was probably the most corrupt, unstable and worst organized society in Europe.[7] By the end of the Victorian era (we should not underestimate the importance of a female monarch in a dependency culture) the British had become, apparently, a different people. But the genes had not altered; there was no cosmic shift or mutation. Instead every institution of note, from the political franchise to the Civil Service, had been reworked. The rabble that had so terrified the Duke of Wellington when it burned down a substantial part of Bristol changed its behaviour once its undoubted power was drawn into the constitutional framework. Workers have the power to disrupt production, even in Poland. That inescapable fact demands an intelligently Machiavellian (i.e. realistic) response. You can't beat the power out of them any more than you can, in the role of schoolteacher, reduce the aggressions of irritated teenagers by hitting them.

This, to their eternal credit, the British statesmen of the nineteenth century saw, though with reluctance, and legislated for. It represented effective leadership, even if we suspect that, had there been a standing army to call upon, events might have taken a different turn. In truth, the people at large took the lead, carrying with them the wisdom and scepticism that had accumulated since Magna Carta. The leaders had the sense and the humility to follow.

The Scots connection

Thus, ironically, the English and Scots political philosophers (Hume, Locke, Mill, etc.) provided the intellectual fuel for the German economic miracle long before the British economic surge, begun in Elizabethan times, had started to peter out. Since 1849 the performance curves of British and German industry diverge with a startling regularity, notwithstanding irruptions of political change and war. The observer of the scene can take his pick; either

[7] G. M. Trevelyan, *History of England*, London, Longman, 1973.

German engineers and workers are simply 'better', or the slow emergence of sensible industrial institutions has produced a different kind of *behaviour*, with concomitant economic benefits. German workers' representatives, having a ⅁ structure by which to regulate relations with the bosses, can be chosen on the basis of a ⅁ mentality. British workers' representatives, down on the shop floor where it counts, are chosen for machismo — and why not, when you examine the implicit bases for managerial selection?

It isn't as if the ⅁ approach has been untried in British industry. Robert Owen employed it in the nineteenth century (and he was read by the Germans too), and Wilfred Brown (significantly, a Scot) implemented it at Glacier Metal after the war.[8] This last was probably the most closely observed and carefully constructed experiment in industrial constitutionalism, anywhere. It worked, but nobody, or hardly anybody, in Britain noticed. Nowadays, among the aggressive young MBAs from the new business schools, it is all regarded as a bit *passé*, as if it told us nothing about human nature at all.

I used to harbour a conspiracy theory about the submergence of Glacier among the English, on the assumption that the whole thing was too threatening to take on board precisely because it was all so simple and obvious. The English business community, thinking in the ∞ mode, tried to explain it all in terms of Brown's supposed charisma, as though the man was more important than the institutions he created. To some extent, its prejudices have been borne out by events since Wilfred Brown's retirement, yet this is to deny the part that institutions played in taking the company from a few hundred people to five thousand, competing successfully in a very tough export market and avoiding all but one minor strike in thirty years.

I no longer believe in the conspiracy theory. I think uncompromising intellects like Wilfred Brown's make Englishmen nervous and, to a lesser extent, Australians and

[8] Lord Wilfred Brown, *Explorations in Management*, Harmondsworth, Penguin, 1965.

Americans too. However, in the long run I suspect that many English businessmen are simply incapable of understanding what Glacier was all about (or, for that matter, Owen or the Frankfurt Parliament). Not understanding the principle means that such things must be stereotyped as: (1) 'red tape' and endless meetings, and/or (2) do-goodism and worse still, 'socialism'. Just what the Hofstede data (p. 187) would predict within a determinedly individualistic (and therefore anti-institutional) industrial subculture with a strongly masculine bent. The Scandinavians, suffering from neither of the illusions above, learned as well as the Germans and without the psychological purgative of a fresh start from ruin.

The recent history of industry in general, and of industrial democracy in particular, seems to me to provide evidence as powerful as one could desire of the importance of the ⌐○ mind in high places, not so much because of the psychological reserve of such leaders but because of intellectual capacity. Not to screen out the ○–○ misfits looks like industrial suicide. Of course, I ought to argue that even the individual skewed towards ○–○ can be corralled by a sound institution, but by the time he or she reaches adulthood, I doubt it.

THE PERSON/PRODUCT LINKAGE

If we examine a few of the dominant industrial cultures, we find the ○–○ and ⌐○ assumptive bases disposed in a variety of permutations according to output and human relations. The assumption here is that any employee, no matter how senior, has to associate himself with the people in the organization, in the context of both interpersonal power and institutional authority, and the organization's output or product (or to dissociate himself, if the product is too shameful to contemplate).

This is obvious enough to sound like a truism, yet the psychology of it is fundamental. Distinguishing between objects and people is not always easy; very disturbed people continually confuse the two, as with the self-righteous authoritarian capable of torture and 'political' murder. In order to murder several million Jews, you need to be able to regard certain people as objects, and dangerous objects at that. Conversely, the incompetent may ascribe to inanimate objects the unpredictabilities and mischievousness of certain people.

One of the very first steps in the development of intellect (see chapter 2) is the distinguishing of inner feeling (full tummy) from breast (object) from Mum (person). Clever mums allow their infants to feel 'good enough' while they puzzle out the object/person distinction. One of the classic instances when people were treated as objects was the Industrial Revolution. The point is that the exploitative owners were, in a sense, decent and godly people (if smug). But they had a blind spot, as did the better of the concentration camp guards. Maybe this insensitivity to human feelings, or failure of empathy, was linked with insensitivity to the product as 'good object'. God, for such people, resided in church rather than in the wonders of materials and technological creation.

Victorian exploitative

Some historians have argued that the true origins of the Industrial Revolution lay in the extraordinary inventiveness of the Elizabethan era. The outpourings of Shakespeare and Byrd were paralleled by very vigorous commercial and manufacturing activity. At any rate, by the time the official Industrial Revolution got under way in the late eighteenth century, there were just a few, stunning, mechanical inventions to come (many of them contrived by Northerners and Scotsmen, as were the great parallel works of political and economic philosophy).

But, as Hobsbawn reminds us, the period of greatest wealth coincided with an absence of innovation and with the continued exploitation of old sources, not excluding the Colonies.[9] Britain's main trade rivals – France, Germany and the USA – were pressing on to the second-phase,

[9] E. J. Hobsbawm, *Industry and Empire : 1750 to the Present Day*, Harmondsworth, Penguin, 1969.

'science-based' Industrial Revolution. British industrialists simply eked out existing resources, among which was a relativley expendable commodity – people (or, perhaps more correctly, 'elements of labour' from a 'labour market').

The story requires no retelling. British industrialists, almost uniquely in Europe, strove to educate their off-spring out of industry, perhaps because of a partly con-scious shame about what they were doing to the communities in which they operated. Even Brunel sent his son to Harrow. At any rate, the new and unlovely corps of 'managers' moved in to separate the ownership from its fell misdeeds, bringing with it the *arrivistes* and their contempt for the proletariat. Whatever feel there may have been for the output (☌) or for the employees as citizens was hardly ever handed down from generation to generation.

The result was an industrial subsystem with a binary ○–○ character both as to product and as to human relations. That is, the product was cherished not for itself but only as a means of amassing more money to facilitate the escape to gentility. The constitutional arrangements simply didn't exist at all except in the case of a few Quaker and Quaker-influenced organizations plus, of course, Robert Owen's far-sighted venture in Lanark. While the political system embraced the ☌ principle by steadily extending the fran-chise, the citizen in his occupational role remained a mere unit in a 'market' for labour. Thus the Victorian pattern was (and in many cases still is) that shown in Figure 27.

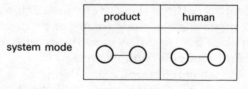

Figure 27

Benign exploitative (USA)

The USA inherited a great many Germanic engineering skills and, along with the English language itself, a certain anti-union bent. As a result, American products tend to be well-made (though not particularly tastefully designed) and labour relations to be persuasive. America is the home of 'motivation' – expressed as a transitive verb. Motivation is, in truth, a ○—○ wolf dressed up in sheep's clothing. To the extent that 'motivation' is blarney, it might be an inheritance from Old Ireland.

There is always a risk in generalizing about so vast and varied a culture, but one way of expressing it is as significantly ☌ as to product and somewhat ○—○ as to Human Relations. (As Drucker points out, it is important that so many American employers introduced stock option and profit-sharing schemes so early.)[10] Although this represents an incorporation rather than a boundary-clarifying constitutional model, it is still a big improvement on the Victorians. For the USA see Figure 28.

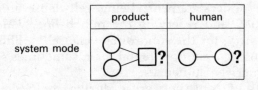

Figure 28

The American benign exploitative approach is quite difficult for others to grasp, just as American leadership styles sometimes baffle foreigners. It all seems so affable on the surface, yet there is a kind of steel in the soul of the superior–subordinate relationship. Bateson explained this in terms of culture and family culture in particular. There is, he argued, much in common between British and American child-rearing practices, but there are also one or two crucial differences. The differences have to do primarily with exhibitionism.

[10] Peter F. Drucker, *Managing in Turbulent Times*, London, Heinemann, 1980.

Among the English middle and upper classes, the linkages are thus:

Parents	Children
succouring	dependence
dominance	submission
exhibitionism	spectatorship

Among the American middle classes the pattern is:

Parents	Children
succouring	dependence
dominance (slight)	submission (slight)
spectatorship	exhibitionism

The difference leads to odd and sometimes amusing miscommunication. The American speaker tends to seem boastful or obstreperous to the English, asserting the rights of the small (the child) over those of the larger and stronger. The English speaker, on the other hand, 'makes his points by understatement, being self-deprecatory in the major clause, and reserving the punch-line, which asserts his superiority, for the subordinate clause'.[11] Thus English speakers, using a calm, parental tone, sometimes seem arrogant to American audiences.

All sorts of confusion arose during the Second World War Alliance, in which the British stylized the relationship as an equal tennis partnership – 'Well played, partner!' – and the Americans as an unequal *business* relationship.

When Churchill said to his partner the American, 'Give us the tools and we'll finish the job,' his assumpton of equal status was misread by Americans as an expression of the superiority of the British. And when the British boasted of their American partners, and congratulated the Americans on the anti-aircraft guns that had saved Britain, they were affronted to find that instead of replying with some courteous, 'Well shot, partner!', and praise for the Normandy landing platforms, the Americans simply blazoned the British praise of our anti-aircraft guns throughout the American press.[12]

[11] Margaret Mead, 'End Linkage: a Tool for Cross-Cultural Analysis', in John Brockman (ed.), *About Bateson*, London, Wildwood House, 1978, p. 173.
[12] ibid., p. 180.

So when an Englishman, Geoffrey Gorer, advised the Americans how to approach the post-war reconstruction of Japan, his advice was virtually unintelligible. He suggested that the Americans refrain from impugning the authority of the dependent figure – the Emperor – because he would be needed as a 'good object' after the war, a prophetic recommendation, as things turned out. 'The US should adopt a firm, fatherly tone towards the Japanese', he advised. This was misinterpreted by the Office of the Co-ordinator of Information in a broadcast to Japan which stated: '*The US is your father.* . . .' Margaret Mead admitted afterwards:

After an initial sense of despair over ever being able to communicate in a useful way, we realized that the error was ours. There is no 'firm, fatherly tone' in the United States such as Geoffrey Gorer, as an Englishman, had wished to evoke. The best we could have done to carry out Gorer's intent would have been to say, 'Talk to the Japanese as if they are fourth graders and you are fifth.'[13]

In her autobiography Margaret Mead (who was married to Gregory Bateson during a crucial phase of both of their work) observes that a marriage of an American woman with an Englishman will be characterized by a kind of energy overlap; each will endlessly over-organize the other. The reverse, the Englishwoman married to an American man, results in a virtual absence of normal social life because no organizing is ever done at all.[14]

Japanese paternal

The two principal things to note in Japan are (1) the *homogenization* of family and corporate ideas in the 1920s after the failure of more coercive models and (2) the study of art and crafts in schools.

The typical Japanese child continues to study art and craft until about 18 years of age. It is not, either, the kind

[13] ibid., p. 181.
[14] Margaret Mead, *Blackberry Winter: My Earlier Years*, London, Angus & Robertson, 1973, p. 182.

of anarchic, irreverent art that we cherish. It is the getting of a brush stroke *exactly* right, according to the ancient conventions of form and calligraphy (and according to the absolute authority of a master in the craft). It is, in the argot of industry, a 'zero-defect' culture. Conventional it may be, but it is a million miles from 'Hammertown Boys' (see Chapter 4) and the woodwork class for illiterate dullards. In a typical British school, if you work with your hands at all, you are thought to be dim (as to literacy and formal scholarship).

So in Japan the product or object is at centre-stage, intuitively and for everybody. Go to any Japanese factory and you will see this object-centred aspect of culture working through in the manufacturing process. Quality control is not a technique but a religion. When study tours of American industry took place after the Second World War, the British brought back 'communications', 'motivation' and other such blarney; the Japanese brought back 'quality circles'. (To the uninitiated, the recent emergence of the 'quality circle' religion in the USA and UK is baffling. The inquiry usually goes something like this:

'What is a quality circle?'

'Well, it's working people talking about how to do things better.'

'But isn't that what everybody does anyway?'

'Well, I suppose so, but it's *organized* in the quality circle.'

'But surely that's what managers are for, organizing that sort of thing?'

And so on.)

But as to human relations, the Japanese organization reflects the grossly male-dominated wider society by enhancing dependence and massive sibling rivalry in a family-like milieu. Competition among schoolchildren is fierce – a prime source of personal insecurity despite all the social support and, later on, of the highest suicide rate in the world. The Japanese employee is truly the kamikaze pilot of modern industrial society but, in the process, he produces a nearly perfect object.

One other aspect of Japanese organization deserves

comment, bearing in mind this dependent aspect of Japanese human relations. A large percentage of earnings is often contributed by the annual bonus: in a good year up to seven or eight months' salary. This annual variation has a somewhat agricultural feel, like the result of a successful harvest. Some have even argued that the structural dynamic of Japanese industry owes much to its relatively recent agrarian past and to the particular demands placed by Japanese topography on subsistence farming. The constraints of rice production and irrigation led to a unit of about a dozen families, who had to decide consensually because they shared the ditches. It must have been a good grounding for an industrial sector of collective responsibility, long-term evaluation and 'promotion', non-specialized 'career paths' plus the occasional bonanza. Strictly speaking, it is a clan rather than a family dynamic.

In the end the Japanese configuration of product/people is rather like the American, only more so (see Figure 29).

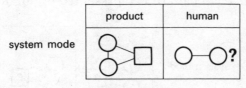

Figure 29

You might argue that the 'family' human relations model ought to be expressed as ⧎. After all, the family is an institutionalized 'third corner'. But we are dealing with a family *model* here – Sony, Mitsubishi, National Matsushita and the rest are not actually the families of their employees, even though they usually behave as if they were. This is human relations by fantasy, and it is already showing signs of fragility in the behaviour of Japanese youth.

Mature Germanic Scandinavian constitutional

Believers in the sanctity of the ⧎ notion must turn to Northern Europe in order to find sympathetic attitudes to both objects and people in the industrial subculture. Here, the engineers hold sway in the boardrooms (symbolizing the centrality of the output), and the constitutional arrangements are actually copied from the nineteenth-century British constitution (see p. 193 above). The Germans have learned it painfully, and the Scandinavians, according to Hofstede's data (see above) are strongly oriented to the feminine pole anyway (where the ♂ mode is usually taken for granted).

The Scandinavians, whatever local difficulties may occur in their economic cycles, are locked into a virtuous circle. Manufacturing directors automatically prefer uncharismatic young hopefuls who care about product. Scandinavian top managers assume constitutional relations between all employees of an enterprise, from the board of directors down, rather than a network of interpersonal power relations. The existence of the institutions begets the right people and the right people, in situ, reinforce the institutions. It all happens without anybody really noticing. The Scandinavian pattern is represented by Figure 30.

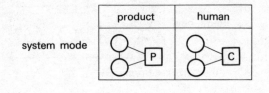

C = constitution
P = product

Figure 30

The important thing is perhaps the psychological harmony. Interpersonal relations at work are mediated by *two* 'third corners' – the product itself and the constitutional structure. The ♂ assumptive base is constantly reinforced by the relationship between the output system and the human system. It is as if maleness (projecting the output to the environment) and femaleness (human beings containing, even loving, the gestation) are harmonized by a single felicitous image.

If all this sounds a little romantic, it can't really be helped. When work, and especially the making of things, loses all its romance we are doomed. It is not necessary to argue that Scandinavian industrial life is perfect – that would be far from the truth. It is necessary to ask only why such quiet, decent, uncharismatic, dedicated and solid characters adorn so many Scandinavian boardrooms, and to compare them with the flashy and shallow (though energetic) emotional misfits one meets occasionally in the boardrooms of English-speaking countries.[15]

As a postscript, I have considered the fourth possibility as to the o–o and 𝔇 dispositions vs. product and human systems (see Figure 31). It would be nice to think that such

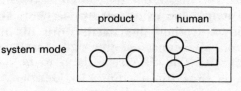

Figure 31

an organization could not exist, but I fear that the British Civil Service might qualify at certain points. That is to say, the Service is impeccably based on constitutional rules and conventions internally, but its relations with its 'masters' (the elected representatives of the people) have an uncomfortably o–o character. For example, when the Fulton Royal Commission pronounced on the much needed reforms in the Civil Service, especially as to the background and experience of recruits, the Service cynically and quite consciously subverted the proposals.

In fact, the chief architect of the subversion, the late Sir William Armstrong, the head of the Civil Service at the time and a distinctly o–o character, cheerfully admitted to a reporter afterwards that it was all quite conscious and deliberate. Sir William, having been closely involved with the Heath Government's handling of the three-day week crisis suffered a nervous breakdown and retired early.

[15] Alistair Mant, 'Authority and Task in Manufacturing Operations of Multinational Firms', in *Manufacturing and Management*, London, HMSO, 1978.

Instead of proceeding to the decent obscurity of an academic post, he re-emerged as chairman of one of the great British clearing banks – the kind of move officially frowned on (for obvious reasons) but unofficially achieved with increasing frequency by top civil servants. In the end Sir William was one of the best-paid people in the country, pulling in his service pension as well as the munificent bank salary.

Of course, some of the top civil servants are stratum 6 (see p. 215) and 7 people having to deal with stratum 4 (and worse) politicians. But that, as the man said, is democracy. It is the worst system possible, apart from all the alternatives. As the gentlemanly corruption in the product system persists, the constitutional understandings in the human relations system have begun to be infected; civil servants are starting to demand pay parity, absolute job security, inflation-proof pensions *and* the right to strike whenever they feel like it. The Service's claim to be a service, let alone civil, is thus diminishing. In Germany, of course, *beamter* status spells out the quid pro quo for absolute security in key jobs. The right to strike is not included. Train drivers, logically, are civil servants and *beamte*. To that extent the constitutional arrangements for public service in Britain are incomplete.

There is a considerable, and growing, industry in the making of international industrial comparisons. In fact, this industry grows a lot more quickly than 'industry' itself these days. The attraction of the mode of comparison above is that it offers some hope of helpful cross-fertilization. It is highly unlikely that the British, for example, can alter their attitudes to manufacturing without a root and branch reworking of their schools. Here we find a pernicious circle, for you cannot remove an incompetent head teacher; his employers cannot even force him to teach a standard curriculum. We must accept, therefore, that most children will enter industry both ignorant and twisted (this applies as well, naturally, to the pampered 'ear-oles' from rarefied private schools).

But the ▷ idea requires no teaching. It has been understood, more or less, in Britain since 1215. It is what Britain retaught the world after the fashion of ancient Greeks. It may well be impossible, in the short term, to learn Japanese quality standards or American competitiveness, but it is quite a different matter to transfer a well understood principle from one aspect of one's life to another. The nub of the matter is the quality of leadership. Good leaders don't do things to people; they release deep-seated urges and understandings. That applies to industrial leaders as well as to any others. The quickest possible start on our most pressing problems lies in understanding why we elevate so many awful ∞ characters to high position and in using every trick we know to allow the solider ⊳ types a clearer or fairer run. To achieve all this we need to use our wits (instincts) for a change and to create a few simple institutions. Chapter 8 examines the issues and the problems.

8
Picking Winners

Once you think you know how to select potential ⧽ leaders, there is a temptation to do it by ∘—∘ means. As with everything else, you have first to create new institutions which allow the people in the system to manage it for themselves. One or two examples of this approach are referred to here, but first there is a re-examination of why we want, sometimes, to be led (in Bullock's unforgettable phrase) by 'moral cretins'.

THE INSPIRATION OF LEADERSHIP

The argument of this book so far is quite simple. There are two discernible modes of thinking, and one of them is disastrous in high office. It is also, apart from being disastrous, a mode of thought which is likely to lead on to career success and thus to a gross contribution to organizational inefficiency and madness. Of course, nothing is every quite that simple. We all harbour ∘—∘ and ⧽ bits, and there are undeniably times when the ∘—∘ mode is not merely useful but crucial for survival. We use games, for example, to fantasize about survival. Because a game has rules and conventions, it is a ⧽ institution, but once we have adopted the role of players, we can do and be anything we like, and in the ∘—∘ mode.

In fact, in normal life we oscillate between the two modes. If we don't take a conscious decision to spend periods in a kind of survival mode (through worship, art, games or a retreat to therapy), then those survival needs will emerge, unbidden, from the unconscious to complicate our own working lives and those of our colleagues and subordinates.

Some people, and some of the most conventionally successful people, are emotional cripples in this sense – doomed to spend most of life in the survival mode and usually quite unaware of the costs to others of this skewed psychology. To understand it all, you need a mind capable of paradoxical leaps, and that is exactly what the fixedly o–o mind cannot do because there is no 'third corner' to observe *from*. So far as it is concerned, paradox is not fun; it is simply chaos. Slipping from one abstractional level to another involves letting go, losing control for a moment. Any skier or rally driver will tell you that the secret of changing direction in unknown terrain lies in the controlled (sort of) skid.

There is the further implication that although (as the reader may well have discovered) the o–o and ⫐ modes are difficult to describe, they are not all that difficult to recognize. As they say, you know it when you see it. How do you describe, in suitably scientific terms, sexual attraction? There are, in fact, scientists who are hard at work on this, principally on the olfactory mechanisms; you can't describe it, but you know it when you smell it. It is no less real, as to outcomes, for that.

When it comes to taking decisions of the promotional kind about other people, the problem lies less in the recognition of psychological types than in our distorted views of what is going to be good for us or for the organization. We sometimes promote people we can't stand (as people) because of a misguided belief that a certain kind of driven madness will drive the organization in a sensible direction. We home in on the drive – the motive force – and neglect the direction, like the Ferrari owner with a faulty map who simply gets to the wrong place more quickly.

In other words, we hanker, in a way, after the raw instincts of survival behaviour. When we are frightened, we are also excited. Our lives, these days, tend to lack real excitement; those dear dead days of the Second World War were not exactly pleasant for most people, but they were hardly boring either. Nostalgia for those days still runs strong, as the scenes at the post-Falklands dockside attest. Guilt about our own failures of will and fortitude cause us to project those qualities on to 'hard men' who are supposed to represent them on our behalf.

The Hitlers and Galtieris of this world could not survive, let alone prosper, unless significant numbers of people experienced a certain ambivalent love/hate feeling for them. Deep in the murk of the dictatorial/authoritarian subconscious is a knowledge that part of each person wants to be raped. It is too shameful a desire for consciousness, so it emerges, through the cracks, in the 'accidents' of political in-fighting. Those liberal-minded Tories in Britain who claim that they never really wanted Margaret Thatcher want it both ways; even tactical leadership voting obeys an underlying logic, especially if you don't have to take responsibility for the outcome – like the proud possessors of the post-Watergate bumper stickers 'Don't blame me, I'm from Massachusetts' (the only state to vote Humphrey).

The cold war, the global expression of the ∘–∘ mode of thought, is sustained by this same ambivalent loathing/awe of named power and implacable will. In a brilliant article on the origins of the A bomb, Bruce Page identifies this ambivalence. The nuclear arsenals, he argues, are out of all proportion to their possible *function* in the real world. In fact

they exist to bolster Western psyches against a fear that Soviet power may be intrinsically superior to anything in the West. And that fear comes down not to numbers of tanks, planes and men-in-arms – though such numbers are often cited. It rests on the notion that the Soviet system *must* be more potent because it is more *ruthless*.[1]

Dr Henry Kissinger, one of the main exponents of this central pessimism, is really a closet admirer of the USSR. William Shawcross gives a useful summary of the Kissinger doctrine:

[1] Bruce Page, 'God is Sophisticated – but not Malicious', *New Statesman*, 19–26 December 1980, p. 28.

In *The Necessity for Choice*, Kissinger endorsed the idea that a missile gap existed between the US and the USSR. . . . It has been said that his early experience of the Weimar Republic and then Fascism impressed him with the irreducible will and purpose of totalitarianism. Certainly he appeared to believe that democracy seemed an ineffectual David against dictatorship.[2]

The Soviet achievements were due to 'greater moral toughness, to a greater readiness to run risks, both physical and moral'. The Russians were 'iron-nerved'; they 'analysed events with a ruthless objectivity. . . . they were cold-blooded, logical, without compunction.'[3]

We need not ask what kind of man Henry Kissinger would be inclined to promote to high office in a commercial organization should he, Heaven forfend, sit upon a selection panel. (Perhaps he does.) The falsity of the argument lies in the assumption of superiority. Page suggests that the Germans were actually gifted with most of the brilliant physicists before the war. No one then would have claimed that Frisch and Peierls, who cracked the nuclear code in Birmingham, were necessarily cleverer than Werner Heisenberg or Karl von Weizsacker back in Nazi Germany. Yet Frisch and Peierls, in a flash of creative insight, saw that the A bomb would be easy to make, while Heisenberg concluded: 'After a year we saw clearly that the bomb was so difficult to make that it would be impossible.' Page argues

It was the political wickedness of the Nazis which *caused* their scientific and technical incompetence. Only a terrorist will use weapons indiscriminately, and pure terrorists cannot muster the moral and emotional resources required for free creativity. This does not means that wicked regimes aren't dangerous, and aren't capable of destructive effort: only that their power on the ground may be less than it appears, as the Yugoslavs demonstrated to Stalin.[4]

---

[2] Willaim Shawcross, *Sideshow : Kissinger, Nixon and the Destruction of Cambodia*, New York, Washington Square Press, 1979, quoted in ibid., p. 29.
[3] ibid.
[4] Page, 'God is Sophisticated', p. 27.

Precisely the same argument may be applied to the relatively obscure figures of J. T. Randall and H. A. H. Boot. They sounded, and looked, for all the world like a pair of county cricket opening batsmen, yet they did more, arguably, to defeat the Nazis than anyone else. Radar was less spectacular than the atom bomb but of far greater tactical importance. In fact, Randall and Boot made their great discovery without quite knowing how the resonant-cavity magnetron worked. It was an inspired creative leap by men in the grip of a collective moral outrage, who never produced anything of comparable brilliance afterwards.

It was as if, to quote Page again, they became possessed for a short time of a kind of scientific perfect pitch. Robert Frisch himself, though from a musical family, had never possessed perfect pitch, the hallmark of the true professional musician. Yet when he was growing up in Vienna he conceived himself to be in love with a girl who belonged to a particular choir. This choir, which sang extremely complex unaccompanied music, insisted on perfect pitch in its members. The girl was so devoted to her music that she informed young Robert she would have no time for him unless he joined. Useless, he lamented, I don't have the pitch. All the same, she said, come to a few rehearsals. He did and, after a few sessions, the choirmaster said: 'Robert, you should take the test.' Useless, said Robert. You must, said the girl. So he did and, miraculously, he passed. Frisch (at 70 years of age): 'For a few months, fifty years ago, I had perfect pitch. You should never underestimate the power of sex.' But, as an American visitor observed, Britain in 1940 was like living in Troy.

Frisch and Peierls, Randall and Boot, and any artist lost in creation, has perfect pitch, perhaps fleetingly and perhaps only once in a lifetime. A prerequisite, perhaps, is the belief in such possibilities based on the internalized 'good object'. A further prerequisite, Page would argue, is the rightness of the setting. The Nazi physicists, decent men all and locked in a ∞ war of conquest, were screened in some inexplicable way from the light of their own creative energy. God, perhaps, withheld their genius just for a while. As to art, Eric Ambler's first novel, *The Dark*

Frontier (written in 1934 when he was 25), foresaw the Bomb. 'It was fairly obvious', he said, 'if you had been educated as an engineer, which I was.'

Now, perfect pitch is but another way of referring to the 'peak experience' which Abraham Maslow said is always part of the 'self-actualizing' mode of life. That is, once a person climbs above survival and survival-motivated relationships, he will occasionally find himself lost in experiences which seem to lift him above the base concerns of the world. He feels a oneness with nature and with the cosmos. This is the moment of inspiration. But Maslow was worried about leadership and particularly about the impact of envy on the choice of leaders.

This is a little like Eisenhower–Stevenson . . . where the obvious intellectual *inferior* was chosen in preference to the obvious intellectual superior. Why is this so? I think my phrasing of leadership would lay a little more stress on this counter-hostility, secret resentment, secret jealousy, and accept more realistically the fact that excellence may be loved and admired, but it is also hated and feared.[5]

Maslow was also concerned about the iron grip of the 'management-style' industry in the USA, which was based on the assumption that it is possible to isolate which style 'works' and then to don it like a cloak: it didn't really matter how *good* you were; what mattered was simply how good an actor you were. Of course, goodness, like sexual attraction and ⏧-ness, is not easily defined but is readily recognized. On the matter of recognition Maslow was really quite sanguine:

All of this adds up to *functional* leadership in which all personality traits of the general sort are secondary to skill and *capability* and to the general requirements of the *situation*. So also should there be more stress on perception of the truth, the creative cognition of the truth, the creative cognition of new truths, of being correct, of being able to be tough, stubborn, and decisive in terms of the facts; that is, when the facts say 'yes' and the

5 Abraham Maslow, *Eupsychian Management : A Journal*, Homewood, Ill., Irwin, 1965, p. 153.

public says 'no', the good leader ought to be able to stick with the facts against the hostility of the public. . . . I don't think there's any great problem here because I'm sure that all of these people would agree with me that this was desirable and that it's just simply a matter of a slight shift in emphasis and in theoretical organization and communication.[6]

Maybe.

What, then, are we to make of Eisenhower and Stevenson? Did the American people choose the amiable old soldier because they resented Stevenson's brains and uncompromising purpose? Or did they genuinely think Eisenhower was brighter or more capable? Or did they just like him because he dripped with the glory of military victory? Did they plump for Reagan as cowboy for similar reasons, rather than the man who challenged their God-given right to guzzle gas? (It was Eisenhower, of course, who went on mispronouncing the word 'nuclear' to the end of his life, presumably because you just can't point out such things to the President.)

Yet Stevenson, the loser, commanded loyalty of a special kind. It was loyalty not to a party that promised benefits in the ∘–∘ contest for survival but to an ideal. Robert Ardrey recalled:

For many Americans then of voting age, life has offered few experiences so exalting as the one that overcame us on a night in 1952 when, grouped around our television sets, we listened to Adlai Stevenson accept his nomination for the Presidency. Tears flowed without shame. Voices choked, hands in the dark gripped other hands, whatever hand was closest. It was as if, half a continent away, a single man struck a hidden bell, and throughout the forests of the American soul, from this tree or that, from the heart of this thicket, from the crown of that lonely pine, bells reverberated in response, bells that had never found voice before, bells unguessed, joined in a wild, unpredicted clamour of purpose and hope, of resolve and thanksgiving. The Stevenson movement was born.

I was still living in Hollywood at that time. I had published a novel earlier in the year, and out of consequent bankruptcy had a

[6] ibid., p. 152.

few weeks before the nomination accepted a film assignment to
pay for my folly. The contract involved a quite splendid mountain of hard cash. A few days after the nomination I went to the
studio, pleaded a heart attack, varicose veins, and several unex-
pectedly slipped discs, and we tore up the contract. I joined the
Stevenson movement and with many another mad American
went to work on the campaign. I became a *Follower*.[7]

In the end we are stuck with calibre, capacity, talent –
call it what you will. Only Elliott Jaques, so far as I know,
has put forward a scale for its measurement.[8] He says that
the touch of greatness is linked with the 'time-span of dis-
cretion', or people fall into natural 'strata' according to
their spans of concentration. The very best people, those
who ought to be running countries, for example, can
envision very long periods of time and can handle the
multiple abstractions from the front line right up to the
chairman's, general's, archbishop's, etc., desk.

Up to the two-year span, according to Jaques, the work
has a concrete quality and the lines of command are usually
direct. Beyond the two-year span of vision, when 'conceptual modelling' and intuition become important, the work
tends to the abstract and the lines of command become
indirect. By stratum 6 (twenty-year vision) the outstanding
person tends to create new institutions rather than simply
to manage them. On this basis, the boss of the medium-
sized business (five-year span) is the equivalent of a brigade
commander in the Army or an Assistant Secretary in the
British Civil Service. The twenty-year person is the head of
an industrial group, an army corps or a Permanent Secretary.

Jaques even claims that these discontinuities in the
capacity for work are a function of organized work itself, so
that the discretionary discontinuities always fall at the same
time boundaries – up to three months for direct workers,
up to one year for the next level (e.g. the ward sister in a
hospital), up to two years for the manager of a small
business who has to develop systems. This level Jaques

[7] Robert Ardrey, *The Social Contract*, London, Collins, 1970, p. 118.
[8] Elliott Jaques, *A General Theory of Bureaucracy*, London, Heinemann, 1976.

calls 'imaginal scanning'. The other discontinuities are at about five years, ten years and twenty years. Beyond that lie strata 7 and 8 and the super-leaders. Jaques thinks that there is probably an inadequate supply of such people for the needs of our biggest bureaucracies. Politicians, of course, tend to have a span of vision as long as an electoral term. Harold Wilson took the view that a week is a long time in politics.

Jaques's importance lies in the exciting attempt to render the selection of leaders a relatively scientific process. But, as we have noted, outstanding people are not always well received. Jesus, for example, must have been infuriatingly clever and saintly. Psychologically, innovative leaders are subject to 'envious attacks'. Melanie Klein's argument was that a 'good object' (for example, a good idea, or even Jesus himself),

which one cannot bear because it is not one's own, may for that reason be turned into something bad, which then becomes a threat through having one's hostility projected on to it. Creativeness is apt to stir up jealous hatred of this kind and the creators all too often become the targets of destructive spite.[9]

We are confronted, then, by two contrary forces if we wish to advance the prospects of clever and saintly people: subconscious envy of good people and a sneaking admiration for bastards. The latter is harder to understand, at any rate on the part of nice people. A partial explanation may lie in the very large number of organizations in our modern world that are devoted to pointless or even pernicious outputs and conducted in shameful ways. Perhaps if all our enterprises were useful, we would have less time for emotional misfits in high places. But in a naughty world there is always going to be a place for the delinquent. Hitler, after all, was an inspired 'selection' if the primary task was genocide.

We know, anyway, that fast social learning occurs only when 'innovation and alphaness coincide'.[10] Robert Ardrey

[9] Eric Trist, *The Evolution of Socio-Technical Systems*, Occasional Paper No. 2, Ontario Quality of Working Life Centre, June 1981.
[10] Ardrey, *The Social Contract*, p. 129.

recounts the famous tale of Imo, the young genius female monkey in a large band on the island of Koshima in Japan.[11] Imo was an 'alpha' as to intellect but, being young and female, her brilliant ideas hardly diffused at all (she was the one who figured out how to clean the sand from sweet potatoes and wheat by panning them in a nearby stream). Her inventions spread to her own family and circle but never to the senior males of the band, the political 'alphas'. It is impossible to recount the story without thinking of certain boards of directors of large enterprises.

The point of the tale is that when the Japanese scientists introduced a new innovation directed at the political leader, the whole band of several hundred monkeys was using the innovation within *four hours*. The question is, in human society can you take the mountain to Mahomet, or must you labour to bring forward young Mahomets to the top in the fullness of time? As I have noted, advancing age and a certain weariness are inclining me to the former view. We ought to try to influence our existing corps of leaders as best we can, but in the nature of things too many of them are stratum 3 people in stratum 6 jobs. In the long run we must find our outstanding people and make sure that we don't waste their talents. But how?

PICKING WINNERS

It is a matter of the greatest simplicity to screen all promotions and selections for the o–o-ness and ⌐-ness of the candidates and to exclude, except in those jobs for which a certain madness seems to be indicated (sales or accountancy, for example), those people irrevocably locked in the survival mode. To put it another way, it is easy to identify those organizations which are already wisely and boldly led and were clearly doing something or other right a few years back, probably quite unconsciously, to ensure an adequate supply of high-stratum people for top-level posts. All that is really necessary is to explain to a top management the

---

[11] ibid., pp. 126–8.

obvious truths about ○-○-ness and ⋻-ness, negotiate a consultancy fee and then help them to get on with it. In a few years the benefits will show through.

Like most important problems, picking winners cannot, in fact, be approached head-on in this fashion. For one thing, too many of the existing corps are ○-○-inclined and have difficulty therefore in distinguishing sheep from goats. Others, the clever Machiavellians with stratum 4 intellect and stratum 1 morals, do see the difference and work with fiendish skill to sustain the existing power network and the prospects of their own protégés within it. If a problem is big and important, you are probably going to have to create at least one sub-institution on the route to its solution.

I discovered this in the course of working as consultant for one major British industrial group. I was invited to join a company taskforce on 'management development'. At my suggestion, the team, all very senior managers, split up to do a little 'research' on various divisions within the group. The primary questions, simple in the extreme but pungent, were:

(1) What do you have to do around here to get things done?

(2) What do you have to do around here to get ahead?

The respondents worked at all levels in the management hierarchy, from brand-new graduates fresh from university to hard-bitten supervisors in the production line. If the answers to these questions seemed to be very different, we reckoned there was a problem in the works.

What emerged from this 'research' was a picture of wildly different assumptions in the various divisions. In some, advancement was seen to flow from serious commitment to authorized task systems and from outstanding performance within them. In others, all work was seen as a series of 'fixed' meetings, covert politics and advancement by informal power-and-influence networks. It was hard to believe that the divisions coexisted in the same organization and under the umbrella of identical personnel policies.

The problem then was: how do you begin to check the otherwise inexorable advance of the power-crazed and inexhaustibly energetic survival types? The answer lies in the surprising activity patterns of typical professional managers. In most organizations, despite the existence of elaborate safeguards and procedures, the actual promotional decisions are rushed, inefficient and based on no serious discussion of the issues behind promotability, as perceived. In short, there is usually no prior (high-quality) argument about the definition of a 'good bloke'. Everybody knows what a good bloke is, but hardly anybody ever examines the assumptions on which this 'knowledge' is based. (Feminists need have no fear; 'good bloke' is here taken to embrace women.)

In this particular company, to quote some of the managers, 'bizarre names come forward' and decisions are based on 'two-minute biographies over the telephone'. The whole elaborate process can be seen, in fact, as a way of *not* exposing prejudices. Most managers, in short, are either extremely confident about who the 'good blokes' are (chaps like themselves) or very nervous of exposing their own uncertainties in making judgements about other people. The latter group are on the right track, of course, but tend to be steamrolled by the former. What is usually lacking is a separate space, properly institutionalized, for having a high-quality argument over conflicting prejudices. Instead, the argument tends to emerge through subconscious cracks to muddle the actual selection process.

Managers need, in other words, to take time and to find a 'space', on a regular basis, in which to explore issues such as the relationship of ∘–∘-ness to ⬠-ness, so that they can either agree on policy or agree to disagree in a sensible fashion when actual names come up for discussion. That 'space' is the sub-institution on the route to a solution. The external consultant is not then faced with committing an impertinence (telling his client whom to prefer); instead he is relying on the existence of an adequacy of decent and intelligent people in the system and permitting them to influence policy adequately. There always does, for some reason, seem to be an adequacy of such people.

Here the external adviser is himself exercising a sophisticated form of management with important implications, at another level, for his client/managers. He is not telling them what to do (which is what people sometimes think management is about) but helping to establish boundary conditions within which residual common sense is likely to emerge triumphant. That approach satisfies the ⟁ rule. The 'space' is the 'third corner' – a safely bounded institution within which high-quality (potentially fruitful) fighting can occur and out of which sensible policy may emerge.

If pressed, I would say that that 'space' is the single most important element in the quest for adequate leadership. But there are other fashionable methods too. Since the Second World War the 'assessment centre' has enjoyed a considerable vogue. Its origins lie in the War Officer Selection Board (WOSB) group activities, based on the belated discovery by the British military that leadership requires *following*, not just a sound pedigree. In the WOSB groups natural group-leadership patterns tended to emerge, and sometimes the most unprepossessing people (as to breeding stock and demeanour) seemed to have the *knack*. It was by no means perfect as a means of selection, but it was a lot more reliable than what had gone before (the *unerring* selection, as N. F. Dixon reminds us, of the wrong people).

The assessment centre usually brings together, for a week or so, hopefuls from the scattered outposts of a large organization and puts them through various hoops (for example, group exercises) under the watchful eyes of senior managers of the organization. There are two important advantages to this method:

(1)   the hopefuls are freed from the power politics and prejudices of their particular subsystems for a while and are able to show their paces in the context of their peers;
(2)   the observing senior managers are placed in a position where they can scarcely fail to learn something about their own unconscious prejudices.

These are not inconsiderable virtues, but against them ought to be set certain disadvantages of the standard 'assessment centre' packages on sale:

(1)   the group exercises are, after all, only exercises;

(2)   the competitive atmosphere positively encourages o—o behaviour, suitably disguised (it is all a bit like a beauty contest, only less beautiful);

(3)   the hopefuls thus depart as recent competitors rather than as colleagues;

(4)   there is commonly a certain secretiveness about the final evaluations and the criteria on which they are based;

(5)   the whole thing is rather an expensive way of selecting people.

Some years ago, in the IBM Corporation, some colleagues and I attempted, with some success, to overcome these problems. This we did by:

(1)   inserting real current and complex business problems in place of standard 'group exercises', so as to evaluate something more (brains, for instance) than game-playing skills (not irrelevant but not everything either);

(2)   turning the tables, in the latter part of the week, by making the hopefuls' top-management group available to them for a half day, to do with as they liked; this was a novel and quite alarming prospect for both sub-groups, calling on skills in policy-making, planning, organization, selection and sheer *management* of an entirely unpredictable situation;

(3)   making the written final evaluation available to line management and to the participants (though each participant also had a confidential end-of-programme interview with a staff member of the assessment centre).[12]

The participants thus had to deal with reality, at one remove in the case of the business problems and directly in the process of 'managing' their own senior management

[12] Alistair Mant, 'A European Look at Assessment Centres', *European Business*, Summer 1974.

interaction. In essence, we democratized, to some extent, a process which is otherwise somewhat less than democratic, and at the same time we rendered the criteria for promotion and selection explicit and visible. The whole assessment centre, in a way, became the 'space' within which personal prejudice was exposed. (This particular model has been copied by others, but without conspicuous success.)

The attraction of the 'space' idea is that you don't really have to do anything about leadership directly – you simply create the requisite conditions for the emergence of intelligent conflict and, ultimately, common sense. The argument here differs not one whit from the philosophical basis for German industrial democracy outlined in Chapter 7: if you create sound institutions, it is quite remarkable how sensibly people will behave in due course. If you fail to create formal institutions which truly reflect the informal reality, then you have no right to blame people when they behave extremely informally or destructively.

One of the great difficulties about leadership arises precisely from this sort of structural failure. All organizations call for an interlocking of *representative* and *managerial* subsystems. There has to be someone (the manager) to keep the bureaucracy running, but there has also to be someone to represent the interests of the whole in policy formulation. The precise equivalent is to be found in the role of citizen in relation to the state. We do not, on the whole, wish to participate in the running of the Civil Service, the police, the Army and so on, but we do wish to participate (through our elected representatives) in the process through which overall policy is set.

When businessmen complain about 'industrial democracy' they sometimes tend to say, 'If we are all to participate in decision-making, then the whole factory is going to grind to a halt every time we hit a decision point.' This view betrays a fundamental misunderstanding of the principle above. Most workers, in my experience, sometimes wish to God their managers would get on with it instead of pretending to 'consult' and playing with all manner of mock 'democratic management' styles. The confusion is between *decision-making* (a managerial function) and *policy formulation* (representative function). Where the Anglo-Saxon managers have failed, on the whole, is in not distinguishing the two subsystems; if the representative system is inadequate, then workers will indeed poke their noses into managerial decisions and much else besides.

Significantly, when the Biendenkopf Commission looked at industrial democracy in parts of Germany,[13] it concluded that most board decisions were in a sense 'fixed' as a result of prior consultation between works council representatives, unions, management and so on. The Commission's conclusion was that this informal arrangement was working extremely well and that it was essential to institutionalize it at once. The British, American and Australian reaction would, I suspect, have been otherwise, something like 'Great! The lads are working it – we don't want all that red tape!' The result in the long run is that where management doesn't give a damn about representation in relation to policy, the representative system, informally and as represented by unions, probably won't give a damn about management either.

Thus the existence of sound institutional arrangements gives rise to a certain kind of leadership – the kind that looks after the constitutional housekeeping and frees workers to get on with the work. Without such arrangements the worker is like a driver who is worried that his wheels are going to fall off – preoccupied and thus incompetent. Hence, it is unhelpful to counterpose the personal (leader) and institutional (constitution) aspects. The ⌘ mind automatically creates institutions, so that there is a 'third corner' for the mediation between forces. Those institutions are no more than an extension of the fundamental thought processes of such a mind, which, we may argue, is in turn no more than a reflection, in the architecture of the human brain, of the 'good object' internalized in very early infancy.

We don't as a matter of fact, have to be terribly clever about these sorts of things. But we have to be clever

[13] Report of the Codetermination Commission, Federal Republic of Germany (1970), Belfast, Queen's University, 1976.

enough to create the useful intervening institutions when we are not quite sure what to do next. In selection, for example, we don't really have to know (via a battery of psychometric tests) who the ideal candidate is. All we have to ensure is that the selection is a success in the long run. We also have to be clever enough to know when and how to initiate 'research' into the mass of mundane data which always surround us.

One of my consultancy assignments involved just this: the task was to improve selection. The temptation was to spend a fortune on a very clever, very complicated testing procedure available from one of the glossier consultancy firms. The solution was to remember that all the records of previous selection rounds (principally for salesmen) were on file. A brief review ('research', if you insist) of the data there revealed that two of the line managers in the system had a genius for selection – not just for choosing the right people but also for representing the organization accurately to them at interview. They were, in short, never wrong.

We could, I suppose, have studied these two men in fine detail, but it wasn't really necessary. All that was needed was to ensure their deployment at selection time and, where possible, to get other (and younger) managers to listen to them. They were, as it happens (and as the reader may guess), somewhat older, wiser, less charismatic and altogether sounder than some of their colleagues. They were, in short, rather ⧟-oriented in their thinking. They were also quite surprised to discover they had a genius at all and gratified ('motivated', if you prefer) to be called on to display it.

DEVELOPING LEADERS FOR THE REAL WORLD

The 'problem' in the case outlined above was cast as one of 'selection', but the outcome, when some of the relative youngsters learned from the two unsung geniuses, was an educational or developmental one. That is to say, somebody learned something (as a by-product) as a result of worrying away at a *real* problem. This is becoming a famil-

iar theme in the world of management: whether anybody
ever learns anything useful except as a result of unpredictable activity designed to solve a problem. The great philosopher R. G. Collingwood set out this principle as a direct
result of worrying what on earth Sir G. Gilbert Scott was
up to in designing the Albert Memorial in London's Hyde
Park.

It . . . began to obsess me. . . . Everything about it was visibly
crawling, verminous; for a time I could not bear to look at it, and
passed with averted eyes; recovering from this weakness, I forced
myself to look, and to face day by day the question: a thing so
obviously, so incontrovertibly, so indefensibly bad, why had
Scott done it? To say that Scott was a bad architect was to burke
the problem with a tautology; to say that there was no accounting
for tastes was to evade it by *suggestio falsi*. What relation was
there, I began to ask myself, between what he had done and what
he had tried to do? Had he tried to produce a beautiful thing; a
thing, I meant, which we should have thought beautiful? If so,
he had of course failed. But had he perhaps been trying to
produce something different? If so, he might possibly have succeeded. If I found the monument merely loathsome, was that
perhaps my fault? Was I looking in it for qualities it did not
possess, and either ignoring or despising those it did?[14]

In the end Collingwood concluded:

You cannot find out what a man means by simply studying his
spoken or written statements, even though he has spoken or
written with perfect command of language and perfectly truthful
intention. In order to find out his meaning you must also know
what the question was (a question in his own mind, and presumed by him to be in yours) to which the thing he has said or
written was meant as an answer.[15]

Collingwood, we must remember, was no Philistine anti-
intellectual but one of the foremost philosophers of the
twentieth century:

[14] R. G. Collingwood, *An Autobiography*, Oxford, Oxford University Press,
1978, pp. 29–30.
[15] ibid., p. 31.

I have never found it easy to learn anything from books, let alone newspapers. When I read my friends' articles about their excavations on the middle page of *The Times*, or the beautifully illustrated handbook that tells me how to look after a certain kind of motor, my brain seems to stop working. But give me half an hour on the excavation, with a student to show me what is what, or leave me alone with the motor and a box of tools, and things go better.[16]

Yet the teaching of management, of all activities, has become rarefied to the point of near disappearance up its own pretensions. In fact, it is assumed that managerial persons, having risen to their Olympian seniorities, ought to be safeguarded from mess, embarrassment, failure or confusion in any educational enterprise upon which they engage. They will expect to 'learn' from 'experts' in as agreeable a fashion as good money can lay on. They may well learn something, but it won't have much to do with managing, not in the real world anyway.

Not surprisingly, R. G. Collingwood was as unpopular and unfashionable a philosopher (until very recently) as Professor R. W. Revans was and is a management educator. Revans got into trouble for espousing similar sentiments, namely that managers usually learn from other managers in a context of trying to solve problems.[17] That, he said, is the reality, whatever the business schools get up to; managers do not in reality learn from experts in the context of 'case studies' (mere *puzzles*, rather than proper problems, in Revans's parlance). The problem in 'management development' is therefore to harness, as best we can, the manager's natural tendency to learn from his own messy experience. Otherwise management development and management education will be cast in a crude ∘–∘ show-biz frame, in which teachers strive to please and students preen themselves on their selection in the first place.

In Revans's world the real problem takes up the 'third corner' in relation to colleagues or the sensible teacher. It is thus a 'good/bad object' (depending on whether it gets

---

[16] ibid., p. 81.
[17] R. W. Revans, *Action Learning*, London, Blond & Briggs, 1980.

solved). If the manager is seriously attached to his work, the problem is inside him, worrying him, as well as 'out there' in the form of a detached, intellectualized problem. The whole process is comparable to the infant's 'stage of concern' (referred to by Winnicott) – that is, the stage at which the baby realizes that mother is both satisfying and frustrating. Real problems are similar; they can cover you with glory or with egg stain, depending on how it goes. If they don't have both potentialities, they aren't real problems,

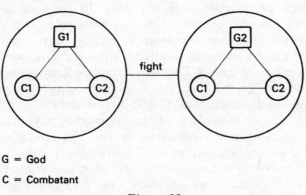

G = God
C = Combatant

Figure 32

It is not, however, easy to promote management development where the outcome cannot be predicted precisely, just as in order to secure research funding it is usually necessary first to demonstrate the pointlessness of the research (by specifying precise outcomes). Saleable management development promises control, from a position of safety. Useful management development is, by definition, threatening. This is another way of saying that the 'management' demands of most managerial jobs are not especially onerous, but leadership (which involves sticking your neck out and some moral fortitude) seems to be a more elusive quality.

Because leadership depends on the 'third corner' (what is striven for), training for leadership has to be constructed on the same ☌ principle. That is perhaps why so many of the new 'leadership' courses for executives, in Britain at least, involve falling off mountains, into rivers and so on; the physical object occupies the 'third corner', and the participants 'take it on'.[18] Most of these enterprises are directed by ex-Strategic Air Services types – that is, the blue-blood, daredevil element of the British Army, where charismatic (hence ∘–∘) ideas about leadership also hold sway. Some confusion in the minds of participants may thus arise within the 'back to nature' school.

But such remedial activities point up only the extent to which reality was lacking in earlier education. We have come to a pretty pass when virtually the only participants in the educational process with a ⋈ view of it (the 'lads' – see Chapter 4) are its rejects. (They were, naturally enough, almost the only pupils to inject a modicum of risk into their school lives.) The arrival on the British scene of a new pressure group, Education for Capability, is especially welcome. Education for Capability argues that if you haven't learned to *make* or *do* in the course of your education, then you aren't educated at all. This is rather bad news for a very large number of professors in the groves of Academe. It will not, unfortunately, be possible for Education for Capability, or anybody else for that matter, to explain all this to them; their circuits aren't wired up that way.

Inevitably, when some colleagues and I were setting up Education for Capability the purposes of the pressure group were misunderstood. It was seen as some kind of attempt to direct the brightest and best of British youth into the trenches of the old ∘–∘ struggle with commercial competitors, especially (dredging up the First World War metaphor) the Germans. My view was, and remains, that teachers ought to advise their pupils as best they can that careers in Government, advertising, academia and the professions are infinitely more acceptable, usually much safer and sometimes better paid than industrial jobs. The Education for Capability message was simpler; its implication

---

[18] Alistair Mant, 'Learning from Experience', in C. L. Cooper (ed.), *Developing Managers for the 1980s*, London, Macmillan, 1981.

was that there is indeed a leadership task of immense pro-
portions to be achieved in modern industry, but it is going
to call for more than a few battalions of ○–○ minds, and the
main battleground anyway is in our schools.

It is just here that the Frasers, Thatchers and Reagans,
bellicose characters all, are inclined to stint. If family life is
a ○–○ survival course, school may be the last ⋈ redoubt for
the young survivor. If that fails too, we have a generation
of survival types in the making. They will take whatever is
going and will give as little as they can. Some will achieve
the status of 'business leaders' and cover themselves with
glory (unless they are found out, of course).

In the meantime, the *real* educational process – that
means by which most people learn whatever it is they really
do learn – will simply bypass the schools. Already it is
happening, partly as a result of new technology; the 'lads'
at Hammertown simply provide the leadership of the
process.

It is a considerable irony that formal management development in recent years has at last begun to extend to executives in industry the felicities enjoyed by schoolchildren in
Friedrich Froebel's first kindergarten in the Thuringian
Forest in 1837. Froebel, who might have founded Education for Capability himself, based the kindergarten on

the belief that little children *already* possessed ideas and skills
which it was the function of education to develop. There was no
need to train or impose; nor could there be any question of
repressing the childishness of children. On the contrary, it was to
be encouraged. The second important principle was vaguer; all
living matter was a unity, a pantheistic oneness which had something to do with the union of Father, Son and Holy Ghost. A
child could only develop, therefore, if he was in tune with nature.

But, as so often in the history of ideas, arguable theory led to
sensible practice. Union with nature meant that children had to
attend classes only in the morning; in the afternoons they went
for walks and studied stamens, grew watercress and so on. The
innate ideas in children were brought out by giving them the
tools and tasks which would elicit them: paper, chalks, paint,
clay, beads to thread, ring-laying, pea-work, balls and blocks to
play with. As a matter of fact, to see his system in practice,

somewhat modified and stripped of its philosophic concepts which are nineteenth-century and German, one has only to look at the infant teaching systems practised in nearly all nursery and primary schools in England and America today.[19]

But, as we have seen, secondary school and (where relevant) university are well capable of eradicating any last vestiges of childlike curiosity about the world of things. By the time the infant strikes 'management development', the odds are he will be disinclined to learn in the same way that he did in infancy – except, that is, for the minority of people who somehow manage, through luck or force of personality, to cling to a secure ⚐ base, a belief, despite the odds, that the 'third corner' may yield up a wondrous prize, even though the getting of it may be fraught with uncertainty and some danger.

In recent years I have had the chance (for research purposes) to offer an unusual opportunity to executives attending a standard curriculum-based ten-week management programme in a major business school. The opportunity is, simply, to sit down once a week with a trained consultant to reflect on the minutiae of work experience in order to understand its meaning a little better. This is a resource-intensive activity that is well beyond the capacity of most business schools to offer.[20] The idea is to help the individual to rise above the dross in order to 'see' himself *in situ*, as subject (trying to get things done) and as object (reacting, sometimes unconsciously, to dynamic forces at work in his organization). For the method to work the individual has to be capable of ascending to the 'third corner' to observe himself at work; indeed, he must comprehend that possibility in order to contract in to the arrangement in the first place.

On the face of it, this would seem to be a very considerable bonus – the chance to complement book learning and

---

[19] Jonathan Gathorne-Hardy, *The Rise and Fall of the British Nanny*, London, Hodder & Stoughton, 1972, p. 177.

[20] Bruce Reed, 'Organizational Role Analysis', in C. L. Cooper (ed.), *Developing Social Skills in Managers*, London, ATM, 1976; see also, for this point and others, Alistair Mant, *The Dynamics of Management Education*, London, Gower Press, 1981.

lectures with a little thoughtful introspection (and especially so in mid-life). The surprise is that, on average, no more than one manager in five volunteers for this option. Those that do will often resort to moral blackmail to make sure they get the opportunity because they know it is what they most need. Indeed, for the volunteers it is what the ten-week course was supposed to be all about in the first place – a 'space' within which one can ask, 'What does it mean to be a manager?' 'What is *my organization for?*' 'How safely can I throw my weight around, knowing what I know now?' And so on. The others, the non-volunteers, are just as certain that they desire the opportunity like a hole in the head.

Of course, the safe big-company men (and women, very occasionally) who are 'sent' on these courses are rarely true entrepreneurs, as the business schools have tacitly recognized. Most of them are motivated in a bland and complaisant way by survival considerations – the swelling pension and the necessity to preserve a clean sheet till the haven of early retirement. They tend to be *nice* people who have split their real motives from work completely. Thus the utility of the company's end products, or the morality of their distribution, is of no concern to them. If the business school were to drag in such matters, these participants might well ask why so much money is being spent by their employers to make them feel so rotten. Here one must sympathize, up to a point, with the business schools. If four out of every five executive students are like this, then the survival of the business school institution will rest on satisfying them and their sponsors, which means colluding in their self-deception.

But this is a book about leadership. We need not concern ourselves with the four, nor need the business schools, beyond a certain show-biz stage management. It is the one in every five we have to worry about; the Pareto principle made flesh. If business schools don't satisfy this minority, its members tend to turn nasty, and inventively so. They are not above brandishing the brochure (the visible and formal 'third corner' which regulates their institutional relationships with staff) in order to point out

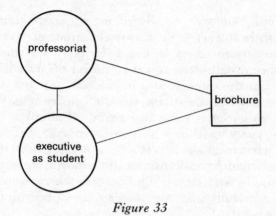

Figure 33

the inconsistencies and hollow promises buried in the PR verbiage (see Figure 33). This subset is the equivalent in a curious way of the 'lads' back at Hammertown (see Chapter 4), though in this case almost invariably middle-class in origin. It knows, from family and school life, about 'third corners' (and the significance therefore of the brochure) and it can spot the show-biz/survival/collusion ∘–∘ model a mile off. The result is a certian contempt for the professors (refer 'Hammertown' again) and a burgeoning 'trouble-maker' reputation.

It doesn't do to be branded a 'troublemaker'; your chair-man might get to hear about it on the top-level grapevine, and it could damage your promotion prospects. Thus is the brave ⌐ mind sometimes frightened into conformity or, more likely, a sullen and private withdrawal to books and the library. Blessed with high intelligence, the possessor of the ⌐ mind grasps that he can't win in so labyrinthine a power system, and so he cuts his losses. As a result, the course as a whole has lost its potential leaders, which is what, you might surmise, was intended (quite unconsciously) by the Faculty (who are after a quiet, agree-able life) in collusion with the other four out of every five participants (who are after a commodity with survival value – the status of alumni of a prestigious institution).

So far my experiments with the one in five, helping them to reflect on experience in a systematic way, have gone rather well. Not only do the ⊃∘ leaders respond with wit and gratitude to the opportunity thus offered, but also the course as a whole 'goes well' (translation: is not bolshie), possibly because its natural leaders are hard at work in a ⊃∘ way (see Figure 34). It is a ⊃∘ subsystem within/straddling a flight ∘—∘ system. This frees everybody else to get on with his or her own largely pointless but 'motivating' pursuits, and to do so without an undue sense of guilt. Still, one wonders what might happen to such courses if all the issues above were made manifest from the outset and worked with relentlessly during the programme. For one thing, the definition of 'capability' among professors would require some adjustment.

By a curious (perhaps divine) inspiration, the 'back-to-nature' school has now infiltrated even these programmes in British business schools. That is to say that, near the beginning of the ten weeks, some of the schools send the whole complement of more or less physically fit and more

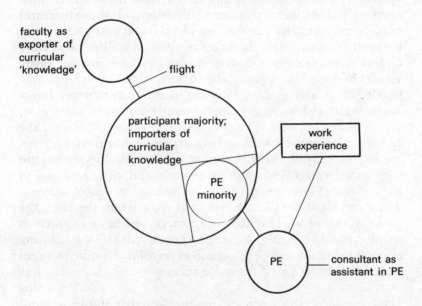

PE = processing of experience

Figure 34: The interlocking of ∘—∘ and ⊃∘ in the business school

or less physically courageous executives to fall off mountains, out of canoes, etc., etc. This is a brilliant, and typically British, fudge. The participants thus have a ⌐ experience, but with a mountain or river as the 'third corner', thus satisfying honour. More important still, the depressive mid-course 'dip', long the bane of such courses, has been eradicated at a stroke. How so? The mid-course 'dip' was an acting out of mid-life – the moment when you discover that the course (or life) hasn't turned out quite as you fantasized and, worse still, that it is too late now to change it much. Result: depression, mourning and guilt.

All surgeons know that patients recover from operations more quickly if the 'crisis of anxiety' is brought forward. It is better to know the truth (i.e. the true risks) beforehand and to process that grim knowledge than to carry an inevitable doubt into the operating theatre. The worst moment for the executives these days is the interview with the doctor to check out the likelihood of pegging out *en bivouac*, so to speak. It is like doing your finals in the first term at university. Once over this hump, the participants tend to stay healthy; in the bad old days one or two people frequently went sick during the 'dip', usually foreigners and/or manufacturing managers deskilled by all the verbiage. The point is, if you feel you have risked your life, you won't feel nearly as bad, later on in the programme, about declining to risk an inspection of your purpose in life.

If this book can be said to contain any helpful hints, they are in this chapter. Our first purpose is to find those people who will get useful work done cleverly and will carry others with them. These people have ⌐ minds, as I have argued. They can fight (∘–∘) like tigers, but only when they see the point of doing so. Having found them, we have to nurture them, mainly simply by appreciating them but also by allowing them a few (high-quality) mistakes. To achieve all this, we have to do a number of things.

(1)   Create a 'third corner' for high-quality fighting about the definition of a 'good bloke'. You can't impose the ⌐ mentality – the survivors won't let you – but you

can enforce a decent space within which the 🐒 argument may flourish. It always will, given that space. This 'third corner' may be a quarterly one-day promotion policy meeting; at another level it may be a form of 'assessment centre'.

(2) Go for the top. Most top people are surprisingly lonely. Surrounded by super-efficient flunkeys, they love cocktail parties and receptions because they meet exciting new people there, some of whom they then wish on to their organizations. Huge energies are expended in neutralizing these outsiders. Still, remember Imo, the genius monkey; avoid young females, except for the gathering of intelligence, and go for the alphas, no matter how far removed from genius.

(3) Build proper constitutional structures, or your interpersonal power system will throw up shallow, flashy charismatics in unpredictable and uncontrollable ways. Structure is not the same thing as red tape. Without proper structures, true 🐒 leaders languish unrecognized or go away and work for somebody else.

(4) Use people who have a genius for character judgement. They may not know how or why they have it, but it doesn't matter. Mistaken appointments and promotions always cost a fortune in the end. A too cautious approach, without genius, is as bad as the bold and silly. Always use people with genius rather than expensive devices peddled by plausible hucksters. Such devices are no safer and make you poorer straight away.

(5) Don't 'train' people at all, unless there is a very clearcut case for the application of a new method or technique to a specific problem area. Instead, help people to understand what goes on, in messy reality, all around them. This calls for much more skill and intelligence than 'training'. It also calls for humility, a somewhat rare quality among the pedagogues.

(6) Above all, try to think of 'lads' (Chapter 4) with some affection and regard. Real talent almost invariably comes in prickly and awkward packages because true

leaders are always aggravated by the existing imper-
fections of the enterprise. Some aggravating people
are just aggressive (o--o); others are kicking against the
pricks. Learn to keep a sensitive eye out for the latter.

Remember, none of these injunctions makes sense in institutions devoted to shameful purposes or in which the processes of work are irredeemably corrupt. Anyone wedded to
such an institution and jealous of his pension should avoid
⊐ ('What's it for?') questions at all costs.

Conclusion

The gist of this book is that competent leaders are born rather than made, and the individual die is probably cast by the onset of latency. The Jesuit boast, 'Give us a boy until seven years of age and we will have him forever', is probably sound. Yet the book's tone is generally optimistic; if we bother to use our wits as to the people we prefer and as to the institutions we create to regulate the preferment process, we can probably exclude quite a few of the cowboys from office – if we really want to.

Still, we live in volatile times. It might be the case that the delicate interweaving of understandings which make up a democracy could come under unbearable strain as economic performance and materialistic aspirations diverge. There is the risk that the book adds up to an implicit approval of the three-part mode and of leaders capable of calm, abstracted thought.

But survival and the survival mode are still important and may get more important. The book's musings are more or less irrelevant, that is to say, for the undernourished dictatorships. It may even prove to be the case that our large Western democracies, as *systems*, are becoming relatively unstable and unsusceptible to leadership of any kind whatever.

The phenomenon of Margaret Thatcher is instructive and so too is that of Ronald Reagan, whom very few Americans believe to have any brains at all. Mrs Thatcher is not only disliked by her opponents to an extent unprecedented in modern British political history, she is also disliked, in a rather different way, by many of the old-school Conservatives – the ones who, secure in their social origins, used to adopt a lordly but still compassionate view of their political responsibilities towards the masses. Confident that they were bound to win any fights going, they pursued consensus and, on the whole, succeeded in achieving it.

But to understand the uprising of Margaret Thatcher, we may have to attend to the system itself. Britain, the model for many of the Western democracies, is a good case study for examination. The country, like some vast mechanical engine, appears to be in the grip of a big wobble or vibration. The oscillations, fuelled by the binary two-party system, geared to the electoral cycle and shaped perhaps by the geography of the country, seem to have been getting more and more violent. Maybe without the *big* wobble (the second-order vibration of war) the system will not be able quite to return to base.

Anyone who has observed an engine with a faulty governor will be familiar with the phenomenon. If the governor is connected to the fuel supply in such a way that the more the arms of the governor diverge, the more the fuel supplied, then the machine will go into runaway, operating faster exponentially until some part breaks or the fuel duct can deliver fuel at no greater rate. There isn't a lot you can do about it unless you have direct access to the fuel supply. In human society that supply is human energy, fuelled in turn by passion, envy, greed and other such volatile chemicals.

In system runaway it is always unwise to interpose your person in the machine, as the 'third-corner' Liberal/Social Democratic Alliance discovered in the 1983 general election; you are likely to get your finger, at least, chopped off. The Alliance must have felt as through they had tried to intervene in a marital squabble. The risk of injury is the same; the protagonists *seem* to be fighting, but they love to fight more than anything else in the world. It is the form their love takes.

In social terms system runaway is a bit like the process which gives more police more equipment and more leeway to duff up anybody they please, which leads to more anti-authoritarian resentment and violence, which leads to a demand for more police, etc, etc.

When a machine starts to vibrate violently the engineer wants to know where it all started, at what point in the time cycle the offending subsystem began to behave unpredictably. In the case of Margaret Thatcher, the answer is quite clear – she isn't supposed to be there at all. The relevant subsystem is, of course, the Conservative Party leadership selection process. Only a very few, perhaps self-flagellatory, Tories wanted her at all. But the vagaries of tactical voting caused something to happen that wasn't in the programme. Once started, the subsystem too went into runaway.

The old-school Tories, pleased and a little bemused by their new lease on life, are actually appalled at the crude and primitive bond which has sprung up between Mrs Thatcher and the little people. She has, as they say ruefully, the common touch. Most commentators were critical of the thinness of her party election manifesto, but the manifesto wasn't important; it was the lady who mattered. She reached out, in her intuitive way, to the meanest, and the communication was, and is, *direct*, untouched by the complexity and doubt of policy-making or, indeed, by politics itself.

This is not supposed to happen. Party leadership conventions exist, in an unconscious sort of way, to ensure it doesn't happen. The operation of the whole system of politics depends on things happening in a *political* way. The British system, in its collective unconscious, does not expect such phenomena as Margaret Thatcher; it does not know how to expect such things. That is not its nature as a system. The compensating selection of the left-wing bibliophile Michael Foot to lead the Labour Opposition was an equally unpolitical happening – a kind of sympathetic vibration or wobble in the machine. Those who were party to that decision were acutely conscious of a kind of lemming-like impulse in the process. To misquote General Bosquet in the Crimea, it was magnificent, but it wasn't politics.

In its way, it was an attempt to break free into some sunlit moral upland after years of squalid party compromise and leaden struggle with the old enemy. That sort of attempt, as Germany discovered in the 1930s, is not simply unrealistic but may lead on to amorality. Hitler, of course, was another of those characters with direct and simple appeal for the declining and rising classes but who appalled the true establishment. The wobble he caused, in the big system, is still rattling around today. We should not forget that, late in 1932, the Nazi momentum was virtually spent, and it took a very deliberate effort, on the part of some of the dimmer nobility, to breathe life into it again.

When the big system goes into a kind of hiccup, it is not easy to be optimistic or coolly and calmly to attend to 'leadership' issues in a businesslike way. The instinct is to get your head down, perhaps in a fall-out shelter, and wait for the wobble to die down. But you have to start somewhere; the key to useful action may lie in one persistent theme of this book – *oscillation*. We can't all be brave and resourceful all the time, especially when faced by an army of well-placed ○–○ survivors in politics, business and industry, unions, schools and so on. The very thought of taking them all on, all the time, is immobilizing.

But we can, if we are clever, work together, some of the time, to discomfit some of them, to some extent. Then we can retreat, occasionally, to the safety of the printed page in order to sneer. Most of all, we must offer some hope to all those good folk in the wings of power who can see the joke and who *know* they could do a more thoughtful and responsible job.

Bibliography

Adler, A., 'Characteristics of the First, Second and Third Child', *Children,* vol. 3, 14 (issue 5), 1956.

Adorno, T. W., *et al., The Authoritarian Personality*, New York, Norton, 1969

Ambler, Eric, *The Dark Frontier,* London, Fontana, 1976.

Ardrey, Robert, *The Social Contract,* London, Collins, 1970

Bateson, Gregory, Mind and Nature – A Necessary Unity, London, Fontana, 1979

Bateson, Gregory, 'Morale and National Character', in *Steps to an Ecology of Mind*, St Albans, Paladin, 1978

Biendenkopf Report, Report of the Codetermination Commission, Federal Republic of Germany (1970), Belfast, Queen's University, 1976

Bion, W. R., *Attention and Interpretation*, London, Tavistock, 1970

Bion, W. R., *Experiences in Groups*, London, Tavistock, 1961

Blumenfeld, Ralph, *et al., Henry Kissinger : The Private and Public Story*, New York, Signet, 1974

Bott, Elizabeth, 'The Concept of Class as a Reference Group', *Human Relations*, vol. 7, 1954

Bower, Tom, *Blind Eye to Murder*, London, André Deutsch, 1981

Brown, Lord Wilfred, *Explorations in Management*, Harmondsworth, Penguin, 1965

Burns, James McGregor, *Leadership*, New York, Harper & Row, 1978

Butler, R. A., *The Art of Memory*, London, Hodder & Stoughton, 1982

Cameron, James, *Guardian*, 31 December 1980

Carlsmith, L., 'Effect of Early Father Absence on Scholastic Aptitude', in Liam Hudson (ed.), *The Ecology of Human Intelligence*, Harmondsworth, Penguin, 1970

Churchill, Winston, *My Early Life*, London, Thornton Butterworth, 1930

Collingwood, R. G., *An Autobiography*, Oxford, Oxford University Press, 1978

Cosgrave, Patrick, *An English Life: R. A. Butler*, London, Quartet, 1983

Dahrendorf, Ralf, 'Not By Bread Alone', *Financial Times*, 30 December 1976

David, Elizabeth, *English Bread and Yeast Cookery*, Harmondsworth, Penguin, 1979

Deeley, Peter, 'Was that Cricket?' *Observer Colour Supplement*, 7 November 1982

Dixon, Norman F., *On the Psychology of Military Incompetence*, London, Futura, 1979

Drucker, Peter F., *Managing in Turbulent Times*, London, Heinemann, 1980

Easterlin, Richard A., *Birth and Fortune*, London, Grant McIntyre, 1980

Egan, D., and Barron, F., 'Leaders and Innovators in Irish Industry', *Journal of Management Studies*, 1968

Ehrenzweig, Anton, *The Hidden Order of Art*, London, Weidenfeld & Nicolson, 1967; St Albans, Paladin, 1970

Erikson, E., 'Identity and the Life Cycle', *Psychological Issues*, vol. 1, 1959

Fest, Joachim C., *Hitler*, Harmondsworth, Penguin, 1977

Fromm, E., *Escape from Freedom*, New York Avon, 1965

Gall, John, *Systemantics*, London, Fontana, 1979

Gathorne-Hardy, Jonathan, *The Rise and Fall of the British Nanny*, London, Hodder & Stoughton, 1972

Grubb Institute, *TWL Network in Practice 1978–81*, report to MSC, London, Grubb Institute of Behavioural Studies, 1981

Heller, Joseph, *Catch-22*, London, Corgi, 1972

Hilsman, Robert, *To Move a Nation*, New York, Doubleday, 1967

Hobsbawm, E. J., *Industry and Empire: 1750 to the Present Day*, Harmondsworth, Penguin, 1969

Hodgson, Godfrey, *In Our time*, London, Macmillan, 1976

Hofstadter, Richard, *The Paranoid Style in American Politics*, London, Cape, 1966

Hofstede, Geert, *Culture's Consequences: International Differences in Work-Related Values*, London, Sage, 1980

Holt, J., *How Children Learn*, Harmondsworth, Penguin, 1970

Hudson, Liam (ed.), *The Ecology of Human Intelligence*, Harmondsworth, Penguin, 1970

Hudson, Liam, *Human Beings*, St Albans, Paladin, 1978

Illingworth, R. S. and Illingworth, C. M., *Lessons from Childhood: Some Aspects of the Early Life of Unusual Men and Women*, Edinburgh, Livingstone, 1966

Jaques, Elliott, *A General Theory of Bureaucracy*, London, Heinemann, 1976

Klein, Melanie, 'Envy and Gratitude', in *Collected Writings*, London, Hogarth Press, 1975

Koestler, Arthur, *The Act of Creation*, New York, Macmillan, 1964

Levinson, Daniel J., *The Seasons of a Man's Life*, New York, Ballantine, 1978

Mant, Alistair, 'Authority and Task in Manufacturing Operations of Multinational Firms', in *Manufacturing and Management*, London, HMSO, 1978

Mant, Alistair, Brown, Lord Wilfred, Hirsch-Weber, Professor W., *Bismarck to Bullock: Conversations about Political and Industrial Contrasts in Britain and Germany*, London, Anglo-German Foundation, 1983

Mant, Alistair, *The Dynamics of Management Education*, London, Gower Press, 1981

Mant, Alistair, 'A European Look at Assessment Centres', *European Business*, Summer 1974

Mant, Alistair, 'Learning from Experience', in C. L. Cooper (ed.), *Developing Managers for the 1980s*, London, Macmillan, 1981

Mant, Alistair, *The Rise and Fall of the British Manager*, London, Pan, 1979

Marr, David, *Barwick*, London, Allen & Unwin, 1980

Maslow, Abraham, *Eupsychian Management: A Journal*, Homewood, Ill., Irwin, 1965

McClelland, D. C., 'On the Psychodynamics of Creative Physical Scientists', in Liam Hudson (ed.), *The Ecology of Human Intelligence*, Harmondsworth, Penguin, 1970

Mead, Margaret, *Blackberry Winter: My Earlier Years*, London, Angus & Robertson, 1973

Mead, Margaret, 'End Linkage: a Tool for Cross-Cultural Analysis', in J. Brockman (ed.), *About Bateson*, London, Wildwood House, 1978

Morris, Roger, *The General's Progress*, London, Ronson Books, 1982

Newman, E., *The Life of Richard Wagner 1848–1860*, New York, Knopf, 1937

Newson, John and Elizabeth, *Four Years Old in an Urban Community*, Harmondsworth, Penguin, 1976

Osgood, Charles E., 'Reciprocal Initiative', in James Roosevelt (ed.), *The Liberal Papers*, New York, Quadrangle Books, 1962

Page, Bruce, 'God is Sophisticated – but not Malicious', *New Statesman*, December 1980

Palazolli, M. S., *Paradox and Counter-Paradox*, New York, Aronson, 1978

Poincaré, H., 'Science et Méthode', in P. E. Vernon, *Creativity*, Harmondsworth, Penguin, 1970

Priestland, Gerald, 'The Ghost that Came to Dinner', *Listener*, 5 November 1981

Raw, Charles, *Slater-Walker*, London, André Deutsch, 1977

Redding, S. G., *The Working-Class Manager*, London, Saxon House, 1979

Reed, Bruce, *The Dynamics of Religion*, London, Darton, Longman, Todd, 1978

Reed, Bruce, 'Organisational Role Analysis', in C. L. Cooper (ed.), *Developing Social Skills in Managers*, London, ATM, 1976

Revans, R. W., *Action Learning*, London, Blond & Briggs, 1980

Richardson, Elizabeth, *The Teacher, the School and the Task of Management*, London, Heinemann, 1973

Schulberg, Bud, *What Makes Sammy Run?*, Harmondsworth, Penguin 1941; repr. 1978

Seligman, Daniel, 'Luck and Careers', *Fortune*, 16 November 1981

Shawcross, William, *Sideshow : Kissinger, Nixon and the Destruction of Cambodia*, New York, Washington Square Press, 1979

Shorter, Edward, *The Making of the Modern Family*, London, Fontana, 1977

Snepp, Frank, *Decent Interval*, Harmondsworth, Penguin, 1980

Stern, J. P., *Hitler : The Führer and the People*, London, Fontana, 1975

Sulloway, F., 'The Role of Cognitive Flexibility in Science', in Liam Hudson (ed.), *The Ecology of Human Intelligence*, Harmondsworth, Penguin, 1970

Tayar, Graham (ed.), *Personality and Power : Studies in Political Achievement*, London, BBC, 1971

Tiger, Lionel, *Men in Groups*, London, Nelson, 1969

Trist, Eric, *The Evolution of Socio-Technical Systems*, Occasional Paper No. 2, Ontario Quality of Working Life Centre, June 1981

Walsh, Maximilian, *Poor Little Rich Country*, Harmondsworth, Penguin, 1979

Watzlawick, Paul, Weakland, John H., and Fisch, Richard *Change : Principles of Problem Formulation and Problem Resolution*, New York, Norton, 1974

Whyte, William F., *Street-Corner Society*, Chicago, Chicago University Press, 1955

Willis, Paul, *Learning to Labour*, London, Gower Press, 1980

Woodham-Smith, Cecil, *The Reason Why*, Harmondsworth, Penguin, 1968

Index